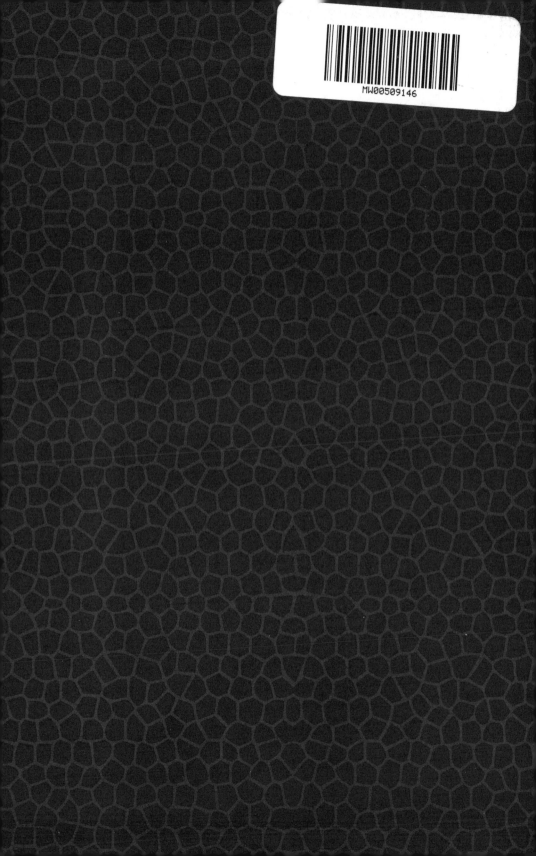

DAVENING
DIVINE

MOSAICA PRESS

RABBI EPHRAIM EPSTEIN

DAVENING DIVINE

A Companion to the
weekly Shabbat Davening

Published by Mosaica Press, Inc.
www.mosaicapress.com
info@mosaicapress.com

In memory of

Henry I. Rothman, ז״ל

And

Bertha G. Rothman, ע״ה

לחמו מלחמת ה׳

Who lived and fought for Torah-true Judaism

Published through the courtesy of the
HENRY, BERTHA AND EDWARD ROTHMAN FOUNDATION
Rochester, N.Y. • Circleville, Ohio • Cleveland

In loving memory of their parents

Aharon and Aziza, *z"l*

and their late brothers

Nachum, Refael, and Zion, *z"l*

תהא נשמתם צרורות בצרור החיים

May their souls be bound up for eternal life.

Dedicated by

JOEL AND MAZI AND THEIR SON YAKIR GOLA

SPONSORS

In honor of

Rabbi Ephraim Epstein

My friend, going back decades

We wish you much success with this new book. You are a great inspiration as a rabbi, friend and advisor. Thank you for all of your guidance, friendship, and insight over our many years. We hope this much needed book has a great impact on all of Klal Yisrael. All our best wishes for health, happiness, and prosperity to Rabbi Ephraim and Debi and the entire family.

Dedicated by
FRAN AND KEN SEGAL

In honor of my patient and loving wife

Rita

our loving children

Jennifer and Jared

our beloved son-in-law

Sean

and our precious grandchildren

Jacob and Madeline

Dedicated by
JEFF AND RITA WILDER

SUPPORTERS

In loving memory of

Elaina and Harry Cohen, *z"l*

and

Darlene and Frank Fleetwood, *z"l*

תנצב״ה.

Dedicated by
DR. AVI AND DAWN COHEN

With best wishes of Mazel Tov and success on the publication
of this *sefer*

Davening Divine

Dedicated by
DRS. FELIX AND MIRIAM GLAUBACH

In loving memory of

Yaakov Layzer ben Baruch Hakohen

Toyba bas Yitzchak

Zalman ben Tzvi

Chaya bas Eliezer

תנצב״ה.

Dedicated by their children
MARLENE AND BRUCE GOLDHAGEN

SUPPORTERS

In honor of

Martin and Gloria Epstein

Who lead and inspire

Dedicated by
RABBI AND MRS. KARASIK

In loving memory of

Harry Farkas, *z"l*

‏ת.נ.צ.ב.ה.‎

Dedicated by
THE MILTZ, MOTELIS, AND FARKAS FAMILIES

In loving memory of

Yitzchak Mordechai ben Avraham Abba, *z"l*

Esther Hinda bas Avraham, *z"l*

Dedicated by their children
MARVIN AND MARCIA RAAB

‏ת.נ.צ.ב.ה.‎

PATRONS

Dedicated by the Fertig Family Foundation
In honor of
Martin and Gloria Epstein

Dedicated by Chaim Leib Kress
In loving memory of his late beloved mother
Malka Sarah bas Yehudah Leib, *z"l*

ת.נ.צ.ב.ה.

Dedicated by Robin Sue and Bill Landsburg
In honor of our extraordinary teacher
Rabbi Ephraim Epstein

Dedicated by Andrea Rauer
In honor of my rabbi
Ephraim Epstein and his *eishes chayil*, Debi

Dedicated by Lorraine and Gerald Reiser
In honor of this worthy venture

The *tefillot* of Shabbat bring light into our lives. Rabbi Epstein's
explanations of these prayers will help us delve deeper into their
meaning and enhance our joy on Shabbat.

שמואל קמנצקי
Rabbi S. Kamenetsky

2018 Upland Way
Philadelphia, PA 19131

Home: 215-473-2798
Study: 215-473-1212

בס"ד א' לסדר ויגש תשע"א

לרום מעלת כבוד בית הוועד רבני שעיר
ספעסין הלוו עזרה לגדיים דיזה דני ואשתו.

אנחנו לשונור בני ישראל דקענין נעלה וזני רבות
שיום ולקבלם בלב שומק דני ואשתו דגאנים פני
ולצית בנים לרבתו שגם שם אל הסם.
יזכי השם שאל תגלות שם ולצליח דתתים
לבחל בגאושם נפשו לעלות מתולין וגילוין
לבל זעט רכי ואלנו זנל מגלף שם.

שא בזכירת לכלתם ואגלת דלת
תשע"א

Rabbi Berel Wein

Prayer is one of the great gifts that the Lord has bestowed upon us. It plays a central role in the daily life of Jews. It is an attempt to conduct our conversation with the Almighty and to recognize the greatness and omnipotence of God. The Sabbath prayer service is especially moving and poignant. It reflects the tranquility of the soul and the purity of the relationship between God and man. Rabbi Epstein has encompassed the ideas of this beautiful set of prayers in a meaningful, enjoyable, and educational manner. It will bring great understanding and insight to our Sabbath day and to our prayer services. It is a must for every Jewish home to have and read.

All blessings,
Berel Wein

TABLE OF CONTENTS

PREFACE

This collection of essays is the culmination of many decades of thought and reflection on the meaning of our prayers and the pursuit of a meaningful prayer experience.

I grew up and attended Jewish day school since kindergarten and attended shul on Shabbat with my father, mother, and brothers from an even younger age. I loved the singing and the warmth of shul and davening, and participated regularly as a leader of *Yigdal* and *Anim Zemirot*. As I began to mature and learned to recite more of the prayers, it began to trouble me that I did not understand what I was saying. I began to ask others in shul if they understood what it was that they were saying every day in davening.

Most people agreed that they did not really understand the words of *tefillah*, even those they recited regularly. They knew that the *tefillot* were important and holy, they enjoyed many of the melodies that were sung during davening, but they did not have even a basic understanding of the prayers they recited on a regular basis.

Although I eventually learned that there is merit in saying *Tehillim* and other *tefillot* even without understanding their meanings, I nevertheless felt uncomfortable that I (and too many other observant Jews), who choose to fulfill the mitzvah of *tefillah*, *"avodah she'balev*—service of the heart," do so without basic understanding of the content and context of our prayers. Even when we daven with a Hebrew-English siddur, who has time to think, consider, and appreciate any of the plain and deeper meanings found in our prayers?

Therefore, already as a teenager, I began to learn the meanings of the *tefillot* and practiced saying them and incorporating these meanings into my thoughts. I found this most rewarding, and it made my *tefillot* much more meaningful and inspirational.

As I continued my studies in yeshivot in America and in Israel, I began to write ideas, insights, and interpretations that I learned into the margins of my siddur. This allowed the words of the *tefillot* to become so much more personal and profound.

Finally, when I became a *rav* in Cherry Hill, New Jersey, in 5761/2001, and was considering a topic for a weekly column to write, "Tefillah Tips" was born. First, I wrote them just for a private email list, and eventually, the OU Synagogue Services, under the guidance of Mr. Frank Buchweitz at the time, began to publish them in their weekly newsletter. This enabled the "Tefillah Tips" to be read far and wide and hopefully created an awareness, and the energy to invest time in preparing for *tefillah*, our daily intimate meeting with Hakadosh Baruch Hu.

I have handpicked many of the essays that relate to the Shabbat *tefillot*, as well as some regarding *Yamim Tovim* for this book. I have read, reread, and edited them, with the hope that others may be able to find more inspiration and meaning in their *tefillah*. I read through dozens of commentaries, which I referenced in the book, and chose to include ones that resonated with me and inspired me. I also have presented my own insights from time to time that I thought were worth sharing.

It is my hope and my prayer that *Davening Divine* will enrich the reader's davening, and that it will encourage more depth and study into the intricacies of our liturgy.

Ephraim Epstein

While Sephardim pronounce the Hebrew letter ת as a *t*, Ashkenazim pronounce it as an *s*. This book uses a *t* to transliterate the letter ת.

ACKNOWLEDGMENTS

I would like to take this opportunity to thank those who have helped make this book a reality.

First and foremost, I would like to humbly thank Hashem for affording me the opportunity to learn, teach, and share His Torah with His children. I only pray that I do so properly and bring honor to His great name.

Thank you to all of the great people at Mosaica Press, especially Rav Yaacov Haber. It has been an honor working with you. Thank you for taking on this project and encouraging me throughout the process.

I want to thank all of my *roshei yeshiva* and *rebbeim* including, but not limited to, HaRav Nachman Bulman, *zt"l*, HaRav Moshe Chait, *zt"l*, HaRav Berel Wein, *shlita*, and HaRav Noach Orlowek, *shlita*, who have inspired and fortified me with their teachings and love of Klal Yisrael.

I want to thank my dear parents, Gloria and Martin Epstein, who have believed in me, supported me, and have provided me with a great example of devoting one's life to ideals greater than oneself.

To my dear father-in-law and mother-in-law, Dr. Howard and Helen Feintuch, who have been there time and time again to provide unending love and support to all of their children, grandchildren, and so many others in need.

To my congregational family, Sons of Israel in Cherry Hill, New Jersey; my local mentors, Rabbi Rothman and Chazzan Horowitz; to my colleague, Rabbi Shalom Shapiro; and to the myriad of families that have shared their lives with me: thank you for inspiring me to share and teach Torah with you. I'd like to especially thank Dr. Sid Goldberg, who encouraged me to start writing these essays almost two decades ago.

I would like to extend a special thank you to Rabbi Yurel Subar, *shlita*, who purchased the *sefer Olas Tamid* over thirty years ago when I shared with him that I wanted to learn more about the siddur. This book has been written on the foundation of that purchase and the many hours we learned together.

To our precious children: Nesanel, Rena and Gedalia and baby Sarah Leah, Atara, Racheli, Nachi, Zev, Yisrael Meir, Yocheved, and Temima—each of you are so special and important to Mommy and me, each in your own ways.

Acharon, acharon chaviv, to my *eishes chayil*, Debi. Thank you for your love, care, and dedication to me, our children, and to Klal Yisrael. I could not have written this book, or accomplished anything else for that matter, without your love and support. May Hashem bless you with long life and with continued *nachas* from our family and from all of your efforts on behalf of Klal Yisrael.

Chapter One

KABBALAT SHABBAT

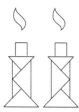

R av Yaakov Kamenetsky was reputed to have said, "When Jews migrated from Europe to America they were able to transport the Shabbos with them, but along the way they lost the Erev Shabbos." Preparing for Shabbat physically, emotionally, and spiritually is vital in order to embrace the quintessential Shabbat experience. The Talmud states it succinctly: "One who prepares for Shabbat, will eat on Shabbat; and one who does not prepare, will not have what to eat."[1]

So let's prepare for Shabbat together by exploring and understanding the beautiful liturgy composed by Chazal—our Sages, in honor of the day, in order to make it as meaningful as possible.

Introduction to Kabbalat Shabbat

Our Friday night *tefillot* differ from all other *tefillot* of the week. In fact, our *tefillot* on Friday night demonstrate the difference between Shabbat and all of the other mitzvot in the *Torah*. The prayer service

---

1   *Avodah Zarah* 3a.

of *Kabbalat Shabbat* is an actual **preparation service** that inspires us to accept Shabbat appropriately. It is rare to find a mitzvah where this phenomenon exists. There is no *kabbalat tzitzit, kabbalat mezuzah,* or *kabbalat tefillin...*just *Kabbalat Shabbat.* Why?

Additionally, Rav Shimshon Pincus writes in *Shabbat Malketa* that unlike all other mitzvot, we treat *Shabbat* as if it has a personality:

- We welcome the Shabbat.
- We escort Shabbat out with a *Melaveh Malkah,* a farewell meal.
- We wear special Shabbat clothing in honor of Shabbat.
- We look forward to when Shabbat will arrive.

How can we understand the nature of Shabbat, and why it is cloaked with such a rich array of unique customs, rituals, and deeds?

Rav Matisyahu Salomon explains in his *sefer Matnat Chaim* the fundamental difference between Shabbat and all other mitzvot:

- The function and task of fulfilling other mitzvot is to sanctify ourselves. Therefore, before performing a mitzvah, one recites the blessing, "*Asher kideshanu b'mitzvotav*—[Hashem] has sanctified **us** with His mitzvot."
- On Shabbat, we not only sanctify ourselves with the mitzvot of the day, we also welcome Hashem's Divine Presence itself and thereby get a glimpse of the world in a state of redemption. Every Friday night we are invited to enter this Sabbatical realm of Godliness. Shabbat is related to the word *shevitah,* which means to come to a complete stop. On Shabbat, the world stops as we know it and transforms into a perfected state.

There are a number of Shabbat customs based on this understanding:

- We chant, "*M'ein Olam Haba Shabbat menuchah,*" which means that Shabbat is tantamount to the World to Come.
- We eat fish and meat on Shabbat because they correspond to the future Messianic celebrations of consuming the *leviatan* (fish) and the *shor ha'bor* (meat).
- On Friday night, we recite *Tehillim, perakim* 95 through 99, which refer to the future Messianic era.

The *Kabbalat Shabbat* service is the portal and the stepping-stone to experiencing *Shabbat kodesh*—the holy Shabbat.

The Six Chapters of Praise

Kabbalat Shabbat begins with six *perakim* of *Tehillim*—95 through 99—and is followed by *Mizmor L'David* (*Tehillim* 29), culminating with *Lechah Dodi*. Rav Yaakov Emden, also known as the *Yaavetz*, explains in his siddur *Beit Yaakov* that the recital of the six *perakim* corresponds to the six days of the week, and *Lechah Dodi* corresponds to Shabbat.

Rav Meir Leibush ben Yehiel Michel Wisser, better known as the *Malbim*, writes that *Tehillim* 95 through 99 reflect the time of Messianic redemption. He explains that at that time there will be two distinct levels of recognition and praise of God.

1. The first level of praise will emanate from the nations of the world because of their new and startling realization and awareness of God's Divine power, strength, and sovereignty over the world.
2. The second and more profound level of praise will be sung by the Jewish People and relates to God as their personal protector and loving King throughout history.

Tehillim 95 introduces both styles of praise. *Tehillim* 96 and 97 are level-1 praises. *Tehillim* 98 and 99 are level-2 praises.

Note the development:

- *Tehillim* 95 introduces both styles of praise.
- *Tehillim* 96 and 97 are level-1 praises.
- *Tehillim* 98 and 99 are level-2 praises.

Interestingly, this approach of the *Malbim* to *Kabbalat Shabbat* reflects the climactic passages in *Hallel* (*Tehillim* 117 and 118) wherein the nations of the world will first praise God, and then Am Yisrael will follow. Let us take a look at them briefly before getting to *Kabbalat Shabbat* itself.

First, *Tehillim* 117:

א הַלְלוּ אֶת ה׳ כָּל גּוֹיִם שַׁבְּחוּהוּ כָּל הָאֻמִּים.	1 *Praise God, all nations, laud Him, all peoples.*
ב כִּי גָבַר עָלֵינוּ חַסְדּוֹ וֶאֱמֶת ה׳ לְעוֹלָם הַלְלוּיָ-הּ.	2 *For His kindness has overwhelmed us, and the truth of God is eternal. Halleluyah!*

Beginning with the entire world and then moving to the Jews, consider *Tehillim* 118:

א הוֹדוּ לַה׳ כִּי טוֹב: כִּי לְעוֹלָם חַסְדּוֹ.	1 *Give thanks to God because He is good, for His kindness is eternal.*
ב יֹאמַר נָא יִשְׂרָאֵל: כִּי לְעוֹלָם חַסְדּוֹ.	2 *Israel shall now say, "For His kindness is eternal."*
ג יֹאמְרוּ נָא בֵית אַהֲרֹן: כִּי לְעוֹלָם חַסְדּוֹ.	3 *The house of Aaron shall now say, "For His kindness is eternal."*
ד יֹאמְרוּ נָא יִרְאֵי ה׳: כִּי לְעוֹלָם חַסְדּוֹ.	4 *Those who fear God shall now say, "For His kindness is eternal."*

So too, in our *Tehillim* of *Kabbalat Shabbat* we see that first the nations of the world will praise God, and then we, Am Yisrael, will express our praise and gratitude, albeit in a different way.

Tehillim 95: *Lechu Neranenah*—Let's Join in Joyful Praise

א לְכוּ נְרַנְּנָה לַה׳ נָרִיעָה לְצוּר יִשְׁעֵנוּ.	1 *Come, let us sing praises to God; let us shout to the Rock of our salvation.*
ב נְקַדְּמָה פָנָיו בְּתוֹדָה בִּזְמִרוֹת נָרִיעַ לוֹ.	2 *Let us greet His presence with thanksgiving; let us shout to Him with songs.*
ג כִּי אֵל גָּדוֹל ה׳ וּמֶלֶךְ גָּדוֹל עַל כָּל אֱלֹהִים.	3 *For God is a great power and a great King over all divine powers.*
ד אֲשֶׁר בְּיָדוֹ מֶחְקְרֵי אָרֶץ וְתוֹעֲפֹת הָרִים לוֹ.	4 *In whose hand are the depths of the earth, and the heights of the mountains are His.*

ה אֲשֶׁר לוֹ הַיָּם וְהוּא עָשָׂהוּ וְיַבֶּשֶׁת יָדָיו יָצָרוּ.	5 *For the sea is His, He made it, and His hands formed the dry land.*
ו בֹּאוּ נִשְׁתַּחֲוֶה וְנִכְרָעָה נִבְרְכָה לִפְנֵי ה׳ עֹשֵׂנוּ.	6 *Come, let us prostrate ourselves and bow; let us kneel before God, our Maker.*
ז כִּי הוּא אֱלֹהֵינוּ וַאֲנַחְנוּ עַם מַרְעִיתוֹ וְצֹאן יָדוֹ הַיּוֹם אִם בְּקֹלוֹ תִשְׁמָעוּ.	7 *For He is our God and we are the people of His pasture, and the flocks of His hand, today, if you hearken to His voice.*
ח אַל תַּקְשׁוּ לְבַבְכֶם כִּמְרִיבָה כְּיוֹם מַסָּה בַּמִּדְבָּר.	8 *Do not harden your heart as [in] Meribah, as [on] the day of Massah in the desert.*
ט אֲשֶׁר נִסּוּנִי אֲבוֹתֵיכֶם בְּחָנוּנִי גַּם רָאוּ פָעֳלִי.	9 *When your ancestors tested Me; they tried Me, even though they had seen My work.*
י אַרְבָּעִים שָׁנָה אָקוּט בְּדוֹר וָאֹמַר עַם תֹּעֵי לֵבָב הֵם וְהֵם לֹא יָדְעוּ דְרָכָי.	10 *Forty years I quarreled with a generation, and I said, "They are a people of erring hearts and they did not know My ways."*
יא אֲשֶׁר נִשְׁבַּעְתִּי בְאַפִּי אִם יְבֹאוּן אֶל מְנוּחָתִי.	11 *For which reason I swore in My wrath, that they would not enter My resting place.*

"Lechu neranenah l'Hashem nariyah l'tzur yisheinu—Let us go and praise God with joy, we will cry out to our Rock of deliverance." The arrival of Mashiach is met with a shofar blast, a *teruah*, to celebrate the historic moment.

The contrast between level-1 praise and level-2 praise is clearly defined in the difference styles of praise in *pesukim* 4 and 5 as opposed to 6 and 7:

- *Pesukim* 4 and 5 speak generally of the wonders of Creation, such as the tall mountains, the depths of the sea, and the types of terrain on earth.
- *Pesukim* 6 and 7 speak more personally and invite Klal Yisrael to come forth and express submission and gratitude to our Maker because He is our God and we are His flock.

The final *pesukim* of *Tehillim* 95 take note of the first generation of Israel that traversed the desert for forty years and did **not** merit entry into Eretz Yisrael.

The Psalmist concludes, "*Al takshu levavchem*—Do not harden your hearts like your forefathers, *im yevo'un el menuchati*—whom I did not allow entry into the promised land."

A DIVINE APPROACH: Before we begin to daven *Tehillim 95, Lechu Neranenah*, let's pause for a moment and imagine the future: a world without war, strife, and terror. Let's envision our world to be a world of total truth, harmony, and beauty. Then, begin the great song of *Lechu Neranenah*.

Tehillim 96: Shiru La'Hashem—Singing a New Song

א שִׁירוּ לַה׳ שִׁיר חָדָשׁ שִׁירוּ לַה׳ כָּל הָאָרֶץ.	1 *Sing to God a new song, sing to God, all the earth.*
ב שִׁירוּ לַה׳ בָּרְכוּ שְׁמוֹ בַּשְּׂרוּ מִיוֹם לְיוֹם יְשׁוּעָתוֹ.	2 *Sing to God, bless His Name, announce His salvation from day to day.*
ג סַפְּרוּ בַגּוֹיִם כְּבוֹדוֹ בְּכָל הָעַמִּים נִפְלְאוֹתָיו.	3 *Tell me of His glory among the nations, among all peoples His wonders.*
ד כִּי גָדוֹל ה׳ וּמְהֻלָּל מְאֹד נוֹרָא הוּא עַל כָּל אֱלֹהִים.	4 *For God is great and very much praised; He is feared over all divine powers.*
ה כִּי כָּל אֱלֹהֵי הָעַמִּים אֱלִילִים וַה׳ שָׁמַיִם עָשָׂה.	5 *For all the gods of the peoples are naught, but God made the heavens.*
ו הוֹד וְהָדָר לְפָנָיו עֹז וְתִפְאֶרֶת בְּמִקְדָּשׁוֹ.	6 *[They ascribe] beauty and majesty before Him; might and glory in His Sanctuary.*
ז הָבוּ לַה׳ מִשְׁפְּחוֹת עַמִּים הָבוּ לַה׳ כָּבוֹד וָעֹז.	7 *Ascribe to God [you] families of peoples, ascribe to God glory and might.*
ח הָבוּ לַה׳ כְּבוֹד שְׁמוֹ שְׂאוּ מִנְחָה וּבֹאוּ לְחַצְרוֹתָיו.	8 *Ascribe to God the glory due His name; carry an offering and come to his courtyards.*
ט הִשְׁתַּחֲווּ לַה׳ בְּהַדְרַת קֹדֶשׁ חִילוּ מִפָּנָיו כָּל הָאָרֶץ.	9 *Prostrate yourselves to God in the majestic Sanctuary; quake before Him, all the earth.*

י אִמְרוּ בַגּוֹיִם ה' מָלָךְ אַף תִּכּוֹן תֵּבֵל בַּל תִּמּוֹט יָדִין עַמִּים בְּמֵישָׁרִים.	10 *Say among the nations, "God has reigned." Also, the inhabited world will be established so that it will not falter; He will judge peoples with equity.*
יא יִשְׂמְחוּ הַשָּׁמַיִם וְתָגֵל הָאָרֶץ יִרְעַם הַיָּם וּמְלֹאוֹ.	11 *The heavens will rejoice, and the earth will exult; the sea and the fullness thereof will roar.*
יב יַעֲלֹז שָׂדַי וְכָל אֲשֶׁר בּוֹ אָז יְרַנְּנוּ כָּל עֲצֵי יָעַר.	12 *The field and all that is therein will jubilate; then all the forest trees will sing praises.*
יג לִפְנֵי ה' כִּי בָא כִּי בָא לִשְׁפֹּט הָאָרֶץ: יִשְׁפֹּט תֵּבֵל בְּצֶדֶק וְעַמִּים בֶּאֱמוּנָתוֹ.	13 *Before God, for He has come, for He has come to judge the earth; He will judge the inhabited world justly and the peoples with His faith.*

Shiru L'Hashem Shir Chadash is about singing a new song, because in the times of Mashiach, the nations of the world will change their outlook about God and, together with Am Yisrael, will therefore "sing a new song."

Let's contemplate for a moment a few of the significant changes that will occur at the time of *geulah*—redemption:

- The entire world population will recognize Hashem as **the** God of the universe.
- The entire world will also realize that there is **no other** power in the universe besides Hashem.
- The physical world will return to its "original shine." Ever since Adam and Chavah's expulsion from Gan Eden, the universe has simply lost its luster. At the time of Mashiach this, too, will return.

In this *perek* of *Tehillim*, King David describes the future redemptive process listed above:

- *Pesukim* 1–3 speak of the world chorus—Jews and non-Jews alike—who together will one day praise Hashem our God, "*Shiru l'Hashem kol ha'aretz.*"
- *Pesukim* 4–10 tell of the nations of the world realizing that God is the only deity of the world. Therefore, David HaMelech states,

"*Se'u minchah…hishtachavu l'Hashem*—Bring gifts to God at His Temple and bow down to Him."

- *Pesukim* 11–13 foretell an exquisite picture of the world itself in the Messianic era, depicting nature in all of its beauty, expressing joy and deliverance, while extolling the greatness of Hashem.

Finally, we note in *pasuk* 13 the double language of "*ki vah, ki vah lishpot ha'aretz*—when God comes, comes…" What is this repetition coming to teach us?

- The *Radak* states that it is purely poetic and merely provides emphasis.
- The *Malbim*, however, teaches that at the time of Mashiach, Hashem will interact with our world both within nature and above nature. The double language announcing the coming of Hashem refers to both dimensions of His perceived presence on earth.

A DIVINE APPROACH: When we look at nature, such as the mountains, oceans, trees, stars, waterfalls, and snow, consider how they are the handiwork of God, and in their own way, they too praise Hashem.

Tehillim 97: *Hashem Malach Tagel Ha'aretz*—When Nature Will Reveal the Hand of God

א ה' מָלָךְ תָּגֵל הָאָרֶץ יִשְׂמְחוּ אִיִּים רַבִּים.	1 *God has reigned, the earth will exult; many islands will rejoice.*
ב עָנָן וַעֲרָפֶל סְבִיבָיו צֶדֶק וּמִשְׁפָּט מְכוֹן כִּסְאוֹ.	2 *Cloud and thick darkness are around Him; righteousness and judgment are the foundation of His throne.*
ג אֵשׁ לְפָנָיו תֵּלֵךְ וּתְלַהֵט סָבִיב צָרָיו.	3 *Fire will go before Him and will burn His enemies all around.*

ד הֵאִירוּ בְרָקָיו תֵּבֵל רָאֲתָה וַתָּחֵל הָאָרֶץ.	4 *His lightnings illuminated the world; the earth saw and quaked.*
ה הָרִים כַּדּוֹנַג נָמַסּוּ מִלִּפְנֵי ה': מִלִּפְנֵי אֲדוֹן כָּל הָאָרֶץ.	5 *Mountains melted like wax from before God, from before the Master of all the earth.*
ו הִגִּידוּ הַשָּׁמַיִם צִדְקוֹ וְרָאוּ כָל הָעַמִּים כְּבוֹדוֹ.	6 *The heavens told His righteousness, and all the earth saw His glory.*
ז יֵבֹשׁוּ כָּל עֹבְדֵי פֶסֶל הַמִּתְהַלְלִים בָּאֱלִילִים הִשְׁתַּחֲווּ לוֹ כָּל אֱלֹהִים.	7 *All worshippers of graven images will be ashamed, those who boast of idols; all gods, prostrate themselves before Him.*
ח שָׁמְעָה וַתִּשְׂמַח צִיּוֹן וַתָּגֵלְנָה בְּנוֹת יְהוּדָה לְמַעַן מִשְׁפָּטֶיךָ ה'.	8 *Zion heard and rejoiced, and the daughters of Judah exulted, because of Your judgments, O God.*
ט כִּי אַתָּה ה' עֶלְיוֹן עַל כָּל הָאָרֶץ מְאֹד נַעֲלֵיתָ עַל כָּל אֱלֹהִים.	9 *For You, O God, are Most High above all the earth; You are very much exalted above all gods.*
י אֹהֲבֵי ה' שִׂנְאוּ רָע: שֹׁמֵר נַפְשׁוֹת חֲסִידָיו מִיַּד רְשָׁעִים יַצִּילֵם.	10 *You who love God, hate evil; He watches the souls of His pious ones, He rescues them from the hands of the wicked.*
יא אוֹר זָרֻעַ לַצַּדִּיק וּלְיִשְׁרֵי לֵב שִׂמְחָה.	11 *A light is sown for the righteous, and for the upright of heart, joy.*
יב שִׂמְחוּ צַדִּיקִים בַּה' וְהוֹדוּ לְזֵכֶר קָדְשׁוֹ.	12 *Rejoice, you righteous, with God, and give thanks to His holy Name.*

In recent years, the world has been barraged with natural disasters. We have witnessed earthquakes and tsunamis, as well as hurricanes, cyclones, and a pandemic. In our current state of exile without prophecy, we are unable to explain exactly why each occurs and why they take place in the countries they do. However, in the times of Mashiach, the purpose of these types of disasters will be understood clearly, as the wicked will be punished and the righteous will praise God.

This third *perek* of *Kabbalat Shabbat* begins with the words, "*Hashem malach tagel ha'aretz, yismechu iyim rabim*—When God will rule, all of the land will rejoice together, even those in more remote places."

The *perek* then explains why in *pasuk* 3, "*Aish l'fanav teileich u'telahet saviv tzarav*—Because clouds of darkness will surround evildoers, fire will jut forth and lightning will strike and consume all the evil nations of the world."

Pasuk 6 then states: "*Higidu ha'shamayim tzidko v'ra'u kol ha'amim kevodo*—The heavens will reveal God's righteousness, and all of the nations of the world will recognize God's glory." The moment of truth will have arrived.

The Psalmist concludes with the famous *pesukim* 11–12: "*Ohr zarua l'tzaddik u'l'yishrei lev simchah. Simchu tzaddikim*—There is a special light sown for the righteous and joy for the straight-hearted. So, rejoice now and give thanks to God."

The *Metzudat David* explains that the word *zarua* is related to the word *zarei'a*, which means planting. This indicates that just as when we plant a seed, a large vegetable grows that is many times its size, so too, we trust and believe that the Divine reward for the righteous who plant seeds of goodness throughout their lives will also be great and abundant.

The *Radak* comments that this *perek* of *Tehillim* was written to combat feelings of hopelessness and strengthen the hearts of those who feel worn out by the long exile. We are subject to daily headlines in the media that depict a world of chaos, terror, and unrest. David HaMelech reminds us each week, "*Hashem malach tagel ha'aretz*"—there is indeed a just and joyful ending to look forward to.

A DIVINE APPROACH: Although we may sometimes witness in our world that the wicked prosper and the righteous suffer, this phenomenon is only temporary. When Mashiach arrives, we will see clearly that the righteousness will be rewarded and evil will finally be eradicated from the world.

Tehillim 98: Mizmor Shiru L'Hashem — The Inner Circle

א מִזְמוֹר שִׁירוּ לַה׳ שִׁיר חָדָשׁ כִּי נִפְלָאוֹת עָשָׂה הוֹשִׁיעָה לּוֹ יְמִינוֹ וּזְרוֹעַ קָדְשׁוֹ.	1 *A song. Sing to God a new song, for He performed wonders; His right hand and His holy arm have saved Him*
ב הוֹדִיעַ ה׳ יְשׁוּעָתוֹ לְעֵינֵי הַגּוֹיִם גִּלָּה צִדְקָתוֹ.	2 *God has made known His salvation; to the eyes of the nations He has revealed His righteousness.*
ג זָכַר חַסְדּוֹ וֶאֱמוּנָתוֹ לְבֵית יִשְׂרָאֵל: רָאוּ כָל אַפְסֵי אָרֶץ אֵת יְשׁוּעַת אֱלֹהֵינוּ.	3 *He remembered His kindness and His faith to the house of Israel; all the ends of the earth have seen the salvation of our God.*
ד הָרִיעוּ לַה׳ כָּל הָאָרֶץ פִּצְחוּ וְרַנְּנוּ וְזַמֵּרוּ.	4 *Shout to God, all the earth, open [your mouths] and sing praises and play music.*
ה זַמְּרוּ לַה׳ בְּכִנּוֹר בְּכִנּוֹר וְקוֹל זִמְרָה.	5 *Play to God with a harp, with a harp and a voice of song.*
ו בַּחֲצֹצְרוֹת וְקוֹל שׁוֹפָר הָרִיעוּ לִפְנֵי הַמֶּלֶךְ ה׳.	6 *With trumpets and the sound of a shofar, raise your voices before the King, God.*
ז יִרְעַם הַיָּם וּמְלֹאוֹ תֵּבֵל וְיֹשְׁבֵי בָהּ.	7 *The sea and the fullness thereof will roar, the inhabited world and the inhabitants thereof.*
ח נְהָרוֹת יִמְחֲאוּ כָף יַחַד הָרִים יְרַנֵּנוּ.	8 *Rivers will clap hands; together mountains will sing praises.*
ט לִפְנֵי ה׳ כִּי בָא לִשְׁפֹּט הָאָרֶץ: יִשְׁפֹּט תֵּבֵל בְּצֶדֶק וְעַמִּים בְּמֵישָׁרִים.	9 *Before God, for He has come to judge the earth; He will judge the inhabited world justly and the peoples with equity.*

Picture this: You are at a close friend's wedding, waiting for the bride and groom to appear in the ballroom. Suddenly, the band leader introduces the couple for the very first time and the opening dance begins. After a few moments of circling the dance floor, the music changes, and the groom and bride each individually takes hold of close family and friends to form an **inner circle**. There is a palpable sense of joy as those in the inner circles sing and dance harmoniously in honor of the royal couple.

In *Tehillim* 98, David HaMelech foretells of another *shir chadash*, a new song, when Hashem will invite his beloved children—*beit Yisrael*, into the **inner circle**. At that moment, the jubilant members of the inner circle will erupt in an unprecedented harmony; notice *pasuk 4*—*"Pitzchu, v'ranenu v'zameiru."*

Together, their voices will play a full orchestra, as in *pasuk 5*—*"Zamru laHashem b'kinor, b'kinor v'kol zimrah."*

The band will play with joy and inspire praise and gratitude in the hearts of all people in the world; see *pasuk 6*—*"B'chatzotzrot v'kol shofar hariyu lifnei ha'melech*—With trumpets and the sound of a shofar, raise your voices before the King, God."

In *pesukim 7–9*, David HaMelech concludes with the description of the world in unparalleled song in front of God, who is arriving to announce the final judgment over all His creations: *"Yiram ha'yam u'mela'o, tevel v'yoshvei vah, neharot yimcha'u chaf yeranenu. Lifnei Hashem ki bah lishpot ha'aretz*—The sea, the earth, and its inhabitants, as well as the rivers will sing in unison as God arrives to judge His world."

The question is, why is this a joyous time? Perhaps it should be an anxious and tense time when Divine justice will be meted out. The answer is that nothing is as uplifting and euphoric as truth, even with its (sometimes difficult) consequences. While we may sometimes think that ignorance is bliss, our souls—endowed unto us by the God of truth—deep down crave truth. In life, genuine happiness and fulfillment is achieved when we experience truth.

Indeed, may we merit experiencing the ultimate truth and happiness soon in our days.

A DIVINE APPROACH: When we daven and do mitzvot let's maintain an awareness that we, Am Yisrael, are in the **inner circle** of Hashem. Being part of the inner circle is a privilege, as well as a responsibility.

Tehillim 99: *Hashem Malach Yirgezu Amim*— The Footstool to Heaven

א ה׳ מָלַךְ יִרְגְּזוּ עַמִּים יֹשֵׁב כְּרוּבִים תָּנוּט הָאָרֶץ.	1 *God has reigned, nations will quake; [before] Him who dwells between the cherubim, the earth will falter.*
ב ה׳ בְּצִיּוֹן גָּדוֹל וְרָם הוּא עַל כָּל הָעַמִּים.	2 *God is great in Zion, and He is high over all the peoples.*
ג יוֹדוּ שִׁמְךָ גָּדוֹל וְנוֹרָא קָדוֹשׁ הוּא.	3 *They will acknowledge Your great and awesome name, [that] it is holy,*
ד וְעֹז מֶלֶךְ מִשְׁפָּט אָהֵב: אַתָּה כּוֹנַנְתָּ מֵישָׁרִים מִשְׁפָּט וּצְדָקָה בְּיַעֲקֹב אַתָּה עָשִׂיתָ.	4 *And the might of the King who loves judgment; You founded equity; judgment and righteousness You made in Yaakov.*
ה רוֹמְמוּ ה׳ אֱלֹהֵינוּ וְהִשְׁתַּחֲווּ לַהֲדֹם רַגְלָיו: קָדוֹשׁ הוּא.	5 *Exalt God, our Lord, and prostrate yourselves to His footstool, it is holy.*
ו מֹשֶׁה וְאַהֲרֹן בְּכֹהֲנָיו וּשְׁמוּאֵל בְּקֹרְאֵי שְׁמוֹ קֹרִאים אֶל ה׳ וְהוּא יַעֲנֵם.	6 *Moshe and Aharon among His priests, and Shmuel among those who call in His name, would call out to God, and He would answer them.*
ז בְּעַמּוּד עָנָן יְדַבֵּר אֲלֵיהֶם שָׁמְרוּ עֵדֹתָיו וְחֹק נָתַן לָמוֹ.	7 *In a pillar of cloud He would speak to them; they kept His testimonies and the statutes He gave them.*
ח ה׳ אֱלֹהֵינוּ אַתָּה עֲנִיתָם: אֵל נֹשֵׂא הָיִיתָ לָהֶם וְנֹקֵם עַל עֲלִילוֹתָם.	8 *God, our Lord, You answered them; You were a forgiving God for them but vengeful for their misdeeds.*
ט רוֹמְמוּ ה׳ אֱלֹהֵינוּ וְהִשְׁתַּחֲווּ לְהַר קָדְשׁוֹ: כִּי קָדוֹשׁ ה׳ אֱלֹהֵינוּ.	9 *Exalt God, our Lord, and prostrate yourselves to the mount of His sanctuary, for God, our Lord, is holy.*

Tehillim 99 is the last of the consecutive *perakim* recited during the Friday night *Kabbalat Shabbat* service. David HaMelech again foretells of the thundering revelation of God's presence on earth amid awe and trembling and invites Klal Yisrael to praise the God of Zion.

There is a fascinating imagery presented in *pasuk* 5 of the *perek*: "*Romemu Hashem Elokeinu v'hishtachavu la'hadom raglav kadosh Hu*—Praise God, our Lord, and bow down toward His **footstool** that is holy." What exactly is God's footstool? Additionally, at the conclusion of the *perek* it states: "*Romemu Hashem...v'hishtachavu l'har kadsho*—Praise God...bow toward the holy mountain." What happened to the footstool?

The commentators remark that God's footstool is a metaphor for the Beit Hamikdash, the Holy Temple in Jerusalem. The question is, why is God's Temple referred to as a footstool?

The *Malbim* explains that when we see an occupied footstool, we understand that connected to the foot resting on the footstool exists a person with legs, a body, arms, and a head. So too, the Beit Hamikdash is referred to as God's "footstool" because it is the earthly connection to the omnipotent presence of God in the heavens above. Just as a footstool provides only a glimpse of the being that rests on it, so too we know that the Shechinah—God's presence in the Temple—is just a taste of the eternal presence of Hashem.

The latter *pasuk* omits reference to the footstool, indicating that in the times of Mashiach, we will no longer be limited to the "footstool experience" of Hashem. We will engage with Hashem directly without limitations and barriers. God's presence will no longer reside in heaven; rather, God will reveal Himself on earth as well.

A DIVINE APPROACH: It is possible to go to shul and pray every morning and evening in order to serve God and completely lose sight of the true aim of prayer. Remember, every shul is likened to the Beit Hamikdash and is therefore our local "footstool" that connects us to God.

Mizmor L'David and *Ana Ba'koach*

א מִזְמוֹר לְדָוִד: הָבוּ לַה' בְּנֵי אֵלִים הָבוּ לַה' כָּבוֹד וָעֹז.	1 *A song of David. Prepare for God, [you] sons of the mighty; prepare for God glory and might.*
ב הָבוּ ה' כְּבוֹד שְׁמוֹ הִשְׁתַּחֲווּ לַה' בְּהַדְרַת קֹדֶשׁ.	2 *Prepare for God the glory due His name; prostrate yourselves to God in the place beautified with sanctity.*
ג קוֹל ה' עַל הַמָּיִם: אֵל הַכָּבוֹד הִרְעִים ה' עַל מַיִם רַבִּים.	3 *The voice of God is upon the waters; the God of glory thunders; God is over the vast waters.*
ד קוֹל ה' בַּכֹּחַ קוֹל ה' בֶּהָדָר.	4 *The voice of God is in strength; the voice of God is in beauty.*
ה קוֹל ה' שֹׁבֵר אֲרָזִים וַיְשַׁבֵּר ה' אֶת אַרְזֵי הַלְּבָנוֹן.	5 *The voice of God breaks the cedars, yea, God breaks the cedars of Lebanon.*
ו וַיַּרְקִידֵם כְּמוֹ עֵגֶל לְבָנוֹן וְשִׂרְיֹן כְּמוֹ בֶן רְאֵמִים.	6 *He causes them to dance like a calf, Lebanon and Sirion like a young wild ox.*
ז קוֹל ה' חֹצֵב לַהֲבוֹת אֵשׁ.	7 *The voice of God cleaves with flames of fire.*
ח קוֹל ה' יָחִיל מִדְבָּר יָחִיל ה' מִדְבַּר קָדֵשׁ.	8 *The voice of God causes the desert to quake; God causes the desert of Kadesh to quake.*
ט קוֹל ה' יְחוֹלֵל אַיָּלוֹת וַיֶּחֱשֹׂף יְעָרוֹת: וּבְהֵיכָלוֹ כֻּלּוֹ אֹמֵר כָּבוֹד.	9 *The voice of God will frighten the hinds and strip the forests, and in His Temple, everyone speaks of His glory.*
י ה' לַמַּבּוּל יָשָׁב וַיֵּשֶׁב ה' מֶלֶךְ לְעוֹלָם.	10 *God sat [enthroned] at the flood; God sat as King forever.*
יא ה' עֹז לְעַמּוֹ יִתֵּן ה' יְבָרֵךְ אֶת עַמּוֹ בַשָּׁלוֹם.	11 *God shall grant strength to His people; God shall bless His people with peace.*
אָנָּא בְּכֹחַ גְּדֻלַּת יְמִינְךָ תַּתִּיר צְרוּרָה:	*We beg You, with the great power of Your right hand, release the bound.*
קַבֵּל רִנַּת עַמְּךָ, שַׂגְּבֵנוּ, טַהֲרֵנוּ, נוֹרָא:	*Accept the supplication of Your people; fortify us, purify us, O Awesome One.*

נָא גִבּוֹר דּוֹרְשֵׁי יְחוּדְךָ כְּבָבַת שָׁמְרֵם:	*Please, O mighty One, guard those who seek Your oneness, as one guards the apple of the eye.*
בָּרְכֵם טַהֲרֵם רַחֲמֵי צִדְקָתְךָ תָּמִיד גָּמְלֵם:	*Bless them, purify them; bestow upon them always Your merciful righteousness.*
חֲסִין קָדוֹשׁ בְּרוֹב טוּבְךָ נַהֵל עֲדָתֶךָ:	*mighty and Holy One, in Your abundant goodness, guide Your congregation.*
יָחִיד גֵּאֶה לְעַמְּךָ פְּנֵה זוֹכְרֵי קְדֻשָּׁתֶךָ:	*Unique and Exalted One, turn to Your people, who recall Your holiness.*
שַׁוְעָתֵנוּ קַבֵּל וּשְׁמַע צַעֲקָתֵנוּ יוֹדֵעַ תַּעֲלֻמוֹת:	*Accept our prayers; hear our cry, Knower of hidden things.*
בָּרוּךְ שֵׁם כְּבוֹד מַלְכוּתוֹ לְעוֹלָם וָעֶד:	*Blessed be the name of His glorious kingdom forever and ever.*

Although we will explore *Tehillim* 29 (*Mizmor L'David* in our section on *Mussaf*), since we recite it during *Kabbalat Shabbat* (and the commentaries stress that it should be recited with vigor and joy!) it is worthwhile for us to comment on it at this point as well.

After we recite the five consecutive *perakim* (95–99) that correspond to the first five days of the week, we rise from our seats and recite *Tehillim* 29, which corresponds to the sixth day, Erev Shabbat. We stand up in honor and awe of the presence of God. We experience His presence now, as Shabbat, the weekly Messianic day of eternity has arrived. We sing joyously, "*Havu laShem b'nei eilim*—You, the children of our Patriarchs, give unto God, Give unto Him your honor and strength, and bow down in this holy space."

The last line of the *perek* reads, "*Hashem oz l'amo yiten, Hashem yevarech et amo ba'shalom*—God gives strength [Torah] to his people, God shall bless us with peace."

Peace is actually one of the names of God, and many of our prayers conclude with the call for peace, such as the *Amidah*, *Birkat Hamazon*, *Birkat Kohanim*, and *Kaddish*. As the last Mishnah in *Uktzin* states:

"There is no greater vessel for blessing then peace."[2] Similarly, *Rashi*[3] states in *Parashat Bechukotai*, "*Im ein shalom ein klum*—If there is no peace, there is nothing at all."[4] In other words, blessings are sustainable amid peace. Since *Tehillim* 29 represents the final day and era before Shabbat, the time of Mashiach, it is accompanied with the blessing of *shalom*—peace.

While standing, we then recite the mystical prayer of the Tanna, Rebbe Nechunia ben HaKana, *Ana Ba'koach*, "We Beg of You." The great Kabbalists considered this prayer to be incredibly powerful, replete with many allusions:

- It contains forty-two words; the first letters of these words form the mystical forty-two-letter name of God.
- These forty-two letters also correspond to the forty-two places mentioned in the Torah where the nation of Israel encamped during the forty years in the desert before entering Eretz Yisrael.
- Traditionally there are also forty-two lines in each column of a *Sefer Torah*.
- The prayer is divided into seven *pesukim* of six words each. These seven lines correspond to the seven *sefirot*: *chessed, gevurah, tiferet, netzach, hod, yesod,* and *malchut*, which translates to kindness, strength, splendor, eternity, glory, foundation, and kingship. These are the seven Kabbalistic dimensions of Godliness that reflect upon His creation.

Therefore, as we conclude the six *perakim* of *Tehillim* that correspond to the six days of the week and the first six thousand years of creation, we welcome the eternal presence of God into the world and into our lives by uttering His Holy Name, constructed within the *tefillah* of *Ana Ba'koach*.

Our preparation is near complete. Shabbat is here!

---

2   *Uktzin* 3:12.
3   Rabbi Shlomo Yitzchaki (1040–1105).
4   *Vayikra* 26:6.

> A DIVINE APPROACH: During the Friday night Shabbat *zemirot* we chant, "*M'ein olam haba yom Shabbat menuchah*—Shabbat tranquility is tantamount to the World to Come." This transforming experience begins during the *tefillah* of *Kabbalat Shabbat*. Close your eyes and experience the sweetness of Shabbat.

Lechah Dodi

לְכָה דוֹדִי לִקְרַאת כַּלָּה. פְּנֵי שַׁבָּת נְקַבְּלָה:	Come, my Beloved, to meet the Bride; let us welcome the Shabbat.
שָׁמוֹר וְזָכוֹר בְּדִבּוּר אֶחָד הִשְׁמִיעָנוּ אֵל הַמְיֻחָד. ה׳ אֶחָד וּשְׁמוֹ אֶחָד. לְשֵׁם וּלְתִפְאֶרֶת וְלִתְהִלָּה:	"Observe" and "Remember," the one and only G-d caused us to hear in a single utterance; God is One and His Name is One, for renown, for glory, and for praise.
לְכָה דוֹדִי לִקְרַאת כַּלָּה. פְּנֵי שַׁבָּת נְקַבְּלָה:	Come, my Beloved, to meet the Bride; let us welcome the Shabbat.
לִקְרַאת שַׁבָּת לְכוּ וְנֵלְכָה. כִּי הִיא מְקוֹר הַבְּרָכָה. מֵרֹאשׁ מִקֶּדֶם נְסוּכָה. סוֹף מַעֲשֶׂה בְּמַחֲשָׁבָה תְּחִלָּה:	Come, let us go to welcome the Shabbat, for it is the source of blessing; from the beginning, from aforetime, it was chosen; last in creation, first in [G-d's] thought.
לְכָה דוֹדִי לִקְרַאת כַּלָּה. פְּנֵי שַׁבָּת נְקַבְּלָה:	Come, my Beloved, to meet the Bride; let us welcome the Shabbat.
מִקְדַּשׁ מֶלֶךְ עִיר מְלוּכָה. קוּמִי צְאִי מִתּוֹךְ הַהֲפֵכָה. רַב לָךְ שֶׁבֶת בְּעֵמֶק הַבָּכָא. וְהוּא יַחֲמוֹל עָלַיִךְ חֶמְלָה:	Sanctuary of the King, royal city, arise, go forth from the ruins; too long have you dwelt in the valley of tears; He will show you abounding mercy.
לְכָה דוֹדִי לִקְרַאת כַּלָּה. פְּנֵי שַׁבָּת נְקַבְּלָה:	Come, my Beloved, to meet the Bride; let us welcome the Shabbat.

הִתְנַעֲרִי מֵעָפָר קוּמִי. לִבְשִׁי בִּגְדֵי תִפְאַרְתֵּךְ עַמִּי: עַל יַד בֶּן יִשַׁי בֵּית הַלַּחְמִי. קָרְבָה אֶל נַפְשִׁי גְאָלָהּ:	*Shake the dust off yourself, arise, don your glorious garments—my people. Through the son of Yishai of Beit Lechem, draw near to my soul and redeem it.*
לְכָה דוֹדִי לִקְרַאת כַּלָּה. פְּנֵי שַׁבָּת נְקַבְּלָה:	*Come, my Beloved, to meet the Bride; let us welcome the Shabbat.*
הִתְעוֹרְרִי הִתְעוֹרְרִי. כִּי בָא אוֹרֵךְ קוּמִי אוֹרִי. עוּרִי עוּרִי שִׁיר דַּבֵּרִי. כְּבוֹד ה' עָלַיִךְ נִגְלָה.	*Arouse yourself, arouse yourself, for your light has come; arise, shine. Awake, awake, utter a song; the glory of God is revealed upon you.*
לְכָה דוֹדִי לִקְרַאת כַּלָּה. פְּנֵי שַׁבָּת נְקַבְּלָה:	*Come, my Beloved, to meet the Bride; let us welcome the Shabbat.*
לֹא תֵבוֹשִׁי וְלֹא תִכָּלְמִי. מַה תִּשְׁתּוֹחֲחִי וּמַה תֶּהֱמִי. בָּךְ יֶחֱסוּ עֲנִיֵּי עַמִּי, וְנִבְנְתָה עִיר עַל תִּלָּהּ:	*Do not be ashamed nor confounded; why are you downcast and why are you agitated? The afflicted of my people will find refuge in you; the city will be rebuilt on its former site.*
לְכָה דוֹדִי לִקְרַאת כַּלָּה. פְּנֵי שַׁבָּת נְקַבְּלָה:	*Come, my Beloved, to meet the Bride; let us welcome the Shabbat.*
וְהָיוּ לִמְשִׁסָּה שֹׁאסָיִךְ. וְרָחֲקוּ כָּל מְבַלְּעָיִךְ. יָשִׂישׂ עָלַיִךְ אֱלֹהָיִךְ. כִּמְשׂוֹשׂ חָתָן עַל כַּלָּה:	*Those who despoil you will be despoiled, and all who would destroy you will be far away. Your God will rejoice over you as a bridegroom rejoices over his bride.*
לְכָה דוֹדִי לִקְרַאת כַּלָּה. פְּנֵי שַׁבָּת נְקַבְּלָה:	*Come, my Beloved, to meet the Bride; let us welcome the Shabbat.*
יָמִין וּשְׂמֹאל תִּפְרוֹצִי. וְאֶת ה' תַּעֲרִיצִי. עַל יַד אִישׁ בֶּן פַּרְצִי. וְנִשְׂמְחָה וְנָגִילָה:	*To the right and to the left you shall spread out, and God you shall extol. And we shall rejoice and exult, through the man who is a descendant of Peretz.*
לְכָה דוֹדִי לִקְרַאת כַּלָּה. פְּנֵי שַׁבָּת נְקַבְּלָה:	*Come, my Beloved, to meet the Bride; let us welcome the Shabbat.*

בּוֹאִי בְשָׁלוֹם עֲטֶרֶת בַּעְלָהּ.	*Come in peace, O crown of her Husband,*
גַּם בְּשִׂמְחָה וּבְצָהֳלָה.	*both with songs and gladness; among the*
תּוֹךְ אֱמוּנֵי עַם סְגֻלָּה. בּוֹאִי	*faithful, the beloved people, come, O Bride,*
כַלָּה, בּוֹאִי כַלָּה:	*come, O Bride.*

לְכָה דוֹדִי לִקְרַאת כַּלָּה.	*Come, my Beloved, to meet the Bride; let us*
פְּנֵי שַׁבָּת נְקַבְּלָה:	*welcome the Shabbat.*

The crescendo of the *Kabbalat Shabbat* service is the beautiful poem called *Lechah Dodi*, "Come, My Beloved." It was composed by Rav Shlomo HaLevi Alkabetz, who lived in Tzfat in the sixteenth century alongside the great scholars and Kabbalists of the day, such as the holy *Ari*, Rav Moshe Cordovero, and Rav Yosef Karo, author of our *Shulchan Aruch*. The first letter of each of the eight *pesukim* spells out the name of the author, "Shlomo HaLevi" as an acrostic style signature. The *tefillah* has been embraced by all walks of Jewish life and can be heard in Ashkenazic, Sephardic, and Chassidic synagogues every Friday night.

Source of the Prayer

The commentators teach that the basis for the *tefillah* is a passage in the Talmud that states: "Rabbi Chanina would wrap himself in his garb Erev Shabbat and proclaim: 'Let us go and greet the Shabbat Queen.' Rabbi Yannai said, 'Please enter, my bride, oh, enter my bride.'"[5]

In fact, it was customary years ago to exit the synagogue at sunset and enter the fields to welcome the Shabbat.

Shabbat, Our Bride

Before we approach the actual content of the poem, we must understand why Shabbat is manifested as a bride or a queen. After all, it is unusual for any of our mitzvot, holidays, or rituals to be portrayed as a personified character.

The *Vilna Gaon* in his Aggadic commentary explains that the reason that Shabbat is referenced as a bride and queen is because all the other

---

5   *Shabbat* 119a.

days of Creation have a partner, while Shabbat was missing its *zivug* (partner):[6]

- Sunday and Wednesday are partners because on both days there was a creation involving light.
- Monday and Thursday are partners because on both days there was a creation involving water.
- Tuesday and Friday are partners because on both days there was a creation involving earth.

The only day missing a natural partner was Shabbat. Hashem remedied the situation and willed that the partner of Shabbat would be us—Am Yisrael. We were destined for each other from the time of Creation; we are a match made in Heaven!

This explains why the three different *tefillot* on Shabbat correspond to the three parts of a wedding:

- On Friday night, we recite, "*Atah Kidashta*," which represents *kiddushin*.
- On Shabbat morning, we recite, "*Yismach Moshe…kelil tiferet…al Har Sinai*," which represents *nisu'in* under a *chuppah*, just as we stood under Har Sinai to receive the Torah.
- On Shabbat afternoon during *Minchah*, we recite, "*Atah echad…u'mi k'amcha beit Yisrael*," which represents *yichud*, marital intimacy, after the *chuppah*.

In keeping with this theme of a wedding, the meals on Shabbat are celebrations of our relationship to the Shabbat. Therefore, we sing, "*Lechah dodi likrat kallah*—Let us go greet our bride," the Shabbat Queen.

The Shabbat Queen

The opening verse and refrain of this poem is: "*Lechah dodi likrat kallah p'nei Shabbat nekablah*—Come, my Beloved, to greet the bride, the Shabbat presence we welcome."

The commentators explain that "*dodi*—my Beloved," is actually God!

---

6   *Bava Kama* 32b.

It seems strange that we invite God to go greet the Shabbat Queen. Who is this mysterious Shabbat Queen?

Rav Pincus explains in *Shabbat Malketa* that the Shabbat Queen represents God's royal, omnipotent, and eternally redemptive presence—the Shechinah. Therefore, we sing, "*Lechah dodi*—Come forth, God; let's go together and transcend this earthly existence and greet the eternity within Shabbat, *p'nei Shabbat.*"

There are several stanzas to the *Lechah Dodi* poem:

- The first stanza recalls the moment at Har Sinai that Hashem commands the Jewish nation to observe Shabbat, "*Shamor v'zachor b'dibbur echad.*" Hashem miraculously voices simultaneously the positive commandment of *zachor* (to remember) and the restriction of *shamor* (to guard). Our tradition teaches that the Torah was actually transmitted on Shabbat itself, which signifies the centrality of Shabbat in Jewish thought and Jewish life.[7] As the famous saying goes: More than the Jews have kept Shabbat, Shabbat has kept the Jews.
- The next stanza is "*Likrat Shabbat lechu v'neilchah ki hi mekor ha'berachah*—Let us go welcome the Shabbat because it is the source of all blessing.*"

There are two significant messages layered within these holy words:

- To engage the majesty of Shabbat, one must extend himself and reach for the Shabbat—"*Likrat Shabbat lechu v'neilchah.*"
- When we celebrate Shabbat correctly, we experience a taste of the World to Come, for it is the source of all blessings.

Consolation and Hope

The remaining stanzas of *Lechah Dodi* include prayers for Yerushalayim, God's throne, and the demise of our oppressors.

What do these have to do with Shabbat? Why do we focus on these ideas now?

---

7   *Shabbat* 86b.

The answer is that these words are not merely referring to our weekly observance of Shabbat, but rather to the time when the entire world will be in a state of Shabbat—the time of Mashiach. In the true future Shabbat, there will be no oppression, and God's glory will be revealed.

The remaining seven stanzas of *Lechah Dodi* are divided into three parts:

1. *Mikdash melech*, *Hitnaari*, and *Hitoreri* all include words of consolation, hope, and renewal of Yerushalayim from a state of exile. We pray that Yerushalayim, the throne of Hashem, will arise from her desolation, cloak herself with splendor, and prepare for the coming of the eternal redemption led by Mashiach ben Yishai, of Beit Lechem.

2. *Lo tevoshi*, *V'hayu limshisah*, and *Yamin u'smol* are a collection of phrases taken from the redemptive prophecies of the *navi* Yeshayahu. These stanzas foretell the eventual rebuilding, celebration, and expansion of the holy city of Yerushalayim.

3. The final stanza, *Bo'i b'shalom*, greets God's presence. It is chanted with true joy and fervor. The custom is to turn around and face the west as the sun is setting and acknowledge the Shechinah's arrival.

In his commentary on the siddur, *Beit Yaakov*, Rav Yaakov Emden writes that at the conclusion of this last stanza, we bow three times:

1. First to the left (toward the right of the Shechinah) and recite, "*Bo'i kallah.*"
2. Then to the right and recite, "*Bo'i kallah.*"
3. Finally, to the center and recite, "*Bo'i Shabbat malketa.*"

He explains that before the Shechinah ascends the throne, she is a *kallah* (a bride), but once she arrives in the palace, she is crowned *malketa* (the queen).

Several times in our discussion of *Kabbalat Shabbat*, we have compared Shabbat to a bride and a queen. It is noteworthy that in the sixth stanza we recite, "*Yasis alayich Elokayich kimsos chattan al kallah*—God will rejoice with you like a groom rejoices with his newly beloved bride." What an image!

Concluding thought: In the *Nefesh Hachaim*,[8] Rav Chaim Volozhiner writes that when we daven, we should not merely focus on our own needs, but also the honor and dignity of Hashem. When Am Yisrael is downtrodden and in exile, it is an embarrassment to God. During *Lechah Dodi*, we not only greet the Shabbat and the Shechinah, we also envision the glory of Hashem revealed: *"kimsos chattan al kallah*—like a groom with his bride."

A DIVINE APPROACH: Our relationship with Shabbat is like a marriage. The more time and energy one invests in their marriage, the better it becomes. So too, the more one learns about, prepares for, and invests energies into Shabbat, the more will be gained. Finally, when we sing *Lechah Dodi*, let's remember that Shabbat is the source of all blessings and provides a true taste of the World to Come.

Tehillim 92: Mizmor Shir L'Yom HaShabbat

א מִזְמוֹר שִׁיר לְיוֹם הַשַּׁבָּת.	1 *A song with musical accompaniment for the Shabbat day.*
ב טוֹב לְהֹדוֹת לַה׳ וּלְזַמֵּר לְשִׁמְךָ עֶלְיוֹן.	2 *It is good to give thanks to God, and to sing to Your name, O Most High.*
ג לְהַגִּיד בַּבֹּקֶר חַסְדֶּךָ וֶאֱמוּנָתְךָ בַּלֵּילוֹת.	3 *To declare in the morning Your kindness and Your faith at night.*
ד עֲלֵי עָשׂוֹר וַעֲלֵי נָבֶל עֲלֵי הִגָּיוֹן בְּכִנּוֹר.	4 *Upon a ten-stringed harp and upon a psaltery, with speech upon a harp.*
ה כִּי שִׂמַּחְתַּנִי ה׳ בְּפָעֳלֶךָ בְּמַעֲשֵׂי יָדֶיךָ אֲרַנֵּן.	5 *For You have made me happy, God, with Your work; with the work of Your hands I shall exult.*
ו מַה גָּדְלוּ מַעֲשֶׂיךָ ה׳ מְאֹד עָמְקוּ מַחְשְׁבֹתֶיךָ.	6 *How great are Your works, God! Your thoughts are very deep.*
ז אִישׁ בַּעַר לֹא יֵדָע וּכְסִיל לֹא יָבִין אֶת זֹאת.	7 *A boorish man does not know; neither does a fool understand this.*

---

8   *Nefesh Hachaim, shaar 2.*

ח בִּפְרֹחַ רְשָׁעִים כְּמוֹ עֵשֶׂב וַיָּצִיצוּ כָּל פֹּעֲלֵי אָוֶן לְהִשָּׁמְדָם עֲדֵי עַד.	8 *When the wicked flourish like grass, and all workers of violence blossom, only to be destroyed to eternity.*
ט וְאַתָּה מָרוֹם לְעֹלָם ה׳.	9 *But You remain on high forever, God.*
י כִּי הִנֵּה אֹיְבֶיךָ ה׳ כִּי הִנֵּה אֹיְבֶיךָ יֹאבֵדוּ: יִתְפָּרְדוּ כָּל פֹּעֲלֵי אָוֶן.	10 *For behold Your enemies, God, for behold Your enemies will perish; all workers of violence will scatter.*
יא וַתָּרֶם כִּרְאֵים קַרְנִי בַּלֹּתִי בְּשֶׁמֶן רַעֲנָן.	11 *But You have raised my horn like that of a wild ox; to soak me with fresh oil.*
יב וַתַּבֵּט עֵינִי בְּשׁוּרָי: בַּקָּמִים עָלַי מְרֵעִים תִּשְׁמַעְנָה אָזְנָי.	12 *My eye has gazed upon those who stare at me [with envy]; when evildoers rise up against me, my ears hear [them].*
יג צַדִּיק כַּתָּמָר יִפְרָח כְּאֶרֶז בַּלְּבָנוֹן יִשְׂגֶּה.	13 *The righteous one flourishes like the palm; as a cedar in Lebanon he grows.*
יד שְׁתוּלִים בְּבֵית ה׳ בְּחַצְרוֹת אֱלֹהֵינוּ יַפְרִיחוּ.	14 *Planted in the house of God, in the courts of our God they will flourish.*
טו עוֹד יְנוּבוּן בְּשֵׂיבָה דְּשֵׁנִים וְרַעֲנַנִּים יִהְיוּ.	15 *They will yet grow in old age; fat and fresh will they be.*
טז לְהַגִּיד כִּי יָשָׁר ה׳ צוּרִי וְלֹא עלתה (עַוְלָתָה) בּוֹ.	16 *To declare that God is upright, my Rock in Whom there is no injustice.*

After the festive singing of *Lechah Dodi* and the ushering in of the Shabbat Queen, we acknowledge our cosmic shift from the mundane week to the holy Shabbat by reciting *Tehillim 92*—"Mizmor Shir L'Yom HaShabbat—the song of Shabbat." This *perek* reflects the future Messianic world of purity, clarity, and eternity. The *perek* contains several themes, which will be explained below.

Teshuvah—Repentance

Shabbat is a time for *teshuvah*, a time to return to God and to one's own inner self; hence the root of the word Shabbat—*shuv*—to return. Regarding the *pasuk*, "*Tov l'hodot laHashem*—It is good to praise God,"

Chazal remark that it was originally stated by the first man of the world, Adam, after he repented from the sin of eating the Forbidden Fruit. It may also be interpreted as *"Tov l'hitvadot laHashem*—It is good to confess to God."[9] Before Shabbat arrives each week, it is a time for all Jews to perform an inner search and attend to any past wrongdoings.

Seeing the Big Picture

"Ish baar lo yeida u'ksil lo yavin et zot—A boor cannot know and a fool will not understand." The Psalmist intimates that the sophisticated understand that evil has a place in our world—temporarily—to endow mankind with freedom of choice.[10] The wise realize that eventually all evil and evildoers will cease to exist. Since God is eternal, we know that eventually all good will be rewarded and all evil will be punished precisely.

When Evil Will Collapse and the Righteous Will Prosper

The *perek* states that *"b'fro'ach resha'im kemo eisev,"* when the wicked prosper, it appears to the masses that there is no ultimate Judge and there is no justice. In the end it will all be clear: *"Yitpardu kol po'alei aven*—The evil will be scattered," and *"Tzaddik k'tamar yifrach k'erez ba'levanon yisgeh*—The righteous will flower like a palm and grow tall like cedars." Since Shabbat provides us a glimpse of the World to Come, we envision the time when Divine justice will be clear to the entire world.

A DIVINE APPROACH: When we do our weekly preparations for Shabbat, let's try to do *teshuvah* by reflecting upon our week and considering areas in which we can actively improve. As we celebrate Shabbat in our finest clothing, enjoying the delicacies of the day, let us remind ourselves that this is only a shadow of the time when all evil will cease, when only goodness will remain, and the world will be in a complete state of Shabbat.

---

9   *Yalkut Shimoni, Tehillim* 92.
10   The *Malbim* commentary on the *pasuk*.

Tehillim 93: Hashem Malach Ge'ut Lavesh

א ה' מָלָךְ גֵּאוּת לָבֵשׁ: לָבֵשׁ ה' עֹז הִתְאַזָּר אַף תִּכּוֹן תֵּבֵל בַּל תִּמּוֹט.	1 *God has reigned; He has attired Himself with majesty; God has attired Himself, He has girded Himself with might. The world also is established that it cannot be moved.*
ב נָכוֹן כִּסְאֲךָ מֵאָז מֵעוֹלָם אָתָּה.	2 *Your throne is established of old; You are from everlasting.*
ג נָשְׂאוּ נְהָרוֹת ה' נָשְׂאוּ נְהָרוֹת קוֹלָם יִשְׂאוּ נְהָרוֹת דָּכְיָם.	3 *The rivers have raised, God, the rivers have raised their voice; the rivers have raised their depths.*
ד מִקֹּלוֹת מַיִם רַבִּים אַדִּירִים מִשְׁבְּרֵי יָם אַדִּיר בַּמָּרוֹם ה'.	4 *More than the voices of great waters and more than the mightiest breakers of the sea is God mighty on high.*
ה עֵדֹתֶיךָ נֶאֶמְנוּ מְאֹד לְבֵיתְךָ נַאֲוָה קֹדֶשׁ ה' לְאֹרֶךְ יָמִים.	5 *Your testimonies are very faithful to Your house, the dwelling of holiness, God, to the length of days.*

The commentators explain that this *perek* is also depicting the future Messianic era—the time when God and the secrets of the universe will be revealed.

The *Malbim* explains that God conducts the world in two different modes: nature and miraculous. One would be inclined to believe that miraculous is a greater state than nature, but this is not so. Miracles take place for a short period of time, but nature is constant and unchanging, which is a greater task. In effect, nature is more miraculous than miracles. Additionally, when Hashem does peform the miraculous, He still maintains nature simultaneously outside of the miracle throughout the rest of the universe.

These concepts are stated in the first *pasuk* of this *perek*. The *Malbim* writes that the word *ge'ut* refers to the miraculous, and the word *oz* refers to nature; the *pasuk* means that in the Messianic era, while God will perform miracles, nature will continue as well.

At that time, all will realize that Hashem created this world and has been sustaining its existence throughout history.

Water is the metaphor used in this *perek* to demonstrate God's dominion over nature and the supernatural simultaneously. While water is natural and rests reliably over a large percentage of the earth, water is also plentiful in some places and sparse in others. Without water we could not live, but with flooding and storms life is endangered. Hashem decides which location receives which amount of water every moment of every day.

The *perek* concludes with the realization that although God is beyond time and space and, in truth, even our comprehension, "*Eidotecha*—Your testimonies," through *Nevi'im* and *Ketuvim*, reveal that God's presence will ultimately be consistently close to us in His dwelling place on earth—the Beit Hamikdash in Yerushalayim in the times of Mashiach.

We look forward to the time when the words of the *Tehillim* of *Kabbalat Shabbat* will materialize in front of our eyes.

A DIVINE APPROACH: When we read of the miracles that Hashem performs in the Torah, let's remember and recognize that while a miracle is unfolding and nature is being suspended, at that time and place, God is simulataneously maintaining nature throughout the rest of the world. This is a great demonstration of Divine Providence and how God interacts simultaneously with all of His creatures and Creation.

Chapter Two

SHABBAT MAARIV

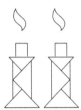

At the conclusion of *Kabbalat Shabbat* and the recital of *Bameh Madlikin* or *K'Gavna*, the custom in many shuls is for the chazzan to physically advance from the *shulchan* toward the bimah to lead *Shabbat Maariv*—the evening prayers for Shabbat. This prayer is recited after sunset, and in many communities the custom is to wait until the stars are visible before beginning. The reason for this is because we recite the evening *Shema* during *Maariv*. The Biblically prescribed time to recite the evening *Shema* is when it is night.

Ha'maariv Aravim

בָּרוּךְ אַתָּה ה׳ אֱלֹהֵינוּ מֶלֶךְ הָעוֹלָם אֲשֶׁר בִּדְבָרוֹ מַעֲרִיב עֲרָבִים בְּחָכְמָה פּוֹתֵחַ שְׁעָרִים	*Blessed are You, God, our Lord, ruler of the universe, who speaks the evening into being, skillfully opens the gates,*
וּבִתְבוּנָה מְשַׁנֶּה עִתִּים וּמַחֲלִיף אֶת הַזְּמַנִּים וּמְסַדֵּר אֶת הַכּוֹכָבִים בְּמִשְׁמְרוֹתֵיהֶם בָּרָקִיעַ כִּרְצוֹנוֹ.	*thoughtfully alters the time and changes the seasons, and arranges the stars in their heavenly courses according to plan.*

בּוֹרֵא יוֹם וָלַיְלָה גּוֹלֵל אוֹר	*You are creator of day and night, rolling light*
מִפְּנֵי חֹשֶׁךְ וְחֹשֶׁךְ מִפְּנֵי אוֹר	*away from darkness and darkness from light,*
וּמַעֲבִיר יוֹם וּמֵבִיא לָיְלָה	*transforming day into night and distinguishing*
וּמַבְדִּיל בֵּין יוֹם וּבֵין לָיְלָה	*one from the other. Hashem Tzeva'ot is*
ה' צְבָאוֹת שְׁמוֹ:	*Your Name.*
אֵל חַי וְקַיָּם תָּמִיד יִמְלוֹךְ	*Ever-living God, may You reign continually over*
עָלֵינוּ לְעוֹלָם וָעֶד:	*us into eternity.*
בָּרוּךְ אַתָּה ה',	*Blessed are You, God, who brings on evening.*
הַמַּעֲרִיב עֲרָבִים:	

All week long, we begin *Maariv* with the two *pesukim* from *Tehillim* 78 and 20: "*V'hu rachum yechaper avon v'lo yashchit*—God is merciful and forgiving of iniquity and frequently He withdraws His anger…may He answer us when we call."

Interestingly, we do not recite these *pesukim* on Shabbat. Why not?

- Since Shabbat is a time of tranquility and earthly Jewish courts are not in session, we do not recite *pesukim* that reflect judgments.
- We are taught that even those who are bearing the painful consequences of their earthly misdeeds after death in Gehinnom are given reprieve on Shabbat; therefore, we also do not mention heavenly judgments and punishments on Shabbat.

The first of the two blessings we recite before *Shema* depict the astounding creation of (and ongoing Divine daily maintenance of) the earth's solar system in general and the generating of sunlight and darkness across the globe each day. While the sun is setting beyond the horizon outside shul in real time, we are chanting, "*Baruch atah*—Blessed are You, *maariv aravim*—who brings forth evenings, organizes nightly the constellations of the stars, removes light, and advances darkness."

The final phrase before the conclusion of the blessing reads: "*Keil chai v'kayam tamid yimloch aleinu l'olam va'ed*—May the Living God continue to rule over us forever; Blessed are You, God, who advances evenings." Traditionally, the penultimate *pasuk* of a lengthy blessing reflects the theme of the entire blessing. For example, in the very next blessing, *"V'ahavatecha...oheiv amo Yisrael,"* the phrase *"Keil chai v'kayam tamid"* seems out of place. Some later authorities actually delete the phrase altogether because of this concern.

Although the phrase does not linguistically present the theme of *maariv aravim*—the coming of evening, it nevertheless does relate to the conceptual theme of our *tefillah*. Namely, the daily travels of the powerful sun from one part of the earth to the opposite side; by gradually advancing—second by second and minute by minute—it demonstrates Hashem's omniscience and omnipotence through his constant involvement, intervention, and orchestration of our world. Therefore, after noting the depth of wisdom and complexity of our solar system, we exclaim, *"Keil chai v'kayam tamid yimloch aleinu l'olam va'ed*—May the Living God continue to rule over us forever [just like God rules over and guides the sunrise and sunset daily], Blessed are You, God, who advances evenings."

A DIVINE APPROACH: Throughout the day, take note of the position of the sun and its daily orbit through the sky above. Reflect on the majesty of Hashem who provides us with the light, warmth, energy, and beauty of the sun, and express gratitude nightly for the benefits we enjoy from the sun and from sunlight.

Ahavat Olam

אַהֲבַת עוֹלָם בֵּית יִשְׂרָאֵל עַמְּךָ אָהָבְתָּ.	*Never-ending love, Israel, Your people, You have loved.*
תּוֹרָה וּמִצְוֹת חֻקִּים וּמִשְׁפָּטִים אוֹתָנוּ לִמַּדְתָּ.	*Torah and mitzvot, decrees and precepts to us You have taught.*
עַל כֵּן ה׳ אֱלֹהֵינוּ בְּשָׁכְבֵנוּ וּבְקוּמֵנוּ נָשִׂיחַ בְּחֻקֶּיךָ וְנִשְׂמַח בְּדִבְרֵי תוֹרָתֶךָ וּבְמִצְוֹתֶיךָ לְעוֹלָם וָעֶד:	*Therefore, God, our Lord, in our laying and in our rising we will meditate on Your laws. And we will rejoice on the words of Your Torah and in Your mitzvot forever and ever.*

כִּי הֵם חַיֵּינוּ וְאֹרֶךְ יָמֵינוּ וּבָהֶם נֶהְגֶּה יוֹמָם וָלָיְלָה:	*For they are our lives and the length of our days, and on them we will study day and night.*
וְאַהֲבָתְךָ אַל תָּסִיר מִמֶּנּוּ לְעוֹלָמִים.	*And may Your love not depart from us for all eternity.*
בָּרוּךְ אַתָּה ה', אוֹהֵב עַמּוֹ יִשְׂרָאֵל:	*Blessed are You, God, who loves His people Israel.*

The second blessing before reciting *Shema* in the evening is "*Ahavat Olam Beit Yisrael*—With an Eternal Love You Have Loved the House of Israel."

There is perhaps no warmer and more secure feeling in the world then feeling loved. A child who knows her parents love her feels secure. A spouse who knows her husband loves and adores her feels strengthened. Even a student in school is fortified by the love and care of a *rebbi* and teacher. We, the Jewish People, should feel infused and inspired, as well as fortified, strengthened, and secure by the eternal love God shares with us. It is because of this love that Hashem has preserved us throughout the millennia, despite the thousands of external and internal threats that have risen up against us.

How does God express this eternal love unto us?

Through sharing and teaching us the elixir of life and afterlife—the Torah, including all the mitzvot: "*Torah u'mitzvot chukim u'mishpatim otanu limadeta*." **This is the gift of the ages; this is what strengthens us and protects us.**

Therefore, we exclaim, "*Ki heim chayeinu v'orech yameinu u'vahem negeh yomam v'laylah*—The precepts of the Torah are our lives and the length of our days; and we will reflect upon them every day and night."

Rav Chaim Twersky once explained the *pasuk* above by comparing a Jew and Torah to a dialysis patient. Dialysis patients take their dialysis quite seriously. They generally do not miss appointments and they wait in line patiently for their turn. Why? Because they know that dialysis is their lifeline; without it they cease to exist. So too, without God's love and the Torah, we, the Jewish people, would cease to exist.

Therefore, we implore Hashem to never remove His eternal love and His Torah from us—"*v'ahavatecha al tasir mimenu l'olamim.*"

"*Baruch atah Hashem oheiv amo Yisrael*—Blessed are You, God, who **loves** His nation, Israel."

A DIVINE APPROACH: We all know from history, as well as from daily life, that there are both pleasant and challenging times in life. When we recite *Ahavat Olam*, we remember that our Father in Heaven loves and cares for us Divinely—more powerfully then anyone else ever could. This gives us the strength and solace to engage with and deal with all we encounter throughout our lives.

After reciting *Maariv Aravim* and reflecting on God having created the beautiful and complex world we live in, and saying *Ahavat Olam* and acknowledging the eternal love God expresses for us with His Torah, we are now ready to recite *Shema Yisrael*.

Shema Yisrael

יָחִיד אוֹמֵר: אֵל מֶלֶךְ נֶאֱמָן:	*One praying alone recites:* God, the trustworthy King.
שְׁמַע יִשְׂרָאֵל ה׳ אֱלֹהֵינוּ ה׳ אֶחָד.	Hear, O Israel, God is our Lord, God is One.
בלחש: בָּרוּךְ שֵׁם כְּבוֹד מַלְכוּתוֹ לְעוֹלָם וָעֶד.	*Recite the following verse in an undertone:* Blessed be the name of the glory of His kingdom forever and ever.
וְאָהַבְתָּ אֵת ה׳ אֱלֹהֶיךָ בְּכָל לְבָבְךָ וּבְכָל נַפְשְׁךָ וּבְכָל מְאֹדֶךָ.	You shall love God, your Lord, with all your heart, with all your soul, and with all your might.
וְהָיוּ הַדְּבָרִים הָאֵלֶּה אֲשֶׁר אָנֹכִי מְצַוְּךָ הַיּוֹם עַל לְבָבֶךָ.	And these words which I command you today shall be upon your heart.
וְשִׁנַּנְתָּם לְבָנֶיךָ וְדִבַּרְתָּ בָּם בְּשִׁבְתְּךָ בְּבֵיתֶךָ וּבְלֶכְתְּךָ בַדֶּרֶךְ וּבְשָׁכְבְּךָ וּבְקוּמֶךָ.	You shall teach them thoroughly to your children, and you shall speak of them when you sit in your house and when you walk on the road, when you lie down, and when you rise.

| וּקְשַׁרְתָּם לְאוֹת עַל יָדֶךָ | You shall bind them as a sign upon your hand, |
| וְהָיוּ לְטֹטָפֹת בֵּין עֵינֶיךָ. | and they shall be for a reminder between your eyes. |

| וּכְתַבְתָּם עַל מְזֻזֹת בֵּיתֶךָ | And you shall write them upon the doorposts of |
| וּבִשְׁעָרֶיךָ. | your house and upon your gates. |

After the recitation of the two blessings preceding it, we fulfill the awesome Biblical commandment to recite the *Shema*. We cover our eyes with our right hands (to block out any distractions and demonstrate that God is not visible) and say out loud the Biblical *pasuk*: "*Shema Yisrael Hashem Elokeinu Hashem Echad*—Hear O Israel, God is our Lord, God is One."

When reciting the *Shema*, we are commanded to accept upon ourselves the yoke of Heaven. Indeed, Chazal refer to the *Shema* as "*kabbalat ol malchut Shamayim*—accepting the yoke of Heaven upon us.*" Rav Avigdor Miller writes that the word *Shema*—to hear, is the word that was also used at the moment of the original acceptance of God and His Torah at Har Sinai, when B'nei Yisrael cried out, "*Naaseh v'nishma*—We will do and we will **hear.**" As our forefathers declared more than 3,330 years ago, so too do we declare today *Shema Yisrael*.

The First Recitation

Chazal teach that although *Shema Yisrael* is an actual *pasuk* in the Torah, in *Devarim*, the first declaration of the *Shema* dates back to when Yaakov Avinu was on his deathbed.[1] In *Bereishit*, we read that Yaakov summons his children to his bedside to say farewell and reveal the secrets of the destiny of Am Yisrael.[2] When he is unable to invoke his Divine insights, he grows despondent and concerned that perhaps his children (the original "B'nei Yisrael") were not faithful to the God of Israel and therefore did not merit hearing his farewell. At that anxiety-filled moment, Yaakov's children recited in unison, "*Shema Yisrael Hashem Elokeinu Hashem Echad*—Hear O Israel, God is our Lord, God

---

1   *Devarim* 6:4.
2   *Bereishit* 49:1.

is One." This provides comfort and fulfillment for Yaakov at the closing moments of his life on this earth.

Since then, *Shema Yisrael* has become the prayer recited by martyrs who died in the name of God before they perished. The Talmud relates the painful story of Rabbi Akiva's death at the hands of the Romans.[3] As his soul was departing from his body, he too recited the *Shema Yisrael*. This reflects our practice until today when Jews say *Shema* every night before going to sleep. As we aim to drift into unconsciousness (which the Talmud compares to death), we faithfully recite *Shema*.

Testimony

The words of the *Shema* are so significant, that they are the chosen texts inside our tefillin boxes and *mezuzot*. We attach the *Shema* to our bodies and our homes to demonstrate our love and commitment to Hashem and His Torah.

In the opening word, the last letter of the word *Shema* is written in the Torah with a large *ayin*, and the last word of the phrase *echad* ends with a large *dalet*. The two letters together spell *eid* which means "testimony." Saying the *Shema* every day in the morning and the evening is a testimony to one's conviction to walk in the ways of God.

The next sentence in *Shema* is "*Baruch shem kevod malchuto l'olam va'ed*—Blessed is the name of His glorious kingdom for all eternity." The reason we don't say *Baruch Shem* out loud is because, unlike the rest of the *Shema*, *Baruch Shem* is nowhere to be found in the Written Torah, and is therefore interrupting two consecutive Biblical sentences. It is, however, mentioned in the Talmud, where it is recorded that Yaakov Avinu said this exact sentence to his children right after they recited *Shema Yisrael* (see above).[4] Therefore, the Talmud concludes it should be said in an undertone.

The *Shema* continues with the words, "*V'ahavta et Hashem Elokecha*—And you shall love God your Lord." How exactly are you to

---

3   *Berachot* 61b.

4   *Pesachim* 56a.

express your love unto Him? *"B'chol levavecha, u'v'chol nafshecha, u'vechol me'odecha*—With all of your heart, your soul, and your might."

The commentators ask, how can the Torah command us to feel? We are generally commanded actions such as to don tefillin, to eat kosher, and to observe the Shabbat—but to **love** God? Emotions are triggered and experienced and not necessarily accessible at will. How then shall we understand the mitzvah to feel *"v'ahavta et Hashem*—you shall love God"?

Rav Baruch HaLevi Epstein, in his work on the siddur, the *Baruch She'amar*, presents two approaches to understanding this *pasuk*. The first approach maintains a literal translation of *"v'ahavta*—you shall love Him." He explains that the mitzvah of *v'ahavta* must be seen in light of the previous prayer in the siddur, *Ahavah Rabbah*. The prayer *Ahavah Rabbah* demonstrates the absolute all-encompassing love that our Creator has for us. *"Ahavah rabbah ahavtanu*—God You have loved us with an abundant love." Once we know, understand, feel, and appreciate God's adoration and love for us, it is only natural for us to experience love for Him in return. Of course, we cannot be commanded to conjure an emotion at will, but we can be commanded to focus on God's love for us that will, over time, trigger in us a deep love for Him in return.

The second approach is based on a passage in the Talmud that interprets *"v'ahavta et"* to mean "God should become beloved through your actions."[5] It is not enough to simply perform mitzvot. We are also obligated to live and behave in a way that creates honor and dignity for Hashem in His world. The way we talk, the way we dress, and the way we relate to our family and colleagues all reflect on our Maker. So the first *pasuk* in the paragraph implores us—*v'ahavta et Hashem*, to love God by making a *kiddush Hashem*, living a noble and ambassadorial life that celebrates the royalty, magnificence, and universality of God and Torah. In our day and age, when the name "Jew" and the name of the Jewish State, "Israel," are not always appreciated and revered by

---

5   *Yoma* 86a.

the nations of the world, fulfilling this mitzvah properly is essential in strengthening and representing the just and eternal nation of Israel.

> A DIVINE APPROACH: It is documented that during the Holocaust the death camp guards knew the first *pesukim* of the *Shema* by heart because they heard millions of Jews chant the *Shema* before dying. When we say *Shema* we carry on their legacy and show that while the evil Nazis are gone, the Jewish People and the reciting of the *Shema* are here to stay.

V'Hayah Im Shamo'a Tishme'u. 1

וְהָיָה אִם שָׁמֹעַ תִּשְׁמְעוּ אֶל מִצְוֹתַי אֲשֶׁר אָנֹכִי מְצַוֶּה אֶתְכֶם הַיּוֹם לְאַהֲבָה אֶת ה' אֱלֹהֵיכֶם וּלְעָבְדוֹ בְּכָל לְבַבְכֶם וּבְכָל נַפְשְׁכֶם.	*And it will be, if you hearken to My commandments that I command you this day to love God, your Lord, and to serve Him with all your heart and with all your soul,*
וְנָתַתִּי מְטַר אַרְצְכֶם בְּעִתּוֹ יוֹרֶה וּמַלְקוֹשׁ וְאָסַפְתָּ דְגָנֶךָ וְתִירֹשְׁךָ וְיִצְהָרֶךָ.	*I will give the rain of your land at its time, the early rain and the latter rain, and you will gather in your grain, your wine, and your oil.*
וְנָתַתִּי עֵשֶׂב בְּשָׂדְךָ לִבְהֶמְתֶּךָ וְאָכַלְתָּ וְשָׂבָעְתָּ.	*And I will give grass in your field for your livestock, and you will eat and be sated.*
הִשָּׁמְרוּ לָכֶם פֶּן יִפְתֶּה לְבַבְכֶם וְסַרְתֶּם וַעֲבַדְתֶּם אֱלֹהִים אֲחֵרִים וְהִשְׁתַּחֲוִיתֶם לָהֶם.	*Beware, lest your heart be misled, and you turn away and worship strange gods and prostrate yourselves before them.*
וְחָרָה אַף ה' בָּכֶם וְעָצַר אֶת הַשָּׁמַיִם וְלֹא יִהְיֶה מָטָר וְהָאֲדָמָה לֹא תִתֵּן אֶת יְבוּלָהּ וַאֲבַדְתֶּם מְהֵרָה מֵעַל הָאָרֶץ הַטֹּבָה אֲשֶׁר ה' נֹתֵן לָכֶם.	*And the wrath of God will be kindled against you, and He will close off the heavens, and there will be no rain, and the ground will not give its produce, and you will perish quickly from upon the good land that God gives you.*

וְשַׂמְתֶּם אֶת דְּבָרַי אֵלֶּה עַל לְבַבְכֶם וְעַל נַפְשְׁכֶם וּקְשַׁרְתֶּם אֹתָם לְאוֹת עַל יֶדְכֶם וְהָיוּ לְטוֹטָפֹת בֵּין עֵינֵיכֶם.	*And you shall set these words of Mine upon your heart and upon your soul, and bind them for a sign upon your hand and they shall be for ornaments between your eyes.*
וְלִמַּדְתֶּם אֹתָם אֶת בְּנֵיכֶם לְדַבֵּר בָּם בְּשִׁבְתְּךָ בְּבֵיתֶךָ וּבְלֶכְתְּךָ בַדֶּרֶךְ וּבְשָׁכְבְּךָ וּבְקוּמֶךָ.	*And you shall teach them to your sons to speak with them, when you sit in your house and when you walk on the way and when you lie down and when you rise.*
וּכְתַבְתָּם עַל מְזוּזוֹת בֵּיתֶךָ וּבִשְׁעָרֶיךָ.	*And you shall inscribe them upon the doorposts of your house and upon your gates,*
לְמַעַן יִרְבּוּ יְמֵיכֶם וִימֵי בְנֵיכֶם עַל הָאֲדָמָה אֲשֶׁר נִשְׁבַּע ה' לַאֲבֹתֵיכֶם לָתֵת לָהֶם כִּימֵי הַשָּׁמַיִם עַל הָאָרֶץ.	*in order that your days may increase and the days of your children, on the land which God swore to your forefathers to give them, as the days of heaven above the earth.*

The second paragraph of *Shema* also originates in the Torah[6] and is referred to as "*Kabbalat ol mitzvot*—the acceptance of the yoke of mitzvot." The passage begins: "*V'hayah im shamo'a **tishme'u** el mitzvotai asher anochi metzaveh **etchem** ha'yom*—And it shall come to pass that if **you** (pl.) listen and adhere to my commandments that I command **you** (pl.) today."

It is noteworthy that the previous section of *Shema*, "*V'ahavta et Hashem Elokecha*—And you shall love God," is written in the singular, and the section of *V'hayah* is in the plural. This demonstrates that the Torah that we learn, the mitzvot we perform, and the loving kindness we express impact us individually, and also as a nation. In fact, we are taught on Rosh Hashanah that Hashem evaluates and judges our deeds as individuals, in addition to judging everyone as part of a greater whole.[7] Although the twenty-first-century societal ethos often smacks of egocentricity—"It's all about me"—the Torah teaches us it's about a lot more than me!

Rav Avigdor Miller writes that we see from the words *"V'hayah im shamo'a"* that the Torah does not demand results; rather it commands listening and adherence: *"V'hayah im shamo'a*—And if you listen." There are times in life that one may simply not be able to follow through due to extenuating circumstances, but one can always listen and resolve to do the best that they can.

The *Baal Shem Tov* was reputed to have said that in heaven we are judged not only by what we did, but rather by what we *desired* to do. Similarly, in *Pirkei Avot* we are taught that it is not our responsibility to complete all tasks, but it most certainly is our responsibility to try and grow and accomplish as much as we can during the years we are granted here on earth.[8] Hashem asks us to do our part, and He will take care of the rest.

Let's analyze the language of the first *pasuk, "V'hayah im* **shamo'a tish-me'u**—And when you **listen, listen.**" Why the double language? Would it not have been sufficient to simply delete either *shamo'a* or *tishme'u*? Why do we need both?

The *Mechilta, Midrash Halachah*[9] explains that from these words, the following lesson is taught: When you listen to one mitzvah, you will be able to listen to many more. The basic understanding of this *Mechilta* is that Torah knowledge is learned and lived by listening and adhering to one mitzvah at a time, and after learning about one mitzvah, we are able to advance toward the next one, as they are all interrelated. Along these lines is the Mishnah in *Avot* that states that the reward of a mitzvah is the opportunity to perform another one.[10]

There is another, deeper, understanding to be learned as well. We know that Torah is layered with multiple levels of knowledge. Another

---

7   *Rosh Hashanah* 16a.

8   *Avot* 2:16.

9   *Mechilta* 19.

10   *Avot* 4:2.

message of this *Mechilta* is that the way to dig deeper and find more meaning in life is by listening to and learning the same piece of Torah over and over again. Each analysis will yield a different lesson to learn from and incorporate. It is incredible that the same *Chumash* and *Rashi* taught to five-year-olds is also expounded upon by the greatest Torah scholars of the generation. This is a reason why we read the same Torah reading over and over each year. Every time we study there is more to discover.

A DIVINE APPROACH: *V'hayah* reminds us how important it is to listen. When we listen carefully, there is so much more to hear, and then apply, to our lives.

V'Hayah Im Shamo'a Tishme'u: 2

"*V'limadetem otam et beneichem l'daber bam b'shivtecha*—You shall teach your children to speak words of Torah in the home, while on the go, when you lie down to sleep, as well as when you arise."

Rashi quotes an alarming *Sifrei*[11] on this *pasuk* that states: "From the moment a child begins to speak, he shall be taught: '*Torah tzivah lanu Moshe*—Moshe has commanded us to abide by the Torah'; if one neglects this opportunity, he is deserving to **bury** the child."

One can readily understand that not teaching children Torah early in life is a missed opportunity, but the tone of the midrash reveals that much more is at stake. Why? If I don't teach my child "*Torah tzivah...*" at two or three, I can do it at age four or five! What's the urgency? What is the message behind this midrash?

Rav Shlomo Wolbe, in his *sefer* on child-rearing states that there are *critical moments* in a child's life. If these critical moments are met with wisdom, tradition, and love, they can result in a profound and long-lasting impact on the child. If, however, these moments are

---

11   *Sifrei, Devarim* 46.

ignored and/or wasted, the opportunities will be lost, buried, and wasted forever.[12]

This spiritual lesson is applicable to an aspect of one's physical health as well. If, God forbid, one breaks a bone, there is a limited amount of time to reset the bone and begin the healing process. If too much time elapses, the opportunity may be lost, and the bone may never heal properly again. It's not just what and how you say and do; it's also *when* you do it.

The passage concludes with a reminder of one of the great rewards for Torah study and mitzvah observance: "*L'maan yirbu yemeichem vimei beneichem*—So that you and your children will live long lives on the holy soil that God promised your forefathers." The *pasuk* states unequivocally that it is specifically Torah knowledge and observance that can provide safety and security for Am Yisrael in Eretz Yisrael.

A DIVINE APPROACH: Since the State of Israel was declared, she has been under constant attack. Israel fought the War of Independence in 1948, the Suez War in 1956, the Six-Day War in 1967, the Yom Kippur War in 1973, in Lebanon in 1982, aside from our recent wars in the north and south, together with ongoing terror attacks and attempts to inspire world hatred and isolation against us. Despite having the most powerful army and weaponry in the Middle East, as well as great influence here in the United States to help our cause, our enemies are as ready and willing as ever to throw us into the sea. The antidote is here in "*V'hayah im shamo'a: V'limaditem otam et beneichem l'daber bam b'shivticha…l'maan yirbu yemeichem vimei beneichem*—You shall teach your children to speak words of Torah so that you and your children will live long lives on the holy soil that God promised your forefathers." The Torah teaches us that the way to ensure national security is through Torah and mitzvot. We have tried everything else and, of course, we need to defend ourselves. However, perhaps it's time to listen and adhere to the Divine words recited each day from the *Shema*.

---

12 *Zeriyah U'Binyan B'Chinuch*, p. 14.

Va'yomer

וַיֹּאמֶר ה׳ אֶל מֹשֶׁה לֵּאמֹר.	*God spoke to Moshe, saying:*
דַּבֵּר אֶל בְּנֵי יִשְׂרָאֵל וְאָמַרְתָּ אֲלֵהֶם וְעָשׂוּ לָהֶם צִיצִת עַל כַּנְפֵי בִגְדֵיהֶם לְדֹרֹתָם וְנָתְנוּ עַל צִיצִת הַכָּנָף פְּתִיל תְּכֵלֶת.	*Speak to the Children of Israel and you shall say to them that they shall make for themselves fringes on the corners of their garments, throughout their generations, and they shall affix a thread of sky blue [wool] on the fringe of each corner.*
וְהָיָה לָכֶם לְצִיצִת וּרְאִיתֶם אֹתוֹ וּזְכַרְתֶּם אֶת כָּל מִצְוֹת ה׳ וַעֲשִׂיתֶם אֹתָם וְלֹא תָתוּרוּ אַחֲרֵי לְבַבְכֶם וְאַחֲרֵי עֵינֵיכֶם אֲשֶׁר אַתֶּם זֹנִים אַחֲרֵיהֶם.	*This shall be fringes for you, and when you see it, you will remember all the commandments of God to perform them, and you shall not wander after your hearts and after your eyes after which you are going astray.*
לְמַעַן תִּזְכְּרוּ וַעֲשִׂיתֶם אֶת כָּל מִצְוֹתָי וִהְיִיתֶם קְדֹשִׁים לֵאלֹהֵיכֶם.	*So that you shall remember and perform all My commandments and you shall be holy to your Lord.*
אֲנִי ה׳ אֱלֹהֵיכֶם אֲשֶׁר הוֹצֵאתִי אֶתְכֶם מֵאֶרֶץ מִצְרַיִם לִהְיוֹת לָכֶם לֵאלֹהִים אֲנִי ה׳ אֱלֹהֵיכֶם.	*I am God, your Lord, who took you out of the land of Egypt to be your Lord; I am God, your Lord.*

The third section of the *Shema* is *Parashat Tzitzit*, which originates in *Bamidbar*.[13] It begins, "*Va'yomer Hashem el Moshe leimor daber el B'nei Yisrael v'amarta aleihem v'asu lahem tzitzit*—And God spoke to Moshe saying that B'nei Yisrael shall make for themselves tzitzit on the corner of their garments."

It concludes, "*Ani Hashem Elokeichem asher hotzeiti etchem mei'Eretz Mitzrayim*—I am God, your Lord, who took you out of Egypt." The Torah commands us to remember *yetziat Mitzrayim* every day.[14] By

---

13   *Bamidbar* 5:37.
14   *Devarim* 16:3.

reciting this paragraph of *Shema*, we fulfill this mitzvah by having in mind the Exodus and reciting *Va'yomer*.

Let's explore the mitzvah of tzitzit and its connection to *yetziat Mitzrayim*.

Rav Shimshon Raphael Hirsch explains that the first *pasuk* of *Parashat Tzitzit* demonstrates the intense devotion that Am Yisrael showed when fulfilling the mitzvah of tzitzit. He explains the *pasuk* the following way: "*Daber el B'nei Yisrael v'amarta aleihem **v'asu lahem** tzitzit*—Speak to the Children of Israel and tell them about the mitzvah and **they will make for themselves** tzitzit." He explains that the Torah did not instruct Jews to make tzitzit; it just informed them of the mitzvah. Because of their love, devotion, and dedication to God and his Torah—***v'asu lahem***—Am Yisrael forged ahead and fulfilled the mitzvah with alacrity. Wearing tzitzit is a unique mitzvah because in the *Shulchan Aruch*[15] it states that unless one is already wearing a four-cornered garment, he is not obligated in the mitzvah of tzitzit at all. Yet it also states[16] that one who is careful to fulfill the mitzvah of tzitzit properly will experience spiritual delight, and a great punishment is in store for those who avoid the mitzvah. We are thereby encouraged to create the obligation by wearing a four-cornered garment in order to fulfill the mitzvah.

Tzitzit symbolize and represent so many fascinating and important lessons. Here are a few:

- The *gematria*—numerical equivalent, of tzitzit equals 600. When we add the eight strings and five knots found on every corner of tzitzit, the total is 613, the number of mitzvot in the Torah that we are required to fulfill.
- Rav Shimon Schwab writes that although the tzitzit are filled with knots, two thirds of each set of strings are left free-flowing. This implies that although there are a significant number of laws

---

15   *Shulchan Aruch* OC 24:1.

16   Ibid., 24:6.

and restrictions in Jewish life, in the end these laws and restrictions unleash an unmatched freedom to live and enjoy life.[17]

• Additionally, the word *tzitz* in Hebrew not only means fringe, but a sprouting flower as well. Wearing tzitzit that extend off of our clothing manifests the unique opportunity for every Jew to grow and develop toward their potential through mitzvot, like a beautiful flower that opens and shares all of its beauty.

The passage concludes: *"Ani Hashem Elokeichem asher hotzeiti etchem mei'Eretz Mitzrayim l'hiyot la'chem l'Elokim*—I am God, your Lord, who took you out of Egypt so that I will be your Master." The commentaries explain why the *parashah* of tzitzit concludes with the memory of *yetziat Mitzrayim*:

• Since tzitzit represent all 613 mitzvot, the message is that God took us out of Egypt specifically so that we can fulfill all the mitzvot.

• The *Ohr Hachaim*[18] writes that a four-cornered garment with tzitzit is a type of uniform that indicates that God rules all four directions of the earth: north, south, east and west. Therefore, we wear them as a reminder that we were slaves to Pharaoh, and now we are uniformed servants of Hashem.

A DIVINE APPROACH: It is customary to kiss the tzitzit when we recite the words *"tzitzit"* and *"Hashem Elokeichem emet*—I am your God of truth." Kissing the tzitzit (which represents all mitzvot) demonstrates how beloved are all the mitzvot that emanate from God, who is loving and whose word is true.

---

17   *Rav Shimon Schwab- On Prayer* (ArtScroll, 2001), p. 37.
18   *Ohr Hachaim* on *Bamidbar* 15:39.

Emet V'Emunah

וֶאֱמוּנָה כָּל זֹאת וְקַיָם עָלֵינוּ כִּי הוּא ה׳ אֱלֹהֵינוּ וְאֵין זוּלָתוֹ וַאֲנַחְנוּ יִשְׂרָאֵל עַמוֹ:	*Faithful is all this and it is firmly established for us that He is God, our Lord, and there is none but Him, and we are Israel, His people.*
הַפּוֹדֵנוּ מִיַד מְלָכִים מַלְכֵּנוּ הַגּוֹאֲלֵנוּ מִכַּף כָּל הֶעָרִיצִים.	*He is the One who redeems us from the power of kings, our King who delivers us from the hand of all the cruel tyrants.*
הָאֵל הַנִפְרָע לָנוּ מִצָּרֵינוּ וְהַמְשַׁלֵם גְּמוּל לְכָל אֹיְבֵי נַפְשֵׁנוּ:	*He is the God who exacts vengeance for us from our foes and who repays just retribution upon all the enemies of the soul;*
הָעוֹשֶׂה גְדוֹלוֹת עַד אֵין חֵקֶר נִסִּים וְנִפְלָאוֹת עַד אֵין מִסְפָּר.	*who performs great deeds that are beyond comprehension and wonders that are beyond number.*
הַשָּׂם נַפְשֵׁנוּ בַּחַיִּים וְלֹא נָתַן לַמּוֹט רַגְלֵנוּ:	*Who set our soul in life and did not allow to falter our foot.*
הַמַּדְרִיכֵנוּ עַל בָּמוֹת אוֹיְבֵינוּ וַיָּרֶם קַרְנֵנוּ עַל כָּל שׂוֹנְאֵינוּ:	*Who led us upon the heights of our enemies and raised our pride above all who hate us.*
הָעוֹשֶׂה לָנוּ נִסִּים וּנְקָמָה בְּפַרְעֹה אוֹתוֹת וּמוֹפְתִים בְּאַדְמַת בְּנֵי חָם.	*Who wrought for us miracles and vengeance upon Pharaoh, signs and wonders in the land of the offspring of Ham.*
הַמַּכֶּה בְעֶבְרָתוֹ כָּל בְּכוֹרֵי מִצְרָיִם וַיּוֹצֵא אֶת עַמּוֹ יִשְׂרָאֵל מִתּוֹכָם לְחֵרוּת עוֹלָם:	*Who struck in His anger all the firstborn of Egypt and removed His people Israel from their midst to everlasting freedom.*
הַמַּעֲבִיר בָּנָיו בֵּין גִּזְרֵי יַם סוּף אֶת רוֹדְפֵיהֶם וְאֶת שׂוֹנְאֵיהֶם בִּתְהוֹמוֹת טִבַּע.	*Who brought His children through the split parts of the Sea of Reeds while those who pursued them and those [who] hated them He sank into the depths.*
וְרָאוּ בָנָיו גְּבוּרָתוֹ שִׁבְּחוּ וְהוֹדוּ לִשְׁמוֹ:	*When His children perceived His power, they praised and gave thanks to His Name.*

וּמַלְכוּתוֹ בְּרָצוֹן קִבְּלוּ עֲלֵיהֶם.	*And His Kingship they accepted willingly upon themselves;*
מֹשֶׁה וּבְנֵי יִשְׂרָאֵל לְךָ עָנוּ שִׁירָה בְּשִׂמְחָה רַבָּה וְאָמְרוּ כֻלָּם:	*Moshe and the Children of Israel to You exclaimed in song with great gladness and said unanimously:*

As opposed to the recital of the *Shema* in the morning (when we recite only one blessing afterward), after *Shema* during *Maariv* in the evening, we recite two blessings. The first blessing is the same as in the morning—"*Baruch atah Hashem ga'al Yisrael*—Blessed are You, God, who redeems Israel."

The prayer after *Shema* begins, "*Emet v'emunah*—Truth and faith," without the word "*baruch*," because it is a continuation of the blessings recited before *Shema* that began with "*baruch*." Like in *Shacharit*, the prayers are arranged utilizing the mechanism of "*berachah ha'semuch l'chaverta*—when one blessing is juxtaposed next to another," the second one need not begin with *baruch*.

"*Emet v'emunah kol zot*"—we declare that every single word, vowel and letter of the *Shema* we just recited is true. The *Etz Yosef* also explains that *Emet V'Emunah* refers to Torah and mitzvot. The Torah is *emet*—truth, and mitzvot are expressions of *emunah*—our faith. This teaches that the way to demonstrate our faith in the truth of God's oneness we just declared in the *Shema* is by (a) studying His Torah, and (b) fulfilling His mitzvot.

After emphasizing the veracity of the *Shema*, the *tefillah* continues and reflects upon *yetziat Mitzrayim*. Rav Yaakov Emden, in his siddur *Beit Yaakov*, notes that the lack of symmetry between the post-*Shema* prayers in the morning and the evening is puzzling. Since the Torah states that we left Egypt in the daytime, it makes perfect sense to invoke the miracles of *yetziat Mitzrayim* after reciting *Shema* in the morning. But why do we mention *yetziat Mitzrayim* at night?

Perhaps the answer can be learned from the final Mishnah in tractate *Berachot*: "*Chayav adam l'varech al ha'ra k'shem she'hu mevarech al ha'tov*—Just as we are commanded to recite a blessing in times of joy, so must we recite a blessing in troubled times."[19] We recite blessings when babies are born, but we also recite a blessing when a loved one passes away. Why? The Talmud explains that it is because *"kol d'avid rachmana l'tav avid*—everything God does is for the good."[20] It may not look good or feel good, but we trust that ultimately it *is* good. Therefore, we even recite a blessing in difficult times. Not only is it good; it brings us a step closer to the *geulah*—the final redemption.

Therefore, we invoke *yetziat Mitzrayim* both in the daytime as well as at night to signify our trust and understanding that even when it seems dark outside or in our lives, the *geulah*—God's loving-kindness and the redemption—are in motion.

A DIVINE APPROACH: It's easy to see the good when everything feels sweet and pleasant in our lives. The challenge is to seek out and experience God's kindness when we experience darkness as well. A way to achieve this is to not only look for the good each day, but also to keep a journal of good and difficult times and look back on it from time to time because in hindsight we may find blessings we did not originally note.

Mi Kamochah Ba'eilim Hashem

מִי כָמֹכָה בָּאֵלִים ה'. מִי כָּמֹכָה נֶאְדָּר בַּקֹּדֶשׁ. נוֹרָא תְהִלֹּת עֹשֵׂה פֶלֶא:	*Who is like You among the heavenly powers, God! Who is like You, mighty in holiness, awesome [beyond] praise, doing wonders!*
מַלְכוּתְךָ רָאוּ בָנֶיךָ. בּוֹקֵעַ יָם לִפְנֵי מֹשֶׁה. זֶה אֵלִי עָנוּ. וְאָמְרוּ: ה' יִמְלֹךְ לְעֹלָם וָעֶד:	*Your majesty did Your children behold as You split the Sea before Moshe. This is my God, they exclaimed and they said: "God will reign forever and ever."*

---

19   *Berachot* 9:5
20   Ibid., 60b.

Our *tefillot* are based on and codified from an array of different sources. Many of our prayers are from *Tehillim*, specifically chosen to be chanted as a form of praise and acknowledgement to God. Other prayers are blessings originally codified in the Talmud that express gratitude to God for all that He does for us each day. Sometimes Chazal include actual *pesukim* from the Torah amid prayers and blessings to emphasize and punctuate a theme of the prayer.

For example, toward the conclusion of *Emet V'Emunah*, the chazzan reads aloud: "*U'malchuto b'ratzon kiblu aleihem Moshe...b'simchah rabbah v'amru kulam*—[B'nei Yisrael] accepted the kingship of God upon them and joyfully shouted in unison." Then the entire congregation says aloud the *pasuk* from *Shemos*: "*Mi kamochah ba'eilim Hashem...nora tehillot oseh fele*—Who is like You God...Your greatness far surpasses our praises!"[21] In the morning during *Shacharit*, we also say aloud *Mi Kamochah* after *Shema*, just before reciting the blessing of *geulah*—redemption, and saying the *Amidah*.

The question is, why does our prayer specifically invoke the *pasuk* from *Shemos*, *Mi Kamochah*? There are nineteen *pesukim* in *Az Yashir*—the Song of the Sea. Why is this particular *pasuk* chosen for us to chant when there are so many other *pesukim* in *Az Yashir* that depict God's strength, providence, and greatness? Why *Mi Kamochah*?

The *Netziv*[22] explains the *pasuk* "*Mi kamochah ba'eilim Hashem*" to mean "Who is like God the great source of **kindness**," because the name of God, *E-l*, refers to kindness, a hallmark of God and Am Yisrael. Perhaps the architects of our siddur wanted us to focus on God's kindness.

The *Malbim* explains that this *pasuk* is unique because it was not only B'nei Yisrael that chanted it, but all the nations of the world also joined in. Chazal remark that the miracles of the Yam Suf—Red Sea, were felt and known all over the world. Therefore, perhaps the *pasuk Mi Kamochah* was chosen because it was chanted universally.

Finally, I would like to suggest that the *pasuk* in question is the one in *Az Yashir* that not only relates to the story of *k'riyat Yam Suf*—the

---

21   *Shemos* 15:11.
22   Rabbi Naftali Zvi Yehudah Berlin.

splitting of the sea, like the previous and subsequent *pesukim*, but can also be relevant to God and His maintaining, sustaining, and guiding the world in our times as well. Therefore, perhaps the intent is that while we reexamine and reflect on *yetziat Mitzrayim* every morning and evening, we must also recognize that the same God who took us out over 3,300 years ago from Egypt demonstrates His strength, kindness, and love to us every single day all across the world. And just as at the time of *yetziat Mitzrayim*, the entire world joined B'nei Yisrael in chanting *Mi Kamochah*, so too in our time we hope, pray for, and look forward to the time that all nations of the world will recognize Hashem as the true and one God of the world.

> A DIVINE APPROACH: When davening from your siddur each day, take note of which specific Biblical *pesukim* are quoted in our prayers and consider why they in particular were chosen to be part of the *tefillot*. This will enable the *tefillot* to be even more personal and meaningful when recited.

V'Ne'emar Ki Fadah Hashem Et Yaakov...Ga'al Yisrael

וְנֶאֱמַר כִּי פָדָה ה' אֶת	*And it is further said: For God has redeemed*
יַעֲקֹב וּגְאָלוֹ מִיַּד חָזָק מִמֶּנּוּ.	*Yaakov and delivered him from the hand of one*
בָּרוּךְ אַתָּה ה' גָּאַל יִשְׂרָאֵל.	*mightier than he. Blessed are You, God, who*
	redeemed Israel.

To experience meaningful prayer is an art as well as a skill. There are many different gateways to meaningful prayer. For some it is the music, the *niggunim*, which lifts their souls and inspires their voices to join in unison to praise and demonstrate gratitude to Hashem. For others, it is the poetry and beauty of the language and expressions in our prayers that inspire attention and reverence to God.

After years of *tefillah* study, one of the gateways I approach in order to achieve potent prayer is concentrating on the sources of the *pesukim* referenced in our *tefillot*.

Let's take a look at the concluding phrase before the blessing of redemption: *"Baruch Atah Hashem ga'al Yisrael."*

We are taught that our Egyptian enslavement and the dramatic events of *yetziat Mitzrayim* were not only the seminal period in the formation of our people, but were also the prototype for all of our future exiles and redemptions. Therefore, so many of our mitzvot and prayers refer to and reflect upon our 210 years in Egypt and our miraculous departure. The mitzvot of tzitzit, tefillin, Kiddush, *Shema*, *pidyon ha'ben*, etc., all relate to *yetziat Mitzrayim*.

The architects of the siddur chose not only to invoke our past glory, but to also instill genuine hope and faith for Jews throughout the millennia. In other words, they masterfully kept our prayers relevant for all times. This *tefillah* is a great example invoking the *pasuk* from *Yirmiyahu*, *"V'ne'emar ki fadah Hashem et Yaakov,"* as it says that God will redeem Yaakov from an even stronger enemy before concluding the blessing, *"Ga'al Yisrael*—Who redeems Israel."

Yirmiyahu 31 tells of *yetziat Mitzrayim*, and then states that just as God redeemed us from Egypt, so too He will redeem us again anew. It says: *"Evneich v'nivneit betulat Yisrael,"*[23] which *Rashi* states is referring to the Third Beit Hamikdash that God will build and will never be destroyed.

At this one moment of prayer during *Maariv*, we reflect on the splitting of the Yam Suf upon our departure from Egypt over 3,300 years ago, and then fast-forward 1,000 years to the redemptive prophecy of Yirmiyahu in Jerusalem in 630 BCE. In this one *tefillah*, we literally travel through history and express our longing for our destiny.

In paintings, the perfect shade of color amid an array of colors creates a masterpiece. A well-timed chord on the piano resonating amid a full orchestra can release the beauty of the entire symphony. So too in our prayers, invoking a specific *pasuk* from *Yirmiyahu* after chanting a highlight of *Az Yashir*, while having just recited the *Shema*, constructs the perfect moment to affirm our past and future redemption.

---

23   31:3.

A DIVINE APPROACH: When we notice in our prayers an array of *pesukim* from disparate sources, let's consider why they have specifically been inserted together. This will lend new meaning to our prayers.

Hashkiveinu

הַשְׁכִּיבֵנוּ ה' אֱלֹהֵינוּ לְשָׁלוֹם וְהַעֲמִידֵנוּ מַלְכֵּנוּ לְחַיִּים וּפְרוֹשׂ עָלֵינוּ סֻכַּת שְׁלוֹמֶךָ וְתַקְּנֵנוּ בְּעֵצָה טוֹבָה מִלְּפָנֶיךָ וְהוֹשִׁיעֵנוּ לְמַעַן שְׁמֶךָ.	*Lay us down, God, our Lord, for peace, and raise us up again, our King, for life. Spread over us Your canopy of peace, and preserve us with good counsel from You, and save us for the sake of Your Name.*
וְהָגֵן בַּעֲדֵנוּ וְהָסֵר מֵעָלֵינוּ אוֹיֵב דֶּבֶר וְחֶרֶב וְרָעָב וְיָגוֹן וְהָסֵר שָׂטָן מִלְּפָנֵינוּ וּמֵאַחֲרֵינוּ וּבְצֵל כְּנָפֶיךָ תַּסְתִּירֵנוּ כִּי אֵל שׁוֹמְרֵנוּ וּמַצִּילֵנוּ אָתָּה כִּי אֵל מֶלֶךְ חַנּוּן וְרַחוּם אָתָּה.	*Shield us, and remove from us, enemy, plague, sword, famine, and sorrow, and remove the Satan from before and behind us. Shelter us in the shadow of Your winged protection, for the power, our protector and savior.*
וּשְׁמוֹר צֵאתֵנוּ וּבוֹאֵנוּ לְחַיִּים וּלְשָׁלוֹם מֵעַתָּה וְעַד עוֹלָם. וּפְרֹשׂ עָלֵינוּ סֻכַּת שְׁלוֹמֶךָ.	*Guard our going out and our coming in, for life and peace, now and forever, and spread Your canopy of peace upon us.*
בָּרוּךְ אַתָּה ה' הַפּוֹרֵשׂ סֻכַּת שָׁלוֹם עָלֵינוּ וְעַל כָּל עַמּוֹ יִשְׂרָאֵל וְעַל יְרוּשָׁלָיִם.	*Blessed are You, God, who spreads Your canopy of peace over us, and over his entire nation, and over Jerusalem.*

The final blessing after the *Shema* in the evening begins, "*Hashkiveinu Hashem Elokeinu l'shalom, v'haamideinu Malkeinu l'chaim*—Lay us down, God, our Lord, for peace, and raise us up again, our King, for life." Since this is the evening prayer, *Maariv*, and we are commanded to recite the *Shema* and its blessings twice a day in the morning and the evening, we pray that God should protect us as we retire for the night and go to sleep *b'shalom*—peacefully.

The word *shalom*—peace, is invoked five times in this prayer. Regarding peace, *Rashi* in *Parashat Bechukotai* writes: "*Im ein shalom, ein klum*—Without peace, one has nothing at all."[24] One could own all the riches, delicacies, and treasures of the world, but without a semblance of peace (internal and external), these blessings are essentially for naught. Therefore, we ask God for peaceful sleep, to provide for us a *sukkat shalom*—a dwelling of peace and that our goings and comings should also be in peace.

Maariv versus Maariv

It is noteworthy that we recite *Hashkiveinu* on Friday night, as well as the rest of the week during *Maariv*. While the rest of the week the other three blessings before and after the *Shema* are exactly the same as the blessings we recite on Shabbat, *Hashkiveinu* has a different ending during the week then it does on Shabbat:

- *Maariv* for weekdays: "*U'shemor tzeiteinu u'vo'einu l'chaim u'l'shalom mei'atah v'ad olam. Baruch…shomer amo Yisrael la'ad*—Protect our goings and comings, for life and for peace, from now until eternity. Blessed God, who protects His people forever."
- *Maariv* on Shabbat: "*U'fros aleinu sukkat shelomecha. Baruch…ha'pores sukkat shalom aleinu v'al kol amo Yisrael v'al Yerushalayim*—Spread over us Your shelter of peace. Blessed…God, who spreads His sukkah of peace upon us, upon all Israel, and upon Jerusalem."

The commentators explain that the theme of the blessing for *Maariv* during the week is **protection**, and the theme for *Maariv* on Shabbat is **peace**. Why is this so?

- The *Kol Bo* explains practically that during the week, we are coming and going amid our daily responsibilities; therefore, we need protection during our travels. On Shabbat we don't travel;

---

24   *Vayikra* 36:6.

we generally stay near our homes and shuls, and therefore we ask only for peace and not protection.

- The *Eliyahu Rabbah* explains that the reason we do not ask for *shemirah*—protection, on Shabbat is because the greatest protection of all time for Am Yisrael is Shabbat observance itself.

> A DIVINE APPROACH: As we observe the Shabbat each week, let's not only observe the mitzvot of Shabbat; let's also aim to be aware of and experience the protective peace of Shabbat as well.

Amidah of *Maariv*: The First Three Blessings

This *Amidah* (silent meditative prayer) includes seven blessings, as opposed to the weekday *Amidah* that contains nineteen. All of the weekday and Shabbat *Amidot* begin with the same three *berachot* of praise, and conclude with the same three *berachot* of gratitude:

- The first *berachah* in all *Amidot* is the blessing of *Avot*—Patriarchs. In *Avot*, we recall the eternal relationships forged by our forefathers Avraham, Yitzchak, and Yaakov with God above, and recognize that our connections to God, Torah, Israel, and each other all rest on these foundational relationships.
- The second *berachah* reveals God's infinite strength—*gevurah*. We acknowledge God's infinite power that not only supports us during our lives, but will restore life unto us even after our death at the time of the ultimate redemption, when Hashem is "*mechayeh ha'meitim*."
- The third blessing in all *Amidot* is the blessing of *Kedushah*—God's holiness. When an *Amidah* is repeated during *Shacharit*, *Minchah*, and *Mussaf*, a communal *Kedushah* is chanted at this point. (Note: We will explore the *Kedushah* formula later in the book. See chapter 3, "*Kedushah* for *Shacharit*.")

After the third blessing we advance with the thematic body of the *Amidah*, which in the Shabbat *Maariv* is "*Atah Kidashta*."

Atah Kidashta

אַתָּה קִדַּשְׁתָּ אֶת יוֹם	You santictifed the seventh day for Your Name,
הַשְּׁבִיעִי לִשְׁמֶךָ תַּכְלִית	the purpose of the makings of Heaven and
מַעֲשֵׂה שָׁמַיִם וָאָרֶץ וּבֵרַכְתּוֹ	earth, and blessed it from among all the days,
מִכָּל הַיָּמִים וְקִדַּשְׁתּוֹ מִכָּל	and sanctified it from among all the times, and
הַזְּמַנִּים וְכֵן כָּתוּב בְּתוֹרָתֶךָ:	so it is written in Your Torah.

As previously mentioned, the *Amidot* on Shabbat differ in content than the *Amidot* during the week. During the week there are nineteen blessings, and on Shabbat there are only seven.

There are several reasons why there are seven:

- Seven reflects the seven times the *Kol Hashem*—the voice of God, is invoked in *Tehillim* 27.
- The twelve middle blessings of the weekday *Amidah* are all requests, and on Shabbat we do not advance personal requests to God.
- Chazal did not want people to have to remain in shul all day, causing *tircha d'tzibbura*—a burden on the community, due to extended *Amidot*.

Nevertheless, if a Jew accidentally prays on autopilot and recites the blessings of the week instead of those for Shabbat, and realizes this in the middle of one of the weekday blessings, he should continue and finish the blessing, and only then go back and begin the section for Shabbat.[25]

There are three phrases in the passage; let's try to understand them.

"Atah kidashta et yom ha'shevi'i li'Shemecha tachlit maaseh shamayim va'aretz—You have sanctified the Shabbat for Your Name, which is the purpose of the creation of the heavens and the earth."

How is it that Shabbat is the purpose of the creation of the world?

The reason God created mankind is to enable them to experience the beauty and joy of the creation, as well as achieve spiritual growth and

---

closeness to God. The day that has been created uniquely for this experience is Shabbat. At this time each week we are actually commanded to
refrain from weekday activities and enjoy God's day of rest and experience the physical and spiritual pleasures of the world He created for us.
Shabbat is truly "*tachlit maaseh shamayim va'aretz*—the purpose of the
creation of the world."

"*U'verachto mi'kol ha'yamim*—**You have blessed Shabbat more than
other days.**"

This phrase refers to the *mann*—manna, that fell in the desert, and
hints to the fact that a double portion fell on Friday so B'nei Yisrael
would not need to collect it on Shabbat.

"*V'kidashto mi'kol ha'zemanim*—**You have sanctified Shabbat more
than any other spiritual time.**"

This phrase also refers to the *mann*. It is saying that since Shabbat is
so holy, the *mann* did not fall on that day. Since on Shabbat the world
is in a state of perfection, we are not permitted to perform any creative
labor, including carrying the *mann* from its place.

Of all the miracles that took place in the desert for forty years, why
does the falling of the *mann* play such a prominent role in our Shabbat
observance, even until today?

Perhaps it is to remind us of the eventual *yom she'kulo Shabbat*, the
Messianic era, when the world will be in a complete state of Shabbat,
and we will see and experience the presence of God as clearly as
B'nei Yisrael did in the desert when they collected and consumed the
holy *mann*.

A DIVINE APPROACH: When we say *Ha'motzi* on the two challot
at each of the three Shabbat meals, let's keep in mind the Divine
gift of the *mann* we ate in the desert. The *mann* was a Divine gift
that demonstrated Hashem's love for us; so too, Shabbat is a gift we
celebrate each week that also demonstrates Hashem's love for us.

Va'yechulu

וַיְכֻלּוּ הַשָּׁמַיִם וְהָאָרֶץ וְכָל צְבָאָם וַיְכַל אֱלֹהִים בַּיּוֹם הַשְּׁבִיעִי מְלַאכְתּוֹ אֲשֶׁר עָשָׂה וַיִּשְׁבֹּת בַּיּוֹם הַשְּׁבִיעִי מִכָּל מְלַאכְתּוֹ אֲשֶׁר עָשָׂה.	*Now the heavens and the earth were completed and all their hosts. And God completed on the seventh day His work that He did, and He abstained on the seventh day from all His work that He did.*
וַיְבָרֶךְ אֱלֹהִים אֶת יוֹם הַשְּׁבִיעִי וַיְקַדֵּשׁ אֹתוֹ כִּי בוֹ שָׁבַת מִכָּל מְלַאכְתּוֹ אֲשֶׁר בָּרָא אֱלֹהִים לַעֲשׂוֹת.	*And God blessed the seventh day and He sanctified it, for on it He abstained from all His work that God created to do.*

After *Atah Kidashta* we recite the Biblical passage *Va'yechulu*,[26] which describes the conclusion of the creation of the world from nothingness, and the infusion of the holy Shabbat into the world. Shabbat is the culmination and the crowned jewel of Creation.

This passage must contain quite a significant message because we recite it three times every Friday night:

1. In the *Amidah*
2. After the *Amidah*
3. During Kiddush on Friday night

Why the repetition?

The *Avudraham* explains that when Shabbat falls together with Yom Tov, the *Amidah* does not contain *Va'yechulu*, but rather *Atah Vechartanu*, so *Va'yechulu* is inserted after the *Amidah* instead. Once it was established that we say it after the *Amidah* on Shabbat of Yom Tov, it was therefore established that we also say it every Friday night. Yet, while this enables the attendees in shul to hear *Va'yechulu*, it doesn't cover the family at home; therefore, we also recite *Va'yechulu* during Kiddush.

Why is *Va'yechulu* so important?

The *Avudraham* explains that the passage of *Va'yechulu* is actually *edut*—testimony. When a Jew recites *Va'yechulu* on Friday night, he

26   *Bereishit* 2:1–3.

is literally testifying in front of the world that Hashem created the heavens and the earth and infused it with the blessings of Shabbat. The Torah mandates that testimony requires witnesses to testify as a two-some while standing.[27] Therefore the custom is that *Va'yechulu* should preferably be recited together with another person while standing in order to provide proper testimony.

A statement in the Talmud also demonstrates the significance of the recital of *Va'yechulu*: Rava once stated, and some say it was Rabbi Yehoshua Ben Levi, that even an individual must recite *Va'yechulu* on Erev Shabbat because Rav Hamnunah stated: "Anyone who prays Friday night and recites *Va'yechulu* is considered to be a partner with God in Creation."[28] The *Maharsha* explains beautifully that just as God created the world with *dibbur*—utterances, so too we become partners with God with our recital of *Va'yechulu*.

The question is, how?

Rav Matisyahu Solomon writes in *Matnat Chaim* that an intrinsic part of the creation of the world was that the greatness and com-plexities of Creation be recognized by God's prized creation—man. Therefore, until Adam and Chavah were created, there was nothing and literally no one in the world that could relate to and understand the beauty and profundity therein. Therefore, just as Adam and Chavah recognized Hashem's incredible handiwork, when we recite *Va'yechulu* on Erev Shabbat, we literally partner with Hashem in the creation of the world.

A DIVINE APPROACH: Notice how we recite *Va'yechulu* three times on Friday night. As we recite it, let's remember that we are literally testifying that God is our Creator and we are doing our part to sus-tain and fulfill the blessings of the creation of our world.

---

27   *Devarim* 19:15.
28   *Shabbat* 119b.

Retzeh Bi'menuchateinu

אֱלֹהֵינוּ וֵאלֹהֵי אֲבוֹתֵינוּ רְצֵה בִמְנוּחָתֵנוּ.	*Our Lord and Lord of our fathers, be pleased with our rest.*
קַדְּשֵׁנוּ בְּמִצְוֹתֶיךָ וְתֵן חֶלְקֵנוּ בְּתוֹרָתֶךָ.	*Sanctify us with Your commandments and give us our portion in Your Torah.*
שַׂבְּעֵנוּ מִטּוּבֶךָ וְשַׂמְּחֵנוּ בִּישׁוּעָתֶךָ וְטַהֵר לִבֵּנוּ לְעָבְדְּךָ בֶּאֱמֶת.	*Satisfy us with Your good, and gladden us with Your deliverance, and purify our hearts to serve You with truth.*
וְהַנְחִילֵנוּ ה' אֱלֹהֵינוּ בְּאַהֲבָה וּבְרָצוֹן שַׁבַּת קָדְשֶׁךָ וְיָנוּחוּ בָה כָּל יִשְׂרָאֵל מְקַדְּשֵׁי שְׁמֶךָ.	*And bestow upon us, God, our Lord, with love and with favor, Your holy Shabbat, and Israel the sanctifiers of Your Name will rest in it.*
בָּרוּךְ אַתָּה ה', מְקַדֵּשׁ הַשַּׁבָּת:	*Blessed are You, God, sanctifier of the Shabbat.*

This *tefillah*, the fourth blessing of the *Amidah*, is the only blessing of the middle section of an *Amidah* that is repeated in all three *tefillot* on Shabbat. If you look carefully, you can find that there is, however, one difference found between *Maariv*, *Shacharit*, and *Minchah*. The difference is in the word after *v'yanuchu* (and they will rest):

- In the *Maariv Amidah*, it is **vah**—feminine singular, meaning **in it**.
- In *Shacharit Amidah*, it is **voh**—masculine singular, meaning **in it**.
- In the *Minchah Amidah*, it is **vam**—masculine plural, meaning **in them**.

What is the reason behind these differences?

I saw two fascinating answers to this question:

1. We are taught that as long as Amalek is in the world, God's name and presence is incomplete; instead of the full *Yud-Hei-Vav-Hei*, we only experience *Yud-Hei*.[29] Since Shabbat is tantamount to *Olam Haba*—the World to Come, on this day, God's

---

29   *Rashi on Shemot* 17:12.

name and presence are complete. Therefore, on Friday night we say *v'yanuchu vah*—adding a **hei**, and Shabbat morning we say *v'yanuchu voh*—thereby adding a **vav** and a **hei** to the *yud* and *hei* we already have, which completes the name of God. On Shabbat *Minchah* we say *v'yanuchu vam* because after Hashem's name is complete, there will be a perpetual state of Shabbat. Therefore, it is fitting that we say *vah*, *voh*, and *vam* during the different prayers.

2. The *Tur*[30] and the *Knesset Hagedolah*[31] explain that since every Shabbat is like a wedding celebration between Hashem, the *chattan*, and the Am Yisrael, the *kallah*, the different expressions in the *tefillot* represent different parts of the celebration. Friday night is representative of the Shabbat of Creation and the first part of a wedding, the *kiddushin*, which often took place in the *kallah*'s father's home. Therefore, it is **v'yanuchu vah**, feminine singular. On Shabbat day, the *tefillah* is representative of the *nisu'in*, reflecting the second part of a wedding service, when Hashem and Klal Yisrael unified through the giving and receiving of the Torah under the *chuppah* of Har Sinai. This is compared to a celebration at the home of the *chattan*. Therefore, the expression is **v'yanuchu voh**, masculine singular. The *Minchah* of Shabbat afternoon is representative of the couple in *yichud* as an established couple. It is a celebration of both the *chattan* and the *kallah*, and therefore, the expression is **vam**, plural.

A DIVINE APPROACH: Just like in the Torah itself, our liturgy, which was authored by prophets and sages, contains meaning in every single word and letter. This is evident in this *tefillah* and the variations of *vah*, *voh* and *vam*.

---

30   Rabbeinu Yaakov (1275–1340).
31   *Orach Chaim* 268:2.

The Last Three Blessings

רְצֵה ה' אֱלֹהֵינוּ בְּעַמְּךָ יִשְׂרָאֵל וּבִתְפִלָּתָם, וְהָשֵׁב אֶת הָעֲבוֹדָה לִדְבִיר בֵּיתֶךָ, וְאִשֵּׁי יִשְׂרָאֵל וּתְפִלָּתָם, בְּאַהֲבָה תְקַבֵּל בְּרָצוֹן, וּתְהִי לְרָצוֹן תָּמִיד עֲבוֹדַת יִשְׂרָאֵל עַמֶּךָ:	*Look with favor, God, our Lord, on Your people Israel and pay heed to their prayer; restore the service to Your Sanctuary and accept with love and favor Israel's fire-offerings and prayer, and may the service of Your people Israel always find favor.*
וְתֶחֱזֶינָה עֵינֵינוּ בְּשׁוּבְךָ לְצִיּוֹן בְּרַחֲמִים:	*May our eyes behold Your return to Zion in mercy.*
בָּרוּךְ אַתָּה ה', הַמַּחֲזִיר שְׁכִינָתוֹ לְצִיּוֹן:	*Blessed are You, God, who restores His Divine Presence to Zion.*
מוֹדִים אֲנַחְנוּ לָךְ, שָׁאַתָּה הוּא ה' אֱלֹהֵינוּ וֵאלֹהֵי אֲבוֹתֵינוּ לְעוֹלָם וָעֶד:	*We thankfully acknowledge that You are God, our Lord and Lord of our fathers, forever.*
צוּר חַיֵּינוּ, מָגֵן יִשְׁעֵנוּ אַתָּה הוּא לְדֹר וָדֹר:	*You are the strength of our life, the shield of our salvation in every generation.*
נוֹדֶה לְּךָ וּנְסַפֵּר תְּהִלָּתֶךָ, עַל חַיֵּינוּ הַמְּסוּרִים בְּיָדֶךָ, וְעַל נִשְׁמוֹתֵינוּ הַפְּקוּדוֹת לָךְ, וְעַל נִסֶּיךָ שֶׁבְּכָל יוֹם עִמָּנוּ, וְעַל נִפְלְאוֹתֶיךָ וְטוֹבוֹתֶיךָ שֶׁבְּכָל עֵת, עֶרֶב וָבֹקֶר וְצָהֳרָיִם:	*We will give thanks to You and recount Your praise, evening, morning, and noon, for our lives that are committed into Your hand, for our souls that are entrusted to You, for Your miracles that are with us daily, and for Your continual wonders and beneficences.*
הַטּוֹב, כִּי לֹא כָלוּ רַחֲמֶיךָ, וְהַמְרַחֵם, כִּי לֹא תַמּוּ חֲסָדֶיךָ, מֵעוֹלָם קִוִּינוּ לָךְ:	*You are the Beneficent One, for Your mercies never cease; the Merciful One, for Your kindnesses never end; for we always place our hope in You.*
וְעַל כֻּלָּם יִתְבָּרַךְ וְיִתְרוֹמַם שִׁמְךָ מַלְכֵּנוּ תָּמִיד לְעוֹלָם וָעֶד:	*And for all these, may Your Name, our King, be continually blessed, exalted, and extolled forever and all time.*

וְכֹל הַחַיִּים יוֹדוּךָ סֶּלָה, וִיהַלְלוּ אֶת שִׁמְךָ בֶּאֱמֶת, הָאֵל יְשׁוּעָתֵנוּ וְעֶזְרָתֵנוּ סֶלָה:	And all living things shall forever thank You, and praise Your great Name eternally, for You are good. God, You are our everlasting salvation and help, O benevolent God.
בָּרוּךְ אַתָּה ה', הַטּוֹב שִׁמְךָ וּלְךָ נָאֶה לְהוֹדוֹת:	Blessed are You, God, Beneficent is Your Name, and to You it is fitting to offer thanks.
שִׂים שָׁלוֹם טוֹבָה וּבְרָכָה, חֵן וָחֶסֶד וְרַחֲמִים, עָלֵינוּ וְעַל כָּל יִשְׂרָאֵל עַמֶּךָ:	Bestow peace, goodness and blessing, life, graciousness, kindness and mercy upon us and upon all Your people Israel.
בָּרְכֵנוּ אָבִינוּ, כֻּלָּנוּ כְּאֶחָד בְּאוֹר פָּנֶיךָ, כִּי בְאוֹר פָּנֶיךָ נָתַתָּ לָּנוּ ה' אֱלֹהֵינוּ, תּוֹרַת חַיִּים, וְאַהֲבַת חֶסֶד, וּצְדָקָה וּבְרָכָה וְרַחֲמִים, וְחַיִּים וְשָׁלוֹם:	Bless us, our Father, all of us as one, with the light of Your countenance. For by the light of Your countenance You gave us, God, our Lord, the Torah of life and loving-kindness, righteousness, blessing, mercy, life, and peace.
וְטוֹב בְּעֵינֶיךָ לְבָרֵךְ אֶת עַמְּךָ יִשְׂרָאֵל בְּכָל עֵת וּבְכָל שָׁעָה בִּשְׁלוֹמֶךָ:	May it be favorable in Your eyes to bless Your people Israel, at all times and at every moment, with Your peace.
בָּרוּךְ אַתָּה ה', הַמְבָרֵךְ אֶת עַמּוֹ יִשְׂרָאֵל בַּשָּׁלוֹם:	Blessed are You, God, who blesses His people Israel with peace.

Retzeh, *Modim* and *V'Al Kulam*, and *Sim Shalom*—the fifth, sixth, and seventh blessings—are the gratitude section of the *Amidah* that is present in every *Amidah* that we recite.

The blessing *Retzeh* asks that we and our prayers be pleasing unto God, and that our service and offerings in the Beit Hamikdash be restored. The blessing concludes: "*Ha'machazir shechinato l'Tzion*—God, who will return His presence to Zion."

The sixth blessing, *Modim*, is our thrice daily prayerful expression of thanksgiving and gratitude to God. This blessing is so important that not only do we say *Modim* in our silent *Amidah*, but there is also a *Modim* to recite during the repetition of the *Amidah* as well as the *Modim D'Rabbanan*. We express our gratitude for every moment of every day that we are gifted here on earth.

The seventh and final blessing is the blessing in which we request peace. Chazal remark that without peace we have nothing.[32] One could live in a palace and be blessed with all life has to offer, but without a state of peace in society, in their home, and in their mind, it is worthless. Therefore, we end so many of our *tefillot*, including the *Amidah*, *Birkat Hamazon*, *Birkat Kohanim*, and *Kaddish* with a request for *shalom*.

Birkat Me'ein Sheva

חזן: בָּרוּךְ אַתָּה ה' אֱלֹהֵינוּ וֵאלֹהֵי אֲבוֹתֵינוּ אֱלֹהֵי אַבְרָהָם אֱלֹהֵי יִצְחָק וֵאלֹהֵי יַעֲקֹב הָאֵל הַגָּדוֹל הַגִּבּוֹר וְהַנּוֹרָא אֵל עֶלְיוֹן קוֹנֵה שָׁמַיִם וָאָרֶץ.	*Chazzan: Blessed are You, God, our Lord and Lord of our fathers, the God of Avraham, the God of Yitzchak, and the God of Yaakov, the powerful, the great, the strong, and the awesome, creator of Heaven and earth.*
חזן וקהל: מָגֵן אָבוֹת בִּדְבָרוֹ מְחַיֶּה מֵתִים בְּמַאֲמָרוֹ הָאֵל הַקָּדוֹשׁ שֶׁאֵין כָּמוֹהוּ.	*Chazzan and Congregation: He was a shield to our fathers with His word; He resurrects the dead by His pronouncement; He is the sacred God Whom none is like Him.*
הַמֵּנִיחַ לְעַמּוֹ בְּיוֹם שַׁבַּת קָדְשׁוֹ כִּי בָם רָצָה לְהָנִיחַ לָהֶם.	*He gives rest to His nation on His holy Shabbat day, for to them He desired to give rest.*
לְפָנָיו נַעֲבוֹד בְּיִרְאָה וָפַחַד וְנוֹדֶה לִשְׁמוֹ בְּכָל יוֹם תָּמִיד מֵעֵין הַבְּרָכוֹת.	*We will serve Him with awe and fear, and offer thanks to His Name every day, continually, in accordance with the blessings [of that day].*
אֵל הַהוֹדָאוֹת אֲדוֹן הַשָּׁלוֹם מְקַדֵּשׁ הַשַּׁבָּת וּמְבָרֵךְ שְׁבִיעִי וּמֵנִיחַ בִּקְדֻשָּׁה לְעַם מְדֻשְּׁנֵי עֹנֶג זֵכֶר לְמַעֲשֵׂה בְרֵאשִׁית:	*He is the God worthy of thanks, the Master of peace, who sanctifies the Shabbat and blesses the Seventh Day and brings rest with holiness to a nation satiated with restful bliss, in remembrance of the work of Creation.*
חזן: אֱלֹהֵינוּ וֵאלֹהֵי אֲבוֹתֵינוּ רְצֵה בִמְנוּחָתֵנוּ.	*Chazzan: Our Lord and Lord of our fathers, be pleased with our rest.*

---

32 *Sifra, Bechukotai.*

קַדְּשֵׁנוּ בְּמִצְוֹתֶיךָ וְתֵן חֶלְקֵנוּ בְּתוֹרָתֶךָ.	Sanctify us with Your commandments and give us our portion in Your Torah.
שַׂבְּעֵנוּ מִטּוּבֶךָ וְשַׂמְּחֵנוּ בִּישׁוּעָתֶךָ וְטַהֵר לִבֵּנוּ לְעָבְדְּךָ בֶּאֱמֶת.	Satisfy us with Your good, and gladden us with Your deliverance, and purify our hearts to serve You with truth.
וְהַנְחִילֵנוּ ה' אֱלֹהֵינוּ בְּאַהֲבָה וּבְרָצוֹן שַׁבַּת קָדְשֶׁךָ וְיָנוּחוּ בָה יִשְׂרָאֵל מְקַדְּשֵׁי שְׁמֶךָ.	And bestow upon us, God, our Lord, with love and with favor, Your holy Shabbat, and Israel the sanctifiers of Your Name will rest in it.
בָּרוּךְ אַתָּה ה' מְקַדֵּשׁ הַשַּׁבָּת:	Blessed are you, our God, who sanctifies the Shabbat.

After the testimonial reciting of *Va'yechulu* by the entire congregation, the leader continues with *Birkat Me'ein Sheva*, the blessing "tantamount to" seven. What is this blessing?

It sounds similar to the blessing we say after consuming cake and cookies: *Al Hamichyah*, which is referred to as *Birkat Me'ein Shalosh* (the blessing tantamount to three). Which blessing is that? *Birkat Hamazon*, which is comprised of three primary blessings. In other words, *Al Hamichyah* is a condensed version of *Birkat Hamazon*. So too, *Birkat Me'ein Sheva* is a condensed version of the *Amidah* we recite on Shabbat, which is comprised of seven blessings.

If we read the words carefuly, we will see how the seven phrases of *Birkat Me'ein Sheva* reflect the seven blessings of the Shabbat *Amidah*:

1. *Magen avot bi'dvaro*—*Magen Avraham*
2. *Mechayeh meitim b'maamaro*—*Mechayeh Ha'meitim*
3. *Ha'keil Ha'kadosh she'ein k'mohu*—*Ha'keil Ha'kadosh*
4. *Ha'meiniach l'amo b'yom Shabbat*—*Mekadesh HaShabbat*
5. *L'fanav naavod b'yirah v'fachad*—*Retzeh*
6a. *V'nodeh lishmo*—*Modim*
6b. *Keil ha'hoda'ot*—*Baruch…L'Hodot*
7. *Adon ha'shalom*—*Sim Shalom*

Since we do not recite a repetition of the *Amidah* for *Maariv* the rest of the week, why do we say the *Birkat Me'ein Sheva* on Friday nights? The Talmud explains that since synagogues were located outside the city in the fields, inevitably there were those who arrived late to the services.[33] There was a concern that the latecomers would be stranded at the shul alone after they finished praying. Therefore, Chazal instituted *Birkat Me'ein Sheva* so that the latecomers would catch up and finish at the same time as the congregation. This Talmudic decree was instituted only for Friday nights; not during the week and not on Yom Tov, unless Yom Tov happened to fall on Friday night, with Pesach being the exception. The *Sefat Emet*[34] explains that the reason why the *berachah* is recited only on Shabbat is because on Yom Tov everyone comes to shul at the same time since Yom Tov does not begin until dark. But on Friday nights, davening begins earlier and people arrive and therefore finish at different times. The halachah states that nowadays we only recite *Birkat Me'ein Sheva* at an established synagogue minyan with a *Sefer Torah* similar to the original decree. If a minyan davens temporarily at a house or hotel, many authorities prescribe not to say *Birkat Me'ein Sheva*.[35] After the leader introduces the blessing, the congregation sings *Magen Avot*, followed by the repetition of *Magen Avot* and the praying of *Elokeinu V'Elokei Avoteinu* and the concluding blessing, *Mekadesh HaShabbat*.

A DIVINE APPROACH: Our prayers are rich with meaning, both in content and in style. The more familiar we become with our prayers, the more we notice the depth and genius therein.

Aleinu L'Shabei'ach

Every single *tefillah* concludes with *Aleinu L'Shabei'ach*, which literally means "It is upon us to praise."

---

33   *Shabbat* 34b.
34   The commentary of the *Sefat Emet* on *Shabbat* 34b.
35   *Shulchan Aruch* 268:10.

עָלֵינוּ לְשַׁבֵּחַ לַאֲדוֹן הַכֹּל לָתֵת גְּדֻלָּה לְיוֹצֵר בְּרֵאשִׁית שֶׁלֹּא עָשָׂנוּ כְּגוֹיֵי הָאֲרָצוֹת וְלֹא שָׂמָנוּ כְּמִשְׁפְּחוֹת הָאֲדָמָה.

It is our duty to praise the Master of all, to acclaim the greatness of the One who forms all creation. For God did not make us like the nations of other lands and did not make us the same as other families of the earth.

שֶׁלֹּא שָׂם חֶלְקֵנוּ כָּהֶם וְגוֹרָלֵנוּ כְּכָל הֲמוֹנָם. (שֶׁהֵם מִשְׁתַּחֲוִים לְהֶבֶל וָרִיק וּמִתְפַּלְלִים אֶל אֵל לֹא יוֹשִׁיעַ.)

God did not place us in the same situations as others, and our destiny is not the same as anyone else's. (For they worship vanity and emptiness and pray to a god who cannot save.)

וַאֲנַחְנוּ כּוֹרְעִים וּמִשְׁתַּחֲוִים וּמוֹדִים לִפְנֵי מֶלֶךְ מַלְכֵי הַמְּלָכִים הַקָּדוֹשׁ בָּרוּךְ הוּא.

And we bend our knees, and bow down, and give thanks, before the Ruler, the Ruler of Rulers, the Holy One, blessed be He.

שֶׁהוּא נוֹטֶה שָׁמַיִם וְיֹסֵד אָרֶץ וּמוֹשַׁב יְקָרוֹ בַּשָּׁמַיִם מִמַּעַל וּשְׁכִינַת עֻזּוֹ בְּגָבְהֵי מְרוֹמִים.

The One who spread out the heavens, and made the foundations of the earth, and whose precious dwelling is in the heavens above, and whose powerful Presence is in the highest heights.

הוּא אֱלֹהֵינוּ אֵין עוֹד.

God is our Lord, there is no one else.

אֱמֶת מַלְכֵּנוּ אֶפֶס זוּלָתוֹ כַּכָּתוּב בְּתוֹרָתוֹ:

Our God is truth, and nothing else compares. As it is written in Your Torah:

וְיָדַעְתָּ הַיּוֹם וַהֲשֵׁבֹתָ אֶל לְבָבֶךָ כִּי ה׳ הוּא הָאֱלֹהִים בַּשָּׁמַיִם מִמַּעַל וְעַל הָאָרֶץ מִתָּחַת אֵין עוֹד:

"And you shall know today, and take to heart, that God is the Lord, in the heavens above and on earth below. There is no other."

וְעַל כֵּן נְקַוֶּה לְךָ ה׳ אֱלֹהֵינוּ לִרְאוֹת מְהֵרָה בְּתִפְאֶרֶת עֻזֶּךָ לְהַעֲבִיר גִּלּוּלִים מִן הָאָרֶץ וְהָאֱלִילִים כָּרוֹת יִכָּרֵתוּן לְתַקֵּן עוֹלָם בְּמַלְכוּת שַׁדָּי.

Therefore, we put our hope in You, God, our Lord, to soon see the glory of Your strength, to remove all idols from the earth, and to completely cut off all false gods; to repair the world, Your holy empire.

וְכָל בְּנֵי בָשָׂר יִקְרְאוּ בִשְׁמֶךָ לְהַפְנוֹת אֵלֶיךָ כָּל רִשְׁעֵי אָרֶץ. יַכִּירוּ וְיֵדְעוּ כָּל יוֹשְׁבֵי תֵבֵל כִּי לְךָ תִּכְרַע כָּל בֶּרֶךְ תִּשָּׁבַע כָּל לָשׁוֹן.	*And for all living flesh to call Your name, and for all the wicked of the earth to turn to You. May all the world's inhabitants recognize and know that to You every knee must bend, and every tongue must swear loyalty.*
לְפָנֶיךָ ה׳ אֱלֹהֵינוּ יִכְרְעוּ וְיִפֹּלוּ וְלִכְבוֹד שִׁמְךָ יְקָר יִתֵּנוּ. וִיקַבְּלוּ כֻלָּם אֶת עֹל מַלְכוּתֶךָ וְתִמְלֹךְ עֲלֵיהֶם מְהֵרָה לְעוֹלָם וָעֶד.	*Before You, God, our Lord, may all bow down, and give honor to Your precious name, and may all take upon themselves the yoke of Your rule. And may You reign over them soon and forever and always.*
כִּי הַמַּלְכוּת שֶׁלְּךָ הִיא וּלְעוֹלְמֵי עַד תִּמְלֹךְ בְּכָבוֹד. כַּכָּתוּב בְּתוֹרָתֶךָ: ה׳ יִמְלֹךְ לְעֹלָם וָעֶד.	*Because all rule is Yours alone, and You will rule in honor forever and ever. As it is written in Your Torah: "God will reign forever and ever."*
וְנֶאֱמַר: וְהָיָה ה׳ לְמֶלֶךְ עַל כָּל הָאָרֶץ בַּיּוֹם הַהוּא יִהְיֶה ה׳ אֶחָד וּשְׁמוֹ אֶחָד:	*And it is said: "God will be Ruler over the whole earth, and on that day, God will be One, and God's name will be One."*

The *Kol Bo* writes that the author of the first section of *Aleinu* is none other than Yehoshua Bin Nun, who was the leader of the Jewish People when they entered Eretz Yisrael, and when the walls of Yericho fell.[36] The latter paragraph is ascribed to Achan as words of repentence before he was punished for taking from the spoils of war at the time of conquering Eretz Yisrael.[37]

This *tefillah* is of such significance that it is recited as the final prayer of every service. It is also said in the middle of the *Mussaf* service on Rosh Hashanah and Yom Kippur and is the only time throughout the year that Jews bow all the way to the ground during prayer. It is also said at the end of a *brit milah*, as well as at the end of *Kiddush Levanah*.

---

36   *Kol Bo, siman* 16.
37   *Yehoshua, perek* 7.

The crux of the *tefillah* is to distinguish the relationship of God and the Jewish People as unique and different than God's relationship with any other nation. "*She'heim mishtachavim l'hevel v'rik*—They bow down to futility...while we bow to the King of kings...*Hu Elokeinu ein od*—He is our God, and there is no other."

Just as in the *Shema* there are raised letters *ayin* and *dalet* that spell out *eid*—testimony, because reciting *Shema* is expressing testimony of *Hashem Echad*, the one and only God, so too, both paragraphs of *Aleinu* begin with an *ayin* and end with a *dalet*. This once again spells *eid* because reciting *Aleinu* at the appointed time testifies to the exclusive relationship between God and Am Yisrael.

Aleinu concludes with the vision of the prophet Zechariah that foretells of the time when all nations will come to the recognition and realization that the God of Israel is the **only** God of the world.[38]

A DIVINE APPROACH: The reason *Aleinu* is recited at the end of each *tefillah* is because Chazal wanted us to leave shul with the messages of *Aleinu* in mind. Let's aim to improve concentration during this incredible *tefillah*.

---

38   *Zecharia*, 14:9.

Chapter Three

SHACHARIT

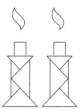

The Shabbat morning prayers begin in a similar manner to the prayers of the rest of the week. They include the opening praises, blessings, and an amalgam of *perakim* from *Tehillim* that prepare us to embrace the yoke of Heaven with *Shema*, and then stand before God during the *Amidah*. We will now discuss the dedicated *Shacharit* service for Shabbat when the *baal Shacharit* ascends to the Amud.

HaKeil B'Taatzumot Uzecha...Shochen Ad

הָאֵל בְּתַעֲצֻמוֹת עֻזֶּךָ הַגָּדוֹל בִּכְבוֹד שְׁמֶךָ הַגִּבּוֹר לָנֶצַח וְהַנּוֹרָא בְּנוֹרְאוֹתֶיךָ הַמֶּלֶךְ הַיּוֹשֵׁב עַל כִּסֵּא רָם וְנִשָּׂא.	*You are the Almighty in the strength of Your power; the Great in the glory of Your Name; the Powerful for eternity, and the Awesome in Your awe-inspiring deeds; the King who sits upon a lofty and sublime throne.*
שׁוֹכֵן עַד מָרוֹם וְקָדוֹשׁ שְׁמוֹ. וְכָתוּב רַנְּנוּ צַדִּיקִים בַּה' לַיְשָׁרִים נָאוָה תְהִלָּה.	*He who dwells for eternity, exalted and holy is His Name. And it is written: "Sing joyously to the Lord, you righteous; it is fitting for the upright to offer praise."*

בְּפִי יְשָׁרִים תִּתְהַלָּל.	By the mouth of the upright You are exalted; by
וּבְדִבְרֵי צַדִּיקִים תִּתְבָּרַךְ.	the lips of the righteous You are blessed; by the
וּבִלְשׁוֹן חֲסִידִים תִּתְרוֹמָם.	tongue of the pious You are hallowed; and in the
וּבְקֶרֶב קְדוֹשִׁים תִּתְקַדָּשׁ.	innermost part of the holy ones You are praised.

These opening lines of Shacharit extol the strength, greatness, and awesomeness of God. We then declare that indeed God shall be praised, blessed, and sanctified by all of Israel, i.e., from the upright, the righteous, the pious, as well as the holy ones.

The *Aruch Hashulchan*[1] writes that in earlier times, the entire *Pesukei D'Zimra*, "Chapters of Praise," was recited without a leader, and the *chazzan* would begin with *Yishtabach*.[2] Nowadays, in the majority of synagogues, a leader begins with the morning blessings and continues through *Pesukei D'Zimrah*, and a different *chazzan* continues at *Yishtabach*.

It is interesting to note that the *chazzan* begins chanting at different places on Shabbat than on the *Shalosh Regalim* (Pesach, Shavuot, and Sukkot) and on the *Yamim Nora'im* (Rosh Hashannah and Yom Kippur). On Shabbat he begins at *Shochen Ad*, on the *Shalosh Regalim* at *HaKeil B'Taatzumot Uzecha*, and on the *Yamim Nora'im* at *Hamelech*. Why?

The *Tashbatz* explains that this is because each of these days is unique; therefore different ideas are accentuated in their respective prayers:[3]

- On the *Yamim Nora'im*, since God judges the world, the *chazzan* begins "*HaMelech*—The King."
- On the *Shalosh Regalim*, we recognize God's strength and involvement in His world through *yetziat Mitzrayim* and *Matan Torah*, so the *chazzan* begins "*HaKeil b'taatzumot uzecha*—God who is intrinsically powerful," which emphasizes God's immeasurable strength and power.

---

1   Rav Yechiel Michel HaLevi Epstein.
2   *Aruch Hashulchan* 53:1.
3   Rav Shimon ben Tzemach Duran.

- On Shabbat, we focus on God as Creator, His giving us the Torah at Sinai, as well as being our Redeemer, so the *chazzan* begins "*Shochen ad*—He dwells on high," which expresses our wonder and awe of God and His presence throughout all of time.

A DIVINE APPROACH: As we begin *Shacharit*, take note from where the *chazzan* begins and understand why he does so with these words in particular.

B'Fi Yesharim

הָאֵל בְּתַעֲצֻמוֹת עֻזֶּךְ הַגָּדוֹל	*You are the Almighty in the strength of Your*
בִּכְבוֹד שְׁמֶךָ הַגִּבּוֹר לָנֶצַח	*power; the great in the glory of Your Name; the*
וְהַנּוֹרָא בְּנוֹרְאוֹתֶיךָ: הַמֶּלֶךְ	*powerful for eternity, and the awesome in Your*
הַיּוֹשֵׁב עַל כִּסֵּא רָם וְנִשָּׂא:	*awe-inspiring deeds; the King who sits upon a*
	lofty and sublime throne.

The same words that are used in our introduction to *Shacharit* match the beginning of the silent *Amidah*—*HaKeil ha'gadol ha'gibor v'ha'nora*—as if to indicate we are beginning the section of *Shacharit* that culminates in our recitation of the *Amidah*, when we speak directly to "*HaKeil ha'gadol ha'gibor v'ha'nora*—The powerful, great, mighty, and awesome One."

בְּפִי יְשָׁרִים תִּתְהַלָּל.	*By the mouth of the upright You are exalted; by*
וּבְדִבְרֵי צַדִּיקִים תִּתְבָּרַךְ.	*the lips of the righteous You are blessed; by the*
וּבִלְשׁוֹן חֲסִידִים תִּתְרוֹמָם.	*tongue of the pious You are hallowed; and in the*
וּבְקֶרֶב קְדוֹשִׁים תִּתְקַדָּשׁ.	*innermost part of the holy ones You are praised.*

In this section, *B'fi Yesharim*, the beginning letter of each second word—*yesharim, tzaddikim, chassidim,* and *kedoshim*—spells out Yitzchak, and the third letter of each third word—*titromam, titbarach, titkadash, and tithallal*—contain the letters that spell out Rivkah. Some commentaries remark that the author of this *tefillah* was a righteous Jew named Yitzchak and his wife was Rivkah.

A DIVINE APPROACH: It is common to find the names of authors of *tefillot*, *zemirot*, and *piyutim* subtly woven into the fabric of the work, as we see here in *B'fi Yesharim*.

U'V'Makhalot Revivot

וּבְמַקְהֲלוֹת רִבְבוֹת עַמְּךָ בֵּית יִשְׂרָאֵל בְּרִנָּה יִתְפָּאַר שִׁמְךָ מַלְכֵּנוּ בְּכָל דּוֹר וָדוֹר.	*Within the assemblies of the myriads of Your nation, the House of Israel, with song they shall glorify Your Name, our King, in every generation.*
שֶׁכֵּן חוֹבַת כָּל הַיְצוּרִים לְפָנֶיךָ ה' אֱלֹהֵינוּ וֵאלֹהֵי אֲבוֹתֵינוּ לְהוֹדוֹת לְהַלֵּל לְשַׁבֵּחַ לְפָאֵר לְרוֹמֵם לְהַדֵּר לְבָרֵךְ לְעַלֵּה וּלְקַלֵּס עַל כָּל דִּבְרֵי שִׁירוֹת וְתִשְׁבְּחוֹת דָּוִד בֶּן יִשַׁי עַבְדְּךָ מְשִׁיחֶךָ.	*For this is the obligation of all created beings, before You, God, our Lord and Lord of our fathers, to offer thanks, to praise, to laud, to glorify, to exalt, to extol, to bless, to magnify, and to acclaim You, beyond all the words of songs of praise and adorations of David, the son of Yishai, Your servant, Your anointed one.*

After the *chazzan* chants, "*B'fi yesharim tithallal*—Through the mouths of the righteous He shall be praised," the congregation continues, "*U'v'makhalot revivot amcha beit Yisrael*—In the tens of thousands of congregations of the House of Israel Your Name shall be glorified from generation to generation."

It is truly fitting that at this moment when the words "Your Name shall be glorified" are chanted in tens of thousands of congregations, it is often the first time in our Shabbat morning prayers that the congregation joins together in song.

Just as all of our prayers have mystical messages interwoven within, here too, the *Anaf Yosef* writes:

- There are precisely forty words in this prayer, reflecting the forty days Moshe Rabbeinu stood at Har Sinai.
- The *tefillah* begins with a *vav*, which has the *gematria* of 6, and ends with a *chaf*, which has the *gematria* of 20. Together this

equals 26, which is the the numerical amount of the ineffable name of God—*Yud-Hei-Vav-Hei*: 10 + 5 + 6 + 5 = 26.

The *Etz Yosef* writes that this *tefillah* foretells of the great day when all of creation will join together in praise of Hashem, "*She'kein chovat kol ha'yetzurim*—It is the obligation of all of His Creations to praise." He also states that the phrase *b'chol dor v'dor* is specifically chosen to reflect the passage in the Torah where God states that until the enemy Amalek falls, His presence will not be fully realized in our world.[4]

The implication is that when Mashiach arrives, our enemies, including Amalek, will indeed be squashed and God's name and presence will be experienced to the fullest. It will be a time of unadulterated joy: "*B'rinah yitpa'er Shemecha*—With joy Your Name will be glorified."

Rav Yaakov Emden in his siddur *Beit Yaakov* explains why there are specifically nine languages of praise invoked in our prayer: *l'hodot, l'hallel, l'shabei'ach, l'fa'er, l'hader, l'varech, l'aleh, l'kales*. The nine forms of praise represent nine of the original ten *maamarot*, the Divine creative expressions God invoked almost six thousand years ago when He created the world anew.[5]

A DIVINE APPROACH: The teachings of the *Anaf Yosef*, the *Etz Yosef*, and the *Beit Yaakov* synthesize a beautiful understanding of our *tefillah*: just as Moshe stood at Har Sinai for forty days and experienced God as never before since the time of Creation, so too every Shabbat morning we sing of the future redemption when all evil will disappear. We will then praise God with all our heart, and the world will again be in a state of perfection.

---

4   *Shemot* 7:16.
5   The tenth of the *maamarot* is represented by the musical instrument, the lyre.

Yishtabach

יִשְׁתַּבַּח שִׁמְךָ לָעַד מַלְכֵּנוּ הָאֵל הַמֶּלֶךְ הַגָּדוֹל וְהַקָּדוֹשׁ בַּשָּׁמַיִם וּבָאָרֶץ.	*May Your Name be praised forever our King, the God, the great and holy King in Heaven and on earth.*
כִּי לְךָ נָאֶה ה׳ אֱלֹהֵינוּ וֵאלֹהֵי אֲבוֹתֵינוּ שִׁיר וּשְׁבָחָה הַלֵּל וְזִמְרָה עֹז וּמֶמְשָׁלָה נֶצַח גְּדֻלָּה וּגְבוּרָה תְּהִלָּה וְתִפְאֶרֶת קְדֻשָּׁה וּמַלְכוּת בְּרָכוֹת וְהוֹדָאוֹת מֵעַתָּה וְעַד עוֹלָם.	*Because for You is appropriate, God, our Lord and Lord of our fathers, song and praise, lauding and hymns, power and dominion, triumph, greatness and strength, praise and splendor, holiness and sovereignty, blessings and thanksgivings from this time and forever.*
בָּרוּךְ אַתָּה ה׳ אֵל מֶלֶךְ גָּדוֹל בַּתִּשְׁבָּחוֹת אֵל הַהוֹדָאוֹת אֲדוֹן הַנִּפְלָאוֹת הַבּוֹחֵר בְּשִׁירֵי זִמְרָה מֶלֶךְ אֵל חֵי הָעוֹלָמִים.	*Blessed are You, God, Lord, King exalted through praises, God of thanksgivings, Master of wonders, who chooses musical songs of praise, King, God, life-giver of the world.*

The *Yishtabach* prayer is the concluding blessing of *Pesukei D'Zimra*, which we recite each morning as we advance toward the *Shema* and the *Amidah*.

The reason the blessing does not contain the normative formula of "*Baruch atah...melech ha'olam*" is because it is a *berachah ha'semuchah l'chavratah*—a blessing that is connected to another one, i.e., the introductory blessing of *Pesukei D'Zimra*, *Baruch She'amar*, which does contain the full Talmudic formula. This same system is utilized after *Yishtabach* with a full formula for *Yotzeir Ohr U'Vorei Choshech*, and then abbreviated blessings for *Yotzeir Ha'me'orot*, *Ha'bocher B'Amo Yisrael B'Ahavah*, and *Ga'al Yisrael*. The system is also utilized during the recitation of *Hallel*, *Birkat HaTorah*, and other places in our liturgy.

Rav Yaakov Emden in his siddur *Beit Yaakov* demonstrates that the first letters of the second, third, fourth, and fifth words of *Yishtabach* spell the name Shlomo, שְׁמְךָ לְעַד מַלְכֵּנוּ הָאֵל, which may indicate that the author of *Yishtabach* is Shlomo HaMelech.

The *Maharal* of Prague[6] explains the significance of the fifteen adulations of God starting from *shir u'shevacha* until *berachot v'hoda'ot*. He writes that it symbolizes:

- The ascending of fifteen spiritual steps that resemble the fifteen steps from the *Ezrat Nashim* section to the *Ezrat Yisrael* section in the Beit Hamikdash.
- The fifteen different *perakim* of *Shir Ha'maalot*—A Song of Ascents in *Tehillim* 120–134.
- The fifteen days from the beginning of the lunar month until the fifteenth of the month as the image of the moon gets larger and brighter each night.

Why specifically fifteen?

Fifteen is the number that corresponds to God's Name—*yud* and *hei* add up to fifteen, which the Talmud teaches are the letters God used to create our world and the World to Come, as it states in *Yeshayahu*: "Ki b'Kah Hashem tzur olamim."[7] Since *Yishtabach* concludes, "*Melech Keil chei ha'olamim*—King and life source **of all worlds**," it is ever so fitting that there are specifically fifteen praises recited.

Finally, Rav Schwab relates that the entire order of the siddur reflects a walk-through of the Beit Hamikdash.[8] It begins with *Mah Tovu* and *Adon Olam* reflecting the entrance at the *Ezrat Nashim* and climaxes in the *Kodesh Hakodashim*—the Holy of Holies, reflecting our recitation of the *Amidah*. He explains that when we recite *Yishtabach*, we are passing from the outer *Ulam* inside the *Heichal* where we can see the three great vessels: the *Shulchan* on the right, the *Menorah* on the left, and the *Mizbei'ach Ha'zahav*—the Golden Altar in the middle. Rav Schwab writes that we can see an allusion to these three great vessels by the three-time usage of the phrase *Keil melech*:

---

6   Rabbi Yehudah Loew (1525–1609).

7   *Yeshayahu* 26:4.

8   *Rav Schwab On Prayer*, p. 247.

- "**HaKeil ha'melech** *ha'gadol v'ha'kadosh*"
- "**Keil melech** *gadol ba'tishbachot*"
- "**Melech Keil** *chei ha'olamim*"

> A DIVINE APPROACH: Each day, we long for the return to the Beit Hamikdash; therefore, every time we daven *Shacharit*, our prayers simulate a personal journey through the Beit Hamikdash.

Barchu

בָּרְכוּ אֶת ה' הַמְבֹרָךְ.	*Bless God, the Blessed One.*
בָּרוּךְ ה' הַמְבֹרָךְ לְעוֹלָם וָעֶד.	*Bless God, the Blessed One, forever and ever.*

A story is told of a father who is trying to wake his son up to go to shul on Shabbat morning. To his chagrin, the son does not budge from his deep slumber. The father exclaims, "You had better be in shul by *Barchu*." The father arrives in shul, davens *Pesukei D'Zimra*, but does not see his son. *Shacharis* begins, but the son is still nowhere to be found. *Barchu* comes and goes, and the son has still not arrived. Thirty minutes later, during the latter section of the Torah reading, the son walks proudly into shul, and sits down innocently next to his father. He is surprised to find that his father is disgruntled and frustrated. The father turns toward the son and says, "Where were you? I told you that you had to be here by *Barchu*!" The son answers, "You didn't say which *Barchu*! There are still a few *Barchus* left in the Torah reading."

This story inspired me to consider exactly when and why we recite *Barchu* in our prayers. Indeed, there are three times in our prayers when *Barchu* is recited.

- Every morning after *Yishtabach*, preceding the blessings before *Shema*.
- Before each *aliyah* read from the Torah.
- At *Maariv*, introducing the blessings before *Shema*.

- Additionally, if one misses saying *Barchu* early in the service, it may be recited at the conclusion by another at the end of *Shacharit* or *Maariv*. This is called a *Barchu Batra*.

There are a number of questions relating to *Barchu*:

- What is the function of *Barchu*?
- Why is it said when it is?
- Why is there no *Barchu* at *Minchah*?

Rav Schwab explains that Barchu is an invitation. The *chazzan* calls out, "*Barchu*—Proclaim God's blessing," inviting the congregation to respond, "*Baruch Hashem ha'mevorach l'olam va'ed...*" describing God's benevolence and blessedness. The Talmud[9] explains that this interchange is based on the *pasuk*, "*Ki Shem Hashem ekra havu godel l'Elokeinu*—To the Name of God I will call, and exclaim greatness toward our God."[10] *Barchu* is only recited as an introduction to passages from the Torah, i.e., the *Shema* or Torah readings in the morning and the evenings, and therefore it is not recited during *Minchah*.

Barchu is a transitional and holy moment of the prayers and is therefore deeply meaningful:

Rav Abraham Azulai, quoted in the *Sefer Levush*, explains that when the *chazzan* chants "*Barchu et Hashem ha'mevorach*—Blessed are You, God, the Blessed," and the congregation answers with alacrity, "*Baruch Hashem ha'mevorach l'olam va'ed*—Blessed are You, God, forever and ever," it is an expression of gratitude that we have been blessed with a soul, the God-like spirit that infuses all mankind with life. The mystics teach us that there are five components of the soul: *nefesh*, *ruach*, *neshamah*, *chayah*, and *yechidah*. Therefore, our response—"*Baruch Hashem ha'mevorach l'olam va'ed*"—contains specifically five words corresponding to the five components of our souls.

---

9   *Berachot* 45a.
10   *Devarim* 32:3.

A DIVINE APPROACH: *Barchu* is recited every morning and night but never at *Minchah* because we do not recite *Shema* or any passage from the Torah at *Minchah*. Additionally, since at night when we sleep our souls depart, and in the morning when we awaken our souls are returned to us, in those two spiritually dynamic moments we recognize the holiness of our souls and recite *Barchu*. However, during the daytime our souls remain within us, so we do not recite *Barchu* at *Minchah*.

Yotzeir Ohr U'Vorei Choshech

בָּרוּךְ אַתָּה ה׳ אֱלֹהֵינוּ מֶלֶךְ הָעוֹלָם יוֹצֵר אוֹר וּבוֹרֵא חֹשֶׁךְ עֹשֶׂה שָׁלוֹם וּבוֹרֵא אֶת הַכֹּל.	*Blessed are You, God, our Lord, King of the universe, who forms light and creates darkness, who makes peace and creates all things.*

This concise blessing contains within it the secrets of the universe. In order to understand it, we must ask a few questions:

- What is the difference between *yotzeir*—fashions, *vorei*—creates, and *oseh*—makes?
- If, in the Torah, darkness exists before light, why does the blessing begin with light?
- Why is it that the first time in the Torah God says, "It is good," this refers to light?[11]

The *Siddur HaGra* explains:

- *Vorei* implies ex nihilo, creating something from nothing.
- *Yotzeir* means to fashion something out of already existing material.
- *Oseh* means to orchestrate and synthesize a myriad of ingredients, even opposing ones, into a whole.

---

11   *Bereishit* 1:4.

Rav Elchanan Wasserman explains that darkness itself is a creation, and not simply the absence of light. It was actually created before light, as it states: "The earth was empty and there was **darkness** over the firmament."[12] Therefore the blessing uses the term *"u'vorei choshech."*

Rav Yaakov Emden explains that the light of the world emanates from the light of God Himself and therefore the appropriate word for creating is *yotzeir*—fashioned, because it emerges from the existing Divine source of light, the original good mentioned in *Bereishit*.

In ancient times, the philosophers believed that different gods presided over different forces in the universe. The Zoroastrians in ancient Persia stated that there was a god of light and a god of darkness.

The Torah teaches us clearly that *"Hashem Echad"*—there is only one God who created and creates **both** light and darkness, good and evil, and synthesizes the different forces of the universe together. That is why the word *oseh*, which implies to **synthesize**, is invoked: *"Oseh shalom u'vorei et ha'kol*—[He] makes peace and creates everything."

Rav Schwab explains that even though darkness existed before light, since we recite *Shacharit* prayers in the morning when the sun rises, the blessing was coined *"yotzeir ohr*—fashioned light," and only then do we mention *"u'vorei choshech*—and created darkness."[13]

He also writes that it was by design that the first time *"Va'yar Hashem ki tov*—God saw it was good" is written in the Torah is regarding the creation of light. This is because the creation of light enhances all future creations to come. The sun has been providing light, energy, warmth, joy, and beauty to the entire world from the third day of Creation until today.

It should also be mentioned that this blessing is based on the *pasuk* in *Yeshayahu*,[14] but one word is specifically changed: *"Oseh shalom u'vorei ra*—God makes peace and creates **evil**" is replaced with *"Oseh shalom u'vorei et ha'kol*—God makes peace and creates **everything**." The Talmud explains that the architects of our siddur chose to use more positive

---

12   *Bereishit* 1:2.
13   *Rav Schwab On Prayer*, p. 259.
14   *Yeshayahu* 45:5.

terminology—*lashon nekiyah*. In fact, the Talmud instructs us to always communicate positively.[15] This is reflected in the Talmudic teaching, "With peace we have it all, and without peace we have nothing."[16]

A DIVINE APPROACH: Every day on earth is a gift, a blessing, and an opportunity. It all starts with a breathtaking sunrise over the horizon. Each morning, when we recite, "*Yotzeir ohr u'vorei choshech oseh shalom u'vorei et ha'kol*," we acknowledge God's handiwork, i.e., the darkness that precedes the dawn, the sun that lights up the world, and the synthesis of the entire solar system.

Ha'kol Yoducha

הַכֹּל יוֹדוּךָ וְהַכֹּל יְשַׁבְּחוּךָ וְהַכֹּל יֹאמְרוּ אֵין קָדוֹשׁ כַּה׳.	*All praise You, all extol You, all declare, "There is none holy like God!"*
הַכֹּל יְרוֹמְמוּךָ סֶּלָה יוֹצֵר הַכֹּל. הָאֵל הַפּוֹתֵחַ בְּכָל יוֹם דַּלְתוֹת שַׁעֲרֵי מִזְרָח וּבוֹקֵעַ חַלּוֹנֵי רָקִיעַ מוֹצִיא חַמָּה מִמְּקוֹמָהּ וּלְבָנָה מִמְּכוֹן שִׁבְתָּהּ וּמֵאִיר לָעוֹלָם כֻּלּוֹ וּלְיוֹשְׁבָיו שֶׁבָּרָא בְּמִדַּת רַחֲמִים.	*All shall exalt You forever, Creator of all, the God who each day opens the doors of the eastern gates [of heaven], who splits the closed windows of the sky, who brings forth the sun from its place and the moon from its abode, and provides light to the whole world, and to its inhabitants which He has created with the Attribute of Mercy.*
הַמֵּאִיר לָאָרֶץ וְלַדָּרִים עָלֶיהָ בְּרַחֲמִים וּבְטוּבוֹ מְחַדֵּשׁ בְּכָל יוֹם תָּמִיד מַעֲשֵׂה בְרֵאשִׁית.	*In mercy He gives light to the earth and to those who dwell upon it, and in His good He renews each day, continuously, the work of Creation.*

---

15 *Pesachim* 3a.
16 *Torat Kohanim* 26:7.

הַמֶּלֶךְ הַמְרוֹמָם לְבַדּוֹ מֵאָז הַמְשֻׁבָּח וְהַמְפֹאָר וְהַמִּתְנַשֵּׂא מִימוֹת עוֹלָם.	*How manifold are Your works, God! You have made them all with wisdom; the earth is full of Your creations. The King, who alone is elevated from aforetime, extolled, glorified, and exalted from the aforetime;*
אֱלֹהֵי עוֹלָם בְּרַחֲמֶיךָ הָרַבִּים רַחֵם עָלֵינוּ אָדוֹן עֻזֵּנוּ צוּר מִשְׂגַּבֵּנוּ מָגֵן יִשְׁעֵנוּ מִשְׂגָּב בַּעֲדֵנוּ.	*God of the universe, in Your abundant mercies have compassion on us. Master of our strength, Rock of our stronghold. Shield of our deliverance, a refuge for us.*
אֵין כְּעֶרְכְּךָ וְאֵין זוּלָתֶךָ אֶפֶס בִּלְתֶּךָ וּמִי דּוֹמֶה לָּךְ.	*There is none comparable to You, and none other than You; there is nothing without You, and who is like You?*
אֵין כְּעֶרְכְּךָ ה׳ אֱלֹהֵינוּ בָּעוֹלָם הַזֶּה וְאֵין זוּלָתְךָ מַלְכֵּנוּ לְחַיֵּי הָעוֹלָם הַבָּא אֶפֶס בִּלְתְּךָ גּוֹאֲלֵנוּ לִימוֹת הַמָּשִׁיחַ וְאֵין דּוֹמֶה לָךְ מוֹשִׁיעֵנוּ לִתְחִיַּת הַמֵּתִים.	*There is none comparable to You, God, our Lord—in this world; and none other than You, our King—in the life of the World to Come; there is nothing without You, our Redeemer—in the days of Mashiach; and there is none like You, our Savior—in the period of the Resurrection of the Dead.*

It is an expanded version of the regular *Ha'me'ir La'aretz*, which we recite during the weekday *Shacharit* service.

Rabbi Jonathan Sacks notes that the *Tefillah* begins with an opening poem that invokes the word *ha'kol*—all, five times.[17] Since the last word of the previous blessing is *ha'kol*, this prayer begins with a reverberating echo of this word.

The *Siddur HaGra* explains the meaning of the four steps of the poem:

1. **"Ha'kol** yoducha—All will thank You,"** when we recognize the good You have done for us.
2. **"V'ha'kol** yeshabchucha—All will praise You,"** even when we experience pain or affliction.

---

17   In the *Koren* siddur.

3. *"V'ha'kol yomru ein kadosh k'Hashem*—All will state nothing is holy like God." While we recognize, praise, and express gratitude to the Almighty, we know that *"ein kadosh k'Hashem*—there is nothing holy like God," whose omnipotent powers and ways transcend our limited understanding.

4. *"Ha'kol yeromamucha selah, yotzeir **ha'kol**—All will exalt you selah, You who forms all."*

Since God and His handiwork are infinite and we are finite, we are unable to properly enumerate and account for even a fraction of His involvement in the world. Therefore, we will exalt Him and express gratitude generally for what we know exists but is beyond us.

The concluding section of the *tefillah*, like the introduction, contains four parts and an elaboration of those four parts. Whereas until now the focus of the *tefillah* has been on God's inimitable Creation of this world and its solar system above and the ecosystems below, the final phrases encapsulate the four stages of life and afterlife for humanity: *Olam Hazeh*—this world; *Olam Haba*—the World to Come; the Messianic era; and *techiyas ha'meisim*—the resurrection of the dead.

1. *"Ein k'erkecha*—There is no one who compares to You" in **this world**.

2. *"Ein zulatecha*—There is no one but You" in the **World to Come**.

3. *"Efes biltecha*—There is none but You" in the **Messianic era**.

4. *"V'ein domeh lecha*—There is no one like You" who can **resurrect the dead**.

Ha'kol Yoducha begins with the acknowledgement and praise of God and His handiwork and concludes with the recognition of our journey throughout the worlds God has created for us, i.e., the four-tiered existence that awaits all mankind.

A DIVINE APPROACH: Prayer enables us to reach beyond the concrete world in front of us and remind ourselves of the eternity that awaits the meritorious. While we acknowledge and praise our Creator throughout our years here on earth, we affirm that there is life after this life that awaits those who will merit to experience it.

Keil Adon Al Kol Ha'maasim

אֵל אָדוֹן עַל כָּל הַמַּעֲשִׂים, בָּרוּךְ וּמְבֹרָךְ בְּפִי כָּל הַנְּשָׁמָה.	*God is the Master of all creations, He is the Blessed One, blessed by the mouths of all life.*
גָּדְלוֹ וְטוּבוֹ מָלֵא עוֹלָם, דַּעַת וּתְבוּנָה סוֹבְבִים אוֹתוֹ.	*His greatness and good fills the universe, insight and understanding surround Him.*
הַמִּתְגָּאֶה עַל חַיּוֹת הַקֹּדֶשׁ, וְנֶהְדָּר בְּכָבוֹד עַל הַמֶּרְכָּבָה.	*He is exalted above the celestial beings, and His Glory is far beyond the Heavenly chariot.*
זְכוּת וּמִישׁוֹר לִפְנֵי כִסְאוֹ, חֶסֶד וְרַחֲמִים לִפְנֵי כְבוֹדוֹ.	*Purity and justice are before His throne, kindness and mercy are full of His Honor.*
טוֹבִים מְאוֹרוֹת שֶׁבָּרָא אֱלֹהֵינוּ, יְצָרָם בְּדַעַת בְּבִינָה וּבְהַשְׂכֵּל.	*Good are the luminaries which our God created, created with insight, understanding, and thought.*
כֹּחַ וּגְבוּרָה נָתַן בָּהֶם, לִהְיוֹת מוֹשְׁלִים בְּקֶרֶב תֵּבֵל.	*Energy and power He gave them, to dominate within the sphere of the universe.*
מְלֵאִים זִיו וּמְפִיקִים נֹגַהּ, נָאֶה זִיוָם בְּכָל הָעוֹלָם.	*Full of brilliant light, and radiating brightness, their brilliance makes the entire world beautiful.*
שְׂמֵחִים בְּצֵאתָם וְשָׂשִׂים בְּבוֹאָם, עוֹשִׂים בְּאֵימָה רְצוֹן קוֹנָם.	*Rejoicing in going out, and exalting in coming in, they fulfill the will of their Creator with reverence.*
פְּאֵר וְכָבוֹד נוֹתְנִים לִשְׁמוֹ, צָהֳלָה וְרִנָּה לְזֵכֶר מַלְכוּתוֹ.	*They give glory and honor to His Name, rejoicing and exuberant gladness in commemoration of His sovereignty,*
קָרָא לַשֶּׁמֶשׁ וַיִּזְרַח אוֹר, רָאָה וְהִתְקִין צוּרַת הַלְּבָנָה.	*He called to the sun and it raised its light, He saw and set the moon's shape.*
שֶׁבַח נוֹתְנִים לוֹ כָּל צְבָא מָרוֹם, תִּפְאֶרֶת וּגְדֻלָּה שְׂרָפִים וְאוֹפַנִּים וְחַיּוֹת הַקֹּדֶשׁ.	*All the Heavenly hosts give Him praise, His beauty and greatness, by different angels: seraphim and ophanim and Holy chayot.*

The *Shulchan Aruch* states that on Shabbat morning, when one is less burdened with worldly responsibilities, it is customary to express greater amounts of praise then we do during the week.[18] This is evident in the next poem we recite: "*Keil Adon Al Kol Ha'maasim*—God is the Master over all of creation."

Keil Adon is an acrostic whereby every phrase of the prayer begins with the next letter of the Hebrew alphabet from *alef* to *tav*.

The *Anaf Yosef* explains that the poem is written in eleven clauses; each clause is made up of two phrases whose opening letters form the acrostic.

- The first clause contains **ten** words.
- The last clause contains **twelve** words.
- The middle **nine** clauses contain **eight** words.

This equals seventy-two words in this section. The *Avudraham*[19] explains the significance of these numbers.

- The opening **ten** words correspond to the *Aseret Ha'dibrot*—Ten Commandments.
- The **twelve** concluding words reflect the *Shevatim*—Twelve Tribes.
- The **seventy-two** letters correspond to the seventy-two-letter ineffable name of God.

The encrypted message is that God, i.e., the seventy-two letters, revealed the Ten Commandments at Har Sinai to the Twelve *Shevatim* of B'nei Yisrael.

The content of the poem expresses:

- The sheer majesty and exquisiteness of the earth's solar system and the heavens above.
- When each of the segments of Creation, i.e., the sun, the moon, and the planets, play their role by rising, setting, orbiting...they are in essence playing a symphony of God's praises.

---

18   *Shulchan Aruch, Orach Chaim* 281:1.
19   Rabbi David Avudraham, Spain (1340).

It has been previously explained[20] that Shabbat is like a wedding between God and Am Yisrael. Rav Yaakov Emden, in the siddur *Beit Yaakov*, addresses the poignant imagery in the phrase, "*Daat u'tevunah sovevim oto*," explaining that knowledge and wisdom encircle God like a *kallah* who encircles her *chattan* under the *chuppah*.

Wedding imagery continues later in the prayer when describing the daily rising and setting of the heavenly luminaries: "***Semeichim** b'tzeitam **v'sosim** b'vo'am osim b'eimah retzon konam*—**Glad** as they go forth, and **joyous** as they return." The commentaries here direct us to a *perek* of *Tehillim* that compares a radiant sunrise to a beaming bridegroom under the wedding canopy.[21]

Finally, The *Baruch She'amar*[22] explains the difference between the words *simchah* and *sasson*—glad and joyous, mentioned above:

- *Simchah* is the joy experienced when beginning a new adventure.
- *Sasson* is the joy experienced when recognizing you have accomplished and fulfilled your goal.

A DIVINE APPROACH: We are able to achieve great inspiration from the great solar system above. In addition to its beauty, complexity, and power, let's recognize the incredible Divine consistency of Hashem's natural order. It is so precise and measurable that throughout the ages, many erred and believed that nature was somehow a force of its own. This beautiful *tefillah* reminds us clearly who the architect, engineer, and manager of all nature is.

---

20   In the section on *Kabbalat Shabbat* above.
21   *Tehillim* 19:7.
22   Rabbi Baruch HaLevi Epstein, Lithuania (1860–1941).

LaKeil Asher Shavat

לָאֵל אֲשֶׁר שָׁבַת מִכָּל הַמַּעֲשִׂים בַּיּוֹם הַשְּׁבִיעִי הִתְעַלָּה וְיָשַׁב עַל כִּסֵּא כְבוֹדוֹ תִּפְאֶרֶת עָטָה לְיוֹם הַמְּנוּחָה עֹנֶג קָרָא לְיוֹם הַשַּׁבָּת.	*To the Almighty, who rested from all activity, on the seventh day He elevated and sat upon His throne of glory. In beauty He garbed the day of rest; blissful restfulness He called the Shabbat day.*
זֶה שֶׁבַח שֶׁל יוֹם הַשְּׁבִיעִי שֶׁבּוֹ שָׁבַת אֵל מִכָּל מְלַאכְתּוֹ.	*This is the praise of the seventh day, that on it the Almighty rested from all His work.*
וְיוֹם הַשְּׁבִיעִי מְשַׁבֵּחַ וְאוֹמֵר: מִזְמוֹר שִׁיר לְיוֹם הַשַּׁבָּת טוֹב לְהֹדוֹת לַה׳.	*And the seventh day offers praise and proclaims, "A Psalm, a Song of the Shabbat day, it is good to praise God."*
לְפִיכָךְ יְפָאֲרוּ וִיבָרְכוּ לָאֵל כָּל יְצוּרָיו.	*Therefore, all His creations shall glorify and bless Him;*
שֶׁבַח יְקָר וּגְדֻלָּה יִתְּנוּ לָאֵל מֶלֶךְ יוֹצֵר כֹּל.	*praise, honor, and greatness shall they give to the Almighty, the King, Creator of all,*
הַמַּנְחִיל מְנוּחָה לְעַמּוֹ יִשְׂרָאֵל בִּקְדֻשָּׁתוֹ בְּיוֹם שַׁבַּת קֹדֶשׁ.	*who endows restfulness to His nation, Israel, in His holiness, on the Shabbat day.*
שִׁמְךָ ה׳ אֱלֹהֵינוּ יִתְקַדַּשׁ וְזִכְרְךָ מַלְכֵּנוּ יִתְפָּאַר בַּשָּׁמַיִם מִמַּעַל וְעַל הָאָרֶץ מִתָּחַת:	*Your Name, God, our Lord, shall be blessed, and Your remembrance, our King, will be glorified, in the Heavens above and on the earth below.*
תִּתְבָּרַךְ מוֹשִׁיעֵנוּ עַל שֶׁבַח מַעֲשֵׂה יָדֶיךָ וְעַל מְאוֹרֵי אוֹר שֶׁעָשִׂיתָ יְפָאֲרוּךָ סֶּלָה:	*You shall be blessed, our Savior, for the praise emerging from Your handiwork, and for the luminaries which You made, they shall glorify You—forever!*

After reciting the great *tefillah Keil Adon*, in which the entire world, i.e., people, the sun, the moon, and the entire Solar System praise God, we begin this prayer by focusing on Whom we have been expressing these praises: "*LaKeil asher shavas*—to the God that rested on Shabbat." The word *tiferet*—splendor, in the latter part of the first *pasuk* reflects the final *pasuk* in *Keil Adon*, "**Tiferet** *u'gedulah seraphim v'ophanim*."

This *tefillah* presents a striking and regal metaphoric image of God Himself ascending toward His Divine throne on the original Shabbat of Creation, endowing the Shabbat with a unique spiritual radiance and proclaiming it a delight:"*Tiferet atah l'yom ha'menuchah oneg kara l'yom haShabbat*."

In the following line, "*V'yom ha'shevi'i meshabei'ach v'omer: mizmor shir l'yom haShabbat*," The **Shabbat itself** then praises God, "*Tov l'hodot l'Hashem*—It is good to praise/thank God."[23]

In Jewish thought, philosophy, and liturgy, Shabbat is sometimes personified. There is a Shabbat Queen, we dress in special clothing to welcome the Shabbat when it arrives, we pray different Shabbat prayers in honor of Shabbat, and we prepare and serve special foods to celebrate Shabbat. It is therefore not surprising that in this *tefillah*, Shabbat itself actually praises God. It is noteworthy that once Shabbat praises God, the rest of the animate and inanimate creatures of the world follow suit. The implication here is that Shabbat contains within it the key to all the blessings of the world. It is the *mekor ha'berachah*—the source of all blessing. If we can somehow connect to and experience the depths, richness, and eternal beauty of Shabbat, the rest of the world will benefit from Shabbat as well.

A DIVINE APPROACH: It is important to understand the meaning of a mitzvah and what it is trying to say to us. Our task as Jews is to not only observe and fulfill the mitzvot of the Torah, but also to try and understand what the mitzvah itself is saying. The mitzvah of Shabbat exclaims, "*Tov l'hodot Lashem*—It is good to praise/ thank God."

---

23   *Tehillim* 92.

Kadosh Kadosh Kadosh

תִּתְבָּרַךְ צוּרֵנוּ מַלְכֵּנוּ וְגוֹאֲלֵנוּ בּוֹרֵא קְדוֹשִׁים.	*Be blessed for eternity, our Rock, our King, and our Redeemer, the Creator of holy beings.*
יִשְׁתַּבַּח שִׁמְךָ לָעַד מַלְכֵּנוּ יוֹצֵר מְשָׁרְתִים וַאֲשֶׁר מְשָׁרְתָיו כֻּלָּם עוֹמְדִים בְּרוּם עוֹלָם וּמַשְׁמִיעִים בְּיִרְאָה יַחַד בְּקוֹל דִּבְרֵי אֱלֹהִים חַיִּים וּמֶלֶךְ עוֹלָם.	*May our name be praised forever, our King who creates ministering angels, and whose ministering angels all stand in the holy heights of the universe and loudly proclaim in awe together the words of the living God, the eternal King.*
כֻּלָּם אֲהוּבִים כֻּלָּם בְּרוּרִים כֻּלָּם גִּבּוֹרִים וְכֻלָּם עֹשִׂים בְּאֵימָה וּבְיִרְאָה רְצוֹן קוֹנָם.	*All of them are beloved, all are pure, all are mighty, all are holy. All carry out the will of their Creator with dread and awe.*
וְכֻלָּם פּוֹתְחִים אֶת פִּיהֶם בִּקְדֻשָׁה וּבְטָהֳרָה בְּשִׁירָה וּבְזִמְרָה וּמְבָרְכִים וּמְשַׁבְּחִים וּמְפָאֲרִים וּמַעֲרִיצִים וּמַקְדִּישִׁים וּמַמְלִיכִים:	*All of them open their mouths in holiness and purity, with song and music, and bless, praise, glorify, extol, sanctify and ascribe kingship:*
אֶת שֵׁם הָאֵל הַמֶּלֶךְ הַגָּדוֹל הַגִּבּוֹר וְהַנּוֹרָא קָדוֹשׁ הוּא.	**To the name of the Almighty, the great, powerful and awesome King, who is holy.**
וְכֻלָּם מְקַבְּלִים עֲלֵיהֶם עֹל מַלְכוּת שָׁמַיִם זֶה מִזֶּה וְנוֹתְנִים רְשׁוּת זֶה לָזֶה לְהַקְדִּישׁ לְיוֹצְרָם בְּנַחַת רוּחַ בְּשָׂפָה בְרוּרָה וּבִנְעִימָה קְדֻשָׁה כֻּלָּם כְּאֶחָד עוֹנִים וְאוֹמְרִים בְּיִרְאָה.	*They all accept upon themselves the yoke of the kingdom of Heaven, one from another and they all lovingly grant permission to each other to sanctify their Maker with a gracious spirit, with refined speech and with sacred melody; together they all exclaim and declare in awe:*
קָדוֹשׁ קָדוֹשׁ קָדוֹשׁ ה' צְבָאוֹת מְלֹא כָל הָאָרֶץ כְּבוֹדוֹ:	*Holy, holy, holy is the God of hosts; the entire earth is filled with His honor.*

"Kadosh kadosh kadosh" is one of the most well-known *pesukim* in Jewish liturgy. We recite it three times each weekday morning: before the *Shema*, during the *Kedushah*, during *U'Va L'Tzion*, twice on Shabbat morning, again at Shabbat *Minchah*, as well as at the conclusion of Shabbat during *V'Yehi No'am*. It is a prophecy revealed to Yeshayahu.[24] When reciting "*Kadosh kadosh kadosh*," we emulate the angels in heaven and praise God with the same words that the angels invoke when they recite their praises.

The Vilna Gaon states that the reason the word *kadosh* is stated three times is for emphasis and to show just how great and distant God is from our understanding, similar to the way we refer to God as *Melech Malchei Ha'melachim*—The King of kings.

The word *kadosh* literally means sanctified and **separate**. When the Torah states, "*Kedoshim tehiyu*—You shall be holy," *Rashi* comments that it means you shall be separate.[25] There are many examples in Jewish life that demonstrate *kadosh* as separate:

- The **Kiddush** we recite on Shabbat separates the Shabbat day as holy and distinct from the other six days of the week.
- When a couple gets married it is called *kiddushin*—it creates a union between husband and wife that separates them as a single unit from the rest of the world. They have a holy bond with each other to the exclusion of every other person.
- When one would dedicate a gift to the Beit Hamikdash, it was called *hekdesh*—holy, because it was separated to be offered as a holy offering.

God is also separate. He is beyond our understanding. The only way we undertake to fulfill His will is through the Torah He presented unto us. Without it we would not know how to live, behave, and relate to Him or to one another in His world.

The *Targum* (Rabbi Yonatan ben Uziel) explains that the three mentions of *kadosh* indicate that God is *Kadosh* on the earth, God is *Kadosh* in the heavenly upper worlds, and God is *Kadosh* for all eternity, from the beginning of time until the end of time.

---

24   *Yeshayahu* 6:3.
25   *Rashi* on *Vayikra* 19:2.

A DIVINE APPROACH: It is important to distinguish that when relating to a human being in person, the less we know of him, the less his presence is felt. However, with God, although He is completely separate and beyond our comprehension, He nevertheless fills up the entire universe with His presence and honor: "*Melo chol ha'aretz kevodo.*" Everywhere we turn we can find God—in nature, in each other, in history, and in our destiny. Every day and in every way He is there, and our job is to perceive Him, emulate Him, and appreciate Him as much as we can.

Baruch Kevod Hashem Mimkomo

וְהָאוֹפַנִּים וְחַיּוֹת הַקֹּדֶשׁ בְּרַעַשׁ גָּדוֹל מִתְנַשְּׂאִים לְעֻמַּת הַשְּׂרָפִים לְעֻמָּתָם מְשַׁבְּחִים וְאוֹמְרִים:	*And the ophanim and the holy chayot, with a mighty sound, rise toward the seraphim, and facing them, offer praise and say:*
בָּרוּךְ כְּבוֹד ה' מִמְּקוֹמוֹ.	***Blessed is Hashem's glory from His place.***

This, too, is a well-known *pasuk* in Jewish liturgy. We recite it three times each weekday morning—before the *Shema*, during the *Kedushah*, during *U'Va L'Tzion*, and on Shabbat day four times. It is a prophecy revealed to Yechezkel.[26]

Rav Avigdor Miller remarks that the *raash*—noise or clamoring of the angels demonstrates how important and significant the act of praising God is.

In contrast, let's consider what people generally *make noise* about in our world? For some it is sports. For others it is politics. For yet others it may be a great sale at the department store.

However, what is really worth making a ruckus over? Yechezkel's prophecy shows that in heaven, the big ruckus is made when praising the King of kings, Hashem.

---

26   *Yechezkel* 3:12.

As opposed to Yeshayahu's "*Kadosh kadosh kadosh melo chol ha'aretz kevodo*," which reveals that the honor and glory of Hashem is present in every corner and crevice of the universe, "*Baruch kevod Hashem mimkomo*" has a totally different meaning. **Mimkomo** means "from His place." The implication of *mimkomo* is that we cannot begin to fathom the essence and the origins of God Himself. "*Kadosh kadosh kadosh melo chol ha'aretz kevodo*" shows us that God is very close to us everywhere we go and with everything we do. "*Baruch kevod Hashem mimkomo*" conveys that no matter how close we feel to God, we must always know that He is Divine and therefore forever unfathomable to us because He is "*mimkomo*—from **His place**."

We often refer to God as Hakadosh Baruch Hu—The Holy One, blessed be He, which is a composite of these two prophecies of Yeshayahu and Yechezkel.

The Talmud states that Yeshayahu and Yechezkel actually saw the same vision, but through different lenses. Yechezkel is compared to a villager on a farm who sees the king, and Yeshayahu is compared to a city dweller who sees the king.[27]

The *Maharal*, referencing a *pasuk* in the beginning of *Shemot*, explains that when God presents Himself to His creations, His presence reflects the particular local mindset.[28] The *pasuk* states that when Moshe was tending his father-in-law's flock, he encountered God's presence at the famous burning thornbush that was not consumed. *Rashi* explains that it is specifically through this image that God appears to demonstrate "*Imo anochi b'tzarah*—I am with My nation Israel in distress."[29] The *Maharal* writes here that despite the fact that God Himself is perfect and omnipotent (i.e., "*Baruch kevod Hashem mimkomo*"), the reason God presents Himself specifically in this lowly bush is to reflect His deep sharing, caring, and concern toward the enslaved and persecuted B'nei Yisrael in Egypt.

---

27   *Chagigah* 13b.

28   In his commentary to *Shemot* 3:2.

29   *Tehillim* 91:13.

A DIVINE APPROACH: Hashem, the Torah, and *tefillah* all relate to us on the level we are at. Although the words are the same, a nine-year-old should not be davening the same *Amidah* when he is a twenty-nine-year-old. So too, each year when we read through the weekly *parashah*, it should reflect different and deeper messages. Finally, as we mature, our relationship with Hashem should deepen and strengthen as well.

Ohr Chadash Al Tzion Ta'ir

לָאֵל בָּרוּךְ נְעִימוֹת יִתֵּנוּ לְמֶלֶךְ אֵל חַי וְקַיָּם זְמִירוֹת יֹאמֵרוּ וְתִשְׁבָּחוֹת יַשְׁמִיעוּ כִּי הוּא לְבַדּוֹ פּוֹעֵל גְּבוּרוֹת עוֹשֶׂה חֲדָשׁוֹת בַּעַל מִלְחָמוֹת זוֹרֵעַ צְדָקוֹת מַצְמִיחַ יְשׁוּעוֹת בּוֹרֵא רְפוּאוֹת נוֹרָא תְהִלּוֹת אֲדוֹן הַנִּפְלָאוֹת הַמְחַדֵּשׁ בְּטוּבוֹ בְּכָל יוֹם תָּמִיד מַעֲשֵׂה בְרֵאשִׁית.	*They offer sweet melodies to the blessed God; to the King, the living and eternal God, they utter hymns and sing praises. For He alone performs mighty deeds and makes new things; He is the master of battle. He sows righteousness, causes deliverance to sprout forth, creates healing; He is awesome in praise, master of wonders, who in His goodness renews each day, continuously, the work of Creation,*
כָּאָמוּר לְעֹשֵׂה אוֹרִים גְּדֹלִים כִּי לְעוֹלָם חַסְדּוֹ.	*as it is said: "To He who makes the great lights, for His kindness is eternal."*
אוֹר חָדָשׁ עַל צִיּוֹן תָּאִיר וְנִזְכֶּה כֻלָּנוּ מְהֵרָה לְאוֹרוֹ.	*Cause a new light to shine on Zion, and we shall all speedily merit its brilliance.*
בָּרוּךְ אַתָּה ה' יוֹצֵר הַמְּאוֹרוֹת.	*Blessed are You, God, who creates the luminaries.*

After the recitation of the *Kedusha D'yeshivah*, *Kadosh Kadosh Kadosh*, and the *Baruch Kevod* before *Shema*, we continue: "*LaKeil baruch ne'imot yiteinu*—They offer sweet melodies to the blessed God." This means that He alone ignites strength, innovates, seeds righteousness, fosters salvation and healing, is awesome and wondrous, and recreates Creation every single day. We then conclude the first of the two blessings that precede *Shema*: "*Ohr chodosh al tzion ta'ir v'nizkeh chulanu meheirah l'orah. Baruch atah Hashem yotzeir ha'me'orot*—A new light will arise in Zion, and we will merit its radiance. Blessed are You, God, who forms light."

There is a dispute as to which light the prayer is referring to:

- Rav Saadiah Gaon states that the subject is our own sun that we see rise and set daily; it will provide a new light.
- An approach based on the opening *pesukim* in *Bereishit* is that the subject matter is a hidden light reserved for the righteous at the time of our awaited redemption.
- The *Rosh*[30] combines the two opinions and states that our *tefillah* is certainly referring to the sun we see rise and set each day, but we also pray that we will merit to see the great spiritual light that awaits us at the time of Mashiach.

The *Anaf Yosef* references the *Kad Hakemach*, which directs our attention to the order of the two blessings that precede *Shema*. The first, *Yotzeir Ha'me'orot*, decribes the luminaries in the sky that brighten our world; the second, *Ahavah Rabbah*, acknowledges the gift of Torah that God has granted the Jewish nation. The *Kad Hakemach* explains that these blessings are specifically in an ascending order. The first, *Yotzeir Ha'me'orot*, is about forces in **this** world; the second, *Ahavah Rabbah*, is about Torah that emanates from God Himself in the heavens and was transmitted at Sinai to this world.

Franz Rozensweig, an early twentieth-century German philosopher who became a *baal teshuvah*, formally referred to the two steps as "Creation and Revelation."

- This structure occurs during the *Maariv* service: First we have *Maariv Aravim*, where God brings darkness and light (Creation), and then in *Ahavat Olam*, we have the blessing of Torah (Revelation).
- It occurs in the order of our Chumash: First is *Bereishit* (Creation), and then *yetziat Mitzrayim* (Revelation).

---

30 Rabbeinu Asher ben Jehiel.

- Our weekly Shabbat celebration is also ordered this way: On Friday night we celebrate the Shabbat of Creation with the words, *"Atah kidashta et yom ha'shevi'i,"* and on Shabbat morning we commemorate our Shabbat at Har Sinai (Revelation) with the words, *"B'omdo lefanecha al Har Sinai."*

Every day a Jew is commanded to recognize and recite the *Shema* and proclaim the **oneness** of God. Chazal have demonstrated through the structure of our *tefillot* that the way to approach declaring God's oneness is by recognizing the wonders of Creation and the eternity of the transcendent revelation at Sinai. After reviewing these two tenets of our faith and history, we are ready to close our eyes and recite the holy *Shema*.

A DIVINE APPROACH: Prayer enables us to notice the brilliance and vastness of the world, as well as to remind ourselves that the best is yet to come: *"Ohr chadash al Tzion ta'ir*—a new and greater light awaits us at the time of redemption."

Ahavah Rabbah

אַהֲבָה רַבָּה אֲהַבְתָּנוּ ה' אֱלֹהֵינוּ חֶמְלָה גְדוֹלָה וִיתֵרָה חָמַלְתָּ עָלֵינוּ.	*You have loved us with a great love, God, our Lord, You have been compassionate with us with a great and abundant compassion.*
אָבִינוּ מַלְכֵּנוּ בַּעֲבוּר אֲבוֹתֵינוּ שֶׁבָּטְחוּ בְךָ וַתְּלַמְּדֵם חֻקֵּי חַיִּים כֵּן תְּחָנֵּנוּ וּתְלַמְּדֵנוּ.	*Our Father, our King, for the sake of our forefathers who trusted in You, and whom You taught the laws of eternal life, be gracious to us as well, and teach us.*
אָבִינוּ הָאָב הָרַחֲמָן הַמְרַחֵם רַחֵם עָלֵינוּ וְתֵן בְּלִבֵּנוּ לְהָבִין וּלְהַשְׂכִּיל לִשְׁמֹעַ לִלְמֹד וּלְלַמֵּד לִשְׁמֹר וְלַעֲשׂוֹת וּלְקַיֵּם אֶת כָּל דִּבְרֵי תַלְמוּד תּוֹרָתֶךָ בְּאַהֲבָה.	*Our Father, the merciful Father who is compassionate, have mercy on us, and grant our heart to comprehend and to discern, to listen, to learn and to teach, to observe, to practice, and to fulfill all that Your Torah teachings include, with love.*

וְהָאֵר עֵינֵינוּ בְּתוֹרָתֶךָ וְדַבֵּק	*Enlighten our eyes in Your Torah, cause our*
לִבֵּנוּ בְּמִצְוֹתֶיךָ וְיַחֵד לְבָבֵנוּ	*hearts to cleave to Your commandments, and*
לְאַהֲבָה וּלְיִרְאָה אֶת שְׁמֶךָ	*unite our hearts to love and fear Your Name;*
וְלֹא נֵבוֹשׁ לְעוֹלָם וָעֶד.	*and may we never be put to shame.*
כִּי בְשֵׁם קָדְשְׁךָ הַגָּדוֹל	*For we have trusted in Your holy, great, and*
וְהַנּוֹרָא בָּטָחְנוּ נָגִילָה	*awesome Name, may we rejoice and exult in*
וְנִשְׂמְחָה בִּישׁוּעָתֶךָ.	*Your salvation.*

The second and concluding blessing before the recitation of the *Shema* is *Ahavah Rabbah*, "With an Abundant Love." *Ahavah Rabbah* expresses our recognition of the immeasurable and overflowing love that God has for His people.

There is a dispute recorded in the Talmud regarding the wording of the opening phrase of this *tefillah*.[31] One opinion is "*Ahavah rabbah ahavtanu*—With an abundant love You have loved us," and the second opinion is "*Ahavat olam beit Yisrael amcha ahavata*—With an eternal love You have loved Your nation." In practice, we utilize both opinions—we say *Ahavah Rabbah* in the morning at *Shacharit* and *Ahavat Olam* in the night at *Maariv*.

The Depth of Love

The *Etz Yosef* writes in his commentary on the siddur that the letter *zayin*, which is numerically seven, is conspicuously missing in both *Ahavat Olam* and *Ahavah Rabbah*. The reason for this is to reference the seven potential types of love available in a family, i.e., a father, mother, brother, sister, son, daughter, and spouse. The missing *zayin* (seven) in these *tefillot* demonstrates that the love that Hashem has for each and every one of us is **more powerful and beyond** even the closest family bonds in life.

Rav Noach Orlowek mentions regularly in his *chinuch* lectures how vital it is to teach our children and remind ourselves of God's infinite love for all of His creations. A child that grows up feeling loved feels

---

31   *Berachot* 11b.

special. There is no love more special and powerful than the love that Hashem, the King of all kings, has for us, His children.

It is logical that before we fulfill the mitzvah in the *Shema* in the morning and the evening of "*V'ahavta et Hashem Elokecha*—You shall love God, your Lord," we first recite with gratitude and appreciation *Ahavah Rabbah/Ahavat Olam*, which tell of God's abundant and immeasurable love for us.

> A DIVINE APPROACH: The human condition and experience throughout life is enhanced and often driven by love. So too, embracing Hashem's love for us will enhance the *tefillot* we recite, and enable us to reflect back our love to Him when we engage in *tefillah* every morning, afternoon, and night.

V'Havi'einu

וַהֲבִיאֵנוּ לְשָׁלוֹם מֵאַרְבַּע	*May You hasten and speedily bring us in peace*
כַּנְפוֹת הָאָרֶץ וְתוֹלִיכֵנוּ	*from the four corners of the earth and lead*
קוֹמְמִיּוּת לְאַרְצֵנוּ כִּי אֵל	*us upright to our land. For You are God who*
פּוֹעֵל יְשׁוּעוֹת אָתָּה וּבָנוּ	*performs acts of deliverance, and us You have*
בָחַרְתָּ מִכָּל עַם וְלָשׁוֹן	*chosen from every nation and tongue. And*
וְקֵרַבְתָּנוּ לְשִׁמְךָ הַגָּדוֹל	*You have brought us close to Your great Name,*
סֶלָה בֶּאֱמֶת לְהוֹדוֹת לְךָ	*forever, in truth, that we may praise You, and*
וּלְיַחֶדְךָ בְּאַהֲבָה.	*proclaim Your Oneness.*
בָּרוּךְ אַתָּה ה' הַבּוֹחֵר בְּעַמּוֹ	*Blessed are You, God, who has chosen His*
יִשְׂרָאֵל בְּאַהֲבָה.	*people Israel with love.*

The *Kitzur Shulchan Aruch* writes that when we recite, "*V'havi'einu l'shalom mei'arba kanfot ha'aretz*," we take the four tzitzit from the four corners of the tallit in our left hand, between the ring finger and the pinky, and hold them close to our hearts.[32] Later in the *tefillah*, we kiss them each time we say the word tzitzit. As we declare that God will

---

32   17:7.

bring us toward peace from the four corners of the earth, we take our *dalet kanfot*, our four-cornered garment, the tzitzit, and bring them together toward our hearts, the place of personal peace.

Why does the verse state that we will not only be brought home to Eretz Yisrael, but first we will be brought to *shalom*—peace? The Vilna Gaon explains that peace and unity is established when we are less concerned with our own wants and desires and instead focus on Divine decrees and desires. When the nations of the world will look upward and devote themselves to what God truly wants and not what each nation or individual wants, *shalom* will be achieved.

Further on in the *tefillah*, we encounter the word *komemiyut*—we will be brought upright. This has several interpretations:

- Rav Baruch HaLevi Epstein explains *komemiyut* to mean we should come back **deserving** to be in our homeland. It should not be only because of the magnanimity of God.

- Rav Schwab explains that *komemiyut* means having reached our potential. While we live in foreign lands with foreign cultures and governments, we are not able to reach our potential. It is only in Eretz Yisrael where we will live under the eternal law of Torah and mitzvot that our potential will be reached.

The *tefillah* ends with a *berachah* that includes the terminology "*Ha'bocheir*—He chooses us."

As opposed to similar blessings when one is called to the Torah, such as "*Asher **bachar** banu*—God **has chosen** us," the concluding blessing of *Ahavah Rabbah* is "***Ha'bocheir** b'amo Yisrael b'ahavah*—Blessed is God who **chooses** His nation with love," which is constructed in the present tense. What does this teach us?

The *Doveir Shalom*[33] explains that this underscores the everpresent, unconditional love God has for His nation. It is well known that the *gematria* of the word *ahavah* is 13, the same numerical equivalent of the word *echad* (which literally means one). This teaches that where there is love, there is oneness between two. It is fascinating that 13 + 13 (double

---

33   Rabbi Yitzchak Eliyahu Landau.

love) = 26, the numeral equivalent of the ineffable name of God, i.e., *Yud-Hei-Vav-Hei*.

A DIVINE APPROACH: Saying the *Shema* each day is a time to stop and focus on the love God has for all of us and in turn how much we love Him—*Ahavah Rabbah*.

Shema Yisrael

See page 34 for commentary.

יָחִיד אוֹמֵר: אֵל מֶלֶךְ נֶאֱמָן:	*One praying alone recites:* **God, the trustworthy King.**
שְׁמַע יִשְׂרָאֵל ה׳ אֱלֹהֵינוּ ה׳ אֶחָד.	*Hear, O Israel, God is our Lord, God is One.*
בלחש: בָּרוּךְ שֵׁם כְּבוֹד מַלְכוּתוֹ לְעוֹלָם וָעֶד.	*Recite the following verse in an undertone:* *Blessed be the name of the glory of His kingdom forever and ever.*
וְאָהַבְתָּ אֵת ה׳ אֱלֹהֶיךָ בְּכָל לְבָבְךָ וּבְכָל נַפְשְׁךָ וּבְכָל מְאֹדֶךָ.	*You shall love God, your Lord, with all your heart, with all your soul, and with all your might.*
וְהָיוּ הַדְּבָרִים הָאֵלֶּה אֲשֶׁר אָנֹכִי מְצַוְּךָ הַיּוֹם עַל לְבָבֶךָ.	*And these words which I command you today shall be upon your heart.*
וְשִׁנַּנְתָּם לְבָנֶיךָ וְדִבַּרְתָּ בָּם בְּשִׁבְתְּךָ בְּבֵיתֶךָ וּבְלֶכְתְּךָ בַדֶּרֶךְ וּבְשָׁכְבְּךָ וּבְקוּמֶךָ.	*You shall teach them thoroughly to your children, and you shall speak of them when you sit in your house and when you walk on the road, when you lie down, and when you rise.*
וּקְשַׁרְתָּם לְאוֹת עַל יָדֶךָ וְהָיוּ לְטֹטָפֹת בֵּין עֵינֶיךָ.	*You shall bind them as a sign upon your hand, and they shall be for a reminder between your eyes.*
וּכְתַבְתָּם עַל מְזֻזוֹת בֵּיתֶךָ וּבִשְׁעָרֶיךָ.	*And you shall write them upon the doorposts of your house and upon your gates.*

וְהָיָה אִם שָׁמֹעַ תִּשְׁמְעוּ אֶל מִצְוֹתַי אֲשֶׁר אָנֹכִי מְצַוֶּה אֶתְכֶם הַיּוֹם לְאַהֲבָה אֶת ה' אֱלֹהֵיכֶם וּלְעָבְדוֹ בְּכָל לְבַבְכֶם וּבְכָל נַפְשְׁכֶם.	*And it will be, if you hearken to My commandments that I command you this day to love God, your Lord, and to serve Him with all your heart and with all your soul,*
וְנָתַתִּי מְטַר אַרְצְכֶם בְּעִתּוֹ יוֹרֶה וּמַלְקוֹשׁ וְאָסַפְתָּ דְגָנֶךָ וְתִירֹשְׁךָ וְיִצְהָרֶךָ.	*I will give the rain of your land at its time, the early rain and the latter rain, and you will gather in your grain, your wine, and your oil.*
וְנָתַתִּי עֵשֶׂב בְּשָׂדְךָ לִבְהֶמְתֶּךָ וְאָכַלְתָּ וְשָׂבָעְתָּ.	*And I will give grass in your field for your livestock, and you will eat and be sated.*
הִשָּׁמְרוּ לָכֶם פֶּן יִפְתֶּה לְבַבְכֶם וְסַרְתֶּם וַעֲבַדְתֶּם אֱלֹהִים אֲחֵרִים וְהִשְׁתַּחֲוִיתֶם לָהֶם.	*Beware, lest your heart be misled, and you turn away and worship strange gods and prostrate yourselves before them.*
וְחָרָה אַף ה' בָּכֶם וְעָצַר אֶת הַשָּׁמַיִם וְלֹא יִהְיֶה מָטָר וְהָאֲדָמָה לֹא תִתֵּן אֶת יְבוּלָהּ וַאֲבַדְתֶּם מְהֵרָה מֵעַל הָאָרֶץ הַטֹּבָה אֲשֶׁר ה' נֹתֵן לָכֶם.	*And the wrath of God will be kindled against you, and He will close off the heavens, and there will be no rain, and the ground will not give its produce, and you will perish quickly from upon the good land that God gives you.*
וְשַׂמְתֶּם אֶת דְּבָרַי אֵלֶּה עַל לְבַבְכֶם וְעַל נַפְשְׁכֶם וּקְשַׁרְתֶּם אֹתָם לְאוֹת עַל יֶדְכֶם וְהָיוּ לְטוֹטָפֹת בֵּין עֵינֵיכֶם.	*And you shall set these words of Mine upon your heart and upon your soul, and bind them for a sign upon your hand and they shall be for ornaments between your eyes.*
וְלִמַּדְתֶּם אֹתָם אֶת בְּנֵיכֶם לְדַבֵּר בָּם בְּשִׁבְתְּךָ בְּבֵיתֶךָ וּבְלֶכְתְּךָ בַדֶּרֶךְ וּבְשָׁכְבְּךָ וּבְקוּמֶךָ.	*And you shall teach them to your sons to speak with them, when you sit in your house and when you walk on the way and when you lie down and when you rise.*
וּכְתַבְתָּם עַל מְזוּזוֹת בֵּיתֶךָ וּבִשְׁעָרֶיךָ.	*And you shall inscribe them upon the doorposts of your house and upon your gates,*

לְמַעַן יִרְבּוּ יְמֵיכֶם וִימֵי
בְנֵיכֶם עַל הָאֲדָמָה אֲשֶׁר
נִשְׁבַּע ה׳ לַאֲבֹתֵיכֶם
לָתֵת לָהֶם כִּימֵי הַשָּׁמַיִם
עַל הָאָרֶץ.

in order that your days may increase and the days of your children, on the land which God swore to your forefathers to give them, as the days of heaven above the earth.

וַיֹּאמֶר ה׳ אֶל מֹשֶׁה לֵּאמֹר.

God spoke to Moshe, saying:

דַּבֵּר אֶל בְּנֵי יִשְׂרָאֵל
וְאָמַרְתָּ אֲלֵהֶם וְעָשׂוּ לָהֶם
צִיצִת עַל כַּנְפֵי בִגְדֵיהֶם
לְדֹרֹתָם וְנָתְנוּ עַל צִיצִת
הַכָּנָף פְּתִיל תְּכֵלֶת.

Speak to the Children of Israel and you shall say to them that they shall make for themselves fringes on the corners of their garments, throughout their generations, and they shall affix a thread of sky blue [wool] on the fringe of each corner.

וְהָיָה לָכֶם לְצִיצִת וּרְאִיתֶם
אֹתוֹ וּזְכַרְתֶּם אֶת כָּל
מִצְוֹת ה׳ וַעֲשִׂיתֶם אֹתָם
וְלֹא תָתוּרוּ אַחֲרֵי לְבַבְכֶם
וְאַחֲרֵי עֵינֵיכֶם אֲשֶׁר אַתֶּם
זֹנִים אַחֲרֵיהֶם.

This shall be fringes for you, and when you see it, you will remember all the commandments of God to perform them, and you shall not wander after your hearts and after your eyes after which you are going astray.

לְמַעַן תִּזְכְּרוּ וַעֲשִׂיתֶם אֶת
כָּל מִצְוֹתַי וִהְיִיתֶם קְדֹשִׁים
לֵאלֹהֵיכֶם.

So that you shall remember and perform all My commandments and you shall be holy to your Lord.

אֲנִי ה׳ אֱלֹהֵיכֶם אֲשֶׁר
הוֹצֵאתִי אֶתְכֶם מֵאֶרֶץ
מִצְרַיִם לִהְיוֹת לָכֶם
לֵאלֹהִים אֲנִי ה׳ אֱלֹהֵיכֶם.

I am God, your Lord, who took you out of the land of Egypt to be your Lord; I am God, your Lord.

Emet V'Yatziv

אֱמֶת וְיַצִּיב וְנָכוֹן וְקַיָּם וְיָשָׁר וְנֶאֱמָן וְאָהוּב וְחָבִיב וְנֶחְמָד וְנָעִים וְנוֹרָא וְאַדִּיר וּמְתֻקָּן וּמְקֻבָּל וְטוֹב וְיָפֶה הַדָּבָר הַזֶּה עָלֵינוּ לְעוֹלָם וָעֶד.	*True, and established, and correct, and enduring, and obviously true, and faithful, and beloved, and cherished, and pleasant, and sweet, and awesome, and mighty, and perfect, and self-evident, and good, and beautiful, is this to us for all eternity.*
אֱמֶת, אֱלֹהֵי עוֹלָם מַלְכֵּנוּ צוּר יַעֲקֹב מָגֵן יִשְׁעֵנוּ לְדֹר וָדֹר הוּא קַיָּם וּשְׁמוֹ קַיָּם וְכִסְאוֹ נָכוֹן וּמַלְכוּתוֹ וֶאֱמוּנָתוֹ לָעַד קַיָּמֶת.	*Truly, the God of the universe is our King; the Stronghold of Yaakov is the shield of our deliverance. He endures and His Name endures; His throne is firmly established, and His sovereignty and the sense of His presence exist forever.*
וּדְבָרָיו חָיִים וְקַיָּמִים נֶאֱמָנִים וְנֶחֱמָדִים לָעַד וּלְעוֹלְמֵי עוֹלָמִים.	*His words are living and eternal, faithful and pleasant, forever and for all eternity.*

Although the *tefillah* begins with the word *emet*, we say *emet* at the conclusion of the third paragraph of *Shema* when we recite, "*Hashem Elokeichem emet.*" There are two reasons presented as to why we do this:

1. It reflects the *pasuk* in *Yirmiyahu*: "*Hashem Elokim emet.*"[34]
2. The Talmud states that the seal of God is truth, so when we mention the name of God, we state He is the God of truth.[35]

Incredible Insight

The *Etz Yosef* presents an unbelievable insight regarding *Emet V'Yatziv*. He begins with the question: The *tefillah* begins with sixteen affirmations, "*Emet, v'yatziv, v'nachon, v'kayam...*" which are all in Hebrew, except for the second word, *v'yatziv*, which is in Aramaic. Why?

He explains that the prayer *Emet V'Yatziv* is a reflection and eluci-dation of the *Shema* itself. There are sixteen *pesukim* in the first two

---

34   *Yirmiyahu* 10:10.
35   *Yerushalmi, Sanhedrin* 2a.

paragraphs of *Shema*. Each one of these sixteen affirmations matches up to the corresponding verse. The first three will be presented here:

- "*Shema Yisrael...echad*—God is one," is represented by the word *emet*—truth, because God's oneness is the ultimate truth.
- "*Baruch shem kevod...l'olam va'ed*—Blessed is the name of His honorable kingdom forever," is represented by the Aramaic word "*v'yatziv*—upright." The reason it is in Aramaic is that Moshe secretly acquired this great angelic verse of praise from the angels while he was in heaven and later shared it with B'nei Yisrael. The angels do not understand Aramaic, so we say this word that reflects *Baruch Shem* in Aramaic so as not to awaken angelic resentment.
- "*V'ahavta et Hashem Elokecha...u'v'chol me'odecha*—You shall love God with all of your heart, soul, and possessions," is represented by "*v'nachon*—correct," reflecting *pesukim* in *Tanach* that associate the word *nachon* with our hearts.[36]

The next verse, "*Emet Elokei olam malkeinu tzur Yaakov magen yisheinu*—It is true that God, our King vis eternal, He is the Rock of Jacob, our shield of salvation," contains the themes of the remaining paragraphs of *birkat k'riat Shema*:

- God is eternal.
- God's connection and protection of Israel is eternal.

The word *emet* is echoed six times from the end of *Shema* until the *Amidah*. It is nearly impossible to state that a fact or an observation is eternally true. What science observes as true today may change in a few years. What society deems as normative in this generation may be altogether different in the next generation. After our recitation of the *Shema*, and the accepting of the yoke of Heaven upon us, we declare that every letter of every word of our *Shema* and the Torah is one hundred percent eternally true.

---

36 *Divrei Hayamim* 29:18; see *Etz Yosef* for the remaining thirteen connections.

> A DIVINE APPROACH: In our world, where realities change from day to day, the recitation of this *tefillah* reminds us that God, the Torah, and our relationship with God through the Torah is eternal and everlasting.

Al Ha'rishonim V'Al Ha'acharonim

עַל אֲבוֹתֵינוּ וְעָלֵינוּ עַל בָּנֵינוּ וְעַל דּוֹרוֹתֵינוּ וְעַל כָּל דּוֹרוֹת זֶרַע יִשְׂרָאֵל עֲבָדֶיךָ.	*Upon our fathers, and upon us, upon our children and upon our descendants, and upon all the generations of the progeny of Israel, Your servants.*
עַל הָרִאשׁוֹנִים וְעַל הָאַחֲרוֹנִים דָּבָר טוֹב וְקַיָּם לְעוֹלָם וָעֶד.	*From the earlier generations to the later generations, this is something that is good and eternal.*
אֱמֶת וֶאֱמוּנָה חֹק וְלֹא יַעֲבֹר.	*In truth and trustworthiness, that will never be abrogated.*
אֱמֶת שָׁאַתָּה הוּא ה' אֱלֹהֵינוּ וֵאלֹהֵי אֲבוֹתֵינוּ מַלְכֵּנוּ מֶלֶךְ אֲבוֹתֵינוּ גּוֹאֲלֵנוּ גּוֹאֵל אֲבוֹתֵינוּ יוֹצְרֵנוּ צוּר יְשׁוּעָתֵנוּ פּוֹדֵנוּ וּמַצִּילֵנוּ מֵעוֹלָם שְׁמֶךָ אֵין אֱלֹהִים זוּלָתֶךָ.	*Truly, You are God, our Lord, and the Lord of our forefathers, our King, the King of our fathers, our Redeemer, the Redeemer of our fathers, our Maker, the Stronghold of our salvation, that You are our Deliverer and Rescuer has always been Your Name; we have no other God besides You.*

Let's examine the final words of the opening line: "The truth of God and His Torah are accepted and affirmed by both the **earlier** and **later** generations." Why don't we simply say: The truth of God and Torah are accepted by the Jewish People **forever**? What is the meaning behind the terminology, "the **earlier** and **later** generations"?

The *Siddur HaGra*[37] in the commentary, *Siach Yitzchak*, explains that while **earlier and later** generations of the Jewish People both experience

---

37   P. 121.

challenges of faith, the challenges are very different. Let's explore the differences between the earlier and later generations:

The Earlier Generations

Many Torah commentaries write about the pure and unadulterated faith of the generation of the Exodus (let's call them Generation E). Generation E witnesses the year-long miracle fest of the ten *makkot*—plagues. They watch the mighty Egyptians drown in the Yam Suf. They participate in the receiving of the Torah at Har Sinai. They see with their own eyes Moshe descend with the first and then second set of *Luchot*—Tablets. Faith is not difficult for them to achieve, but implementation of that faith is a mighty challenge indeed.

The morning after Sinai, Generation E was required to alter their lifestyles, eating habits, relationships, and lives generally **immediately and forever**. No more meat and milk delicacies, no more eating non-kosher animals or even kosher ones without ritual slaughter. Perhaps most difficult was the immediate requirement for Biblically prohibited marriages to end. Some husbands and wives and families that had survived the servitude and persecution in Egypt now needed to separate immediately and forever. Not easy at all!

The Later Generations

The subsequent generations of national Jewish life until today do not face the challenges of extreme and immediate lifestyle changes. These generations have already been exposed to the Torah lifestyle and been raised with Torah as their guide. They face a different set of challenges: namely to uphold and maintain a clear and unwavering belief about what took place generations earlier, despite their distance from the actual revelation experience. Because of this, they also experience the challenges of lethargy and spiritual fatigue.

It is a constant challenge to maintain a freshness and exuberance in daily and weekly rituals we perform; we must put in effort to uphold our beliefs and keep ourselves inspired (hence the goal of this book!).[38]

---

38   The *Vilna Gaon* seems to be referring to the generations of Jews that have continued in the traditions of their ancestors. However, the many in our generation who have been privileged

The remainder of this *tefillah* expresses our affirmation that no matter which generation we live in, it is our task and responsibility to affirm the truth of God as our King, Creator, and Redeemer as a *"chok v'lo yaavor*—inalienable statute."* Rav Schwab writes in his book on prayer that during the Holocaust, when Nazis were leading Jews to be slaughtered, they recited **this** prayer as their final words on earth.[39]

A DIVINE APPROACH: Different generations experience different challenges unique to their times and social surroundings. Nevertheless, while the challenges may differ, our eternal Torah and its teachings remain constant.

Ezrat Avoteinu

עֶזְרַת אֲבוֹתֵינוּ אַתָּה הוּא מֵעוֹלָם מָגֵן וּמוֹשִׁיעַ לִבְנֵיהֶם אַחֲרֵיהֶם בְּכָל דּוֹר וָדוֹר בְּרוּם עוֹלָם מוֹשָׁבֶךָ וּמִשְׁפָּטֶיךָ וְצִדְקָתְךָ עַד אַפְסֵי אָרֶץ אַשְׁרֵי אִישׁ שֶׁיִּשְׁמַע לְמִצְוֹתֶיךָ וְתוֹרָתְךָ וּדְבָרְךָ יָשִׂים עַל לִבּוֹ.	*You have been the help of our fathers from the earliest times, a shield and a deliverer to their children after them in every generation. Your seat is in the heights of the universe, and Your judgments and righteousness extend to the ends of the earth. Fortunate is the person who heeds Your commandments, and Your Torah and Your word he places on his heart.*
אֱמֶת אַתָּה הוּא אָדוֹן לְעַמֶּךָ וּמֶלֶךְ גִּבּוֹר לָרִיב רִיבָם.	*Truly, You are the Master of Your people, and a mighty King to wage their battle.*
אֱמֶת אַתָּה הוּא רִאשׁוֹן וְאַתָּה הוּא אַחֲרוֹן וּמִבַּלְעָדֶיךָ אֵין לָנוּ מֶלֶךְ גּוֹאֵל וּמוֹשִׁיעַ.	*Truly, You are the first and You are the last, and besides You we have no King, Redeemer, and Deliverer.*

to reaffirm their roots and become *baalei teshuvah*, often taking upon themselves dramatic lifestyle changes, may find that their experiences and challenges resemble those of the earlier generations, namely, Generation E.

39 *Rav Schwab on Prayer*, p. 384.

מִמִּצְרַיִם גְּאַלְתָּנוּ ה׳ אֱלֹהֵינוּ וּמִבֵּית עֲבָדִים פְּדִיתָנוּ.	*You redeemed us from Egypt, God, our Lord, and from the house of bondage You took us out,*
כָּל בְּכוֹרֵיהֶם הָרַגְתָּ וּבְכוֹרְךָ גָּאָלְתָּ וְיַם סוּף בָּקַעְתָּ וְזֵדִים טִבַּעְתָּ וִידִידִים הֶעֱבַרְתָּ וַיְכַסּוּ מַיִם צָרֵיהֶם אֶחָד מֵהֶם לֹא נוֹתָר.	*You slew all their firstborn, and Your firstborn you redeemed; You split for them the Sea of Reeds, drowned the wicked, and took Your beloved people across; the waters engulfed their adversaries, not one of them remained.*
עַל זֹאת שִׁבְּחוּ אֲהוּבִים וְרוֹמְמוּ אֵל וְנָתְנוּ יְדִידִים זְמִירוֹת שִׁירוֹת וְתִשְׁבָּחוֹת בְּרָכוֹת וְהוֹדָאוֹת לְמֶלֶךְ אֵל חַי וְקַיָּם.	*For this, the beloved, praised, and exalted God; those in a close bond of love offered hymns, songs, and praises, blessings and thanksgiving to the King, the living and eternal God.*
רָם וְנִשָּׂא. גָּדוֹל וְנוֹרָא מַשְׁפִּיל גֵּאִים וּמַגְבִּיהַּ שְׁפָלִים מוֹצִיא אֲסִירִים וּפוֹדֶה עֲנָוִים וְעוֹזֵר דַּלִּים וְעוֹנֶה לְעַמּוֹ בְּעֵת שַׁוְּעָם אֵלָיו.	*He is lofty and exalted, great and awesome; He humbles the haughty, and raises the lowly; He frees the captives, and redeems the humble, and helps the needy; and answers His people when they cry out to Him.*
תְּהִלּוֹת לְאֵל עֶלְיוֹן בָּרוּךְ הוּא וּמְבֹרָךְ מֹשֶׁה וּבְנֵי יִשְׂרָאֵל לְךָ עָנוּ שִׁירָה בְּשִׂמְחָה רַבָּה וְאָמְרוּ כֻלָּם.	*They offered praises to the ultimate God, blessed be He and He is blessed; Moshe and the Children of Israel responded in song to You with great joy, and they all proclaimed,*
מִי כָמֹכָה בָּאֵלִים ה׳ מִי כָּמֹכָה נֶאְדָּר בַּקֹּדֶשׁ נוֹרָא תְהִלֹּת עֹשֵׂה פֶלֶא.	*"Who is like You among the Gods, God! Who is like You, mighty in holiness, awesome in praise, performing wonders!"*
שִׁירָה חֲדָשָׁה שִׁבְּחוּ גְאוּלִים לְשִׁמְךָ עַל שְׂפַת הַיָּם יַחַד כֻּלָּם הוֹדוּ וְהִמְלִיכוּ וְאָמְרוּ. ה׳ יִמְלֹךְ לְעוֹלָם וָעֶד.	*With a new song, the redeemed ones extolled Your Name at the seashore; together all of them gave thanks and acclaimed Your sovereignty, and said: "God shall reign forever and ever."*

צוּר יִשְׂרָאֵל קוּמָה בְּעֶזְרַת	*Rock of Israel, arise in assistance of Israel, and*
יִשְׂרָאֵל וּפְדֵה כִנְאֻמֶךָ	*redeem Judah and Israel, like Your word. Our*
יְהוּדָה וְיִשְׂרָאֵל גֹּאֲלֵנוּ ה'	*Redeemer, God, Master of Hosts is Your Name,*
צְבָאוֹת שְׁמוֹ קְדוֹשׁ יִשְׂרָאֵל.	*Holy One of Israel.*

בָּרוּךְ אַתָּה ה' גָּאַל יִשְׂרָאֵל.	*Blessed are You, God, who delivered Israel.*

This is the final *tefillah* before reciting the *Shacharit Amidah*. The subject of this *tefillah* is *geulah*—redemption, and therefore concludes with, *"Baruch Atah Hashem ga'al Yisrael*—Blessed are You, God, the Redeemer of Israel." This is in consonance with the Talmudic passage[40] that instructs us to juxtapose the blessing of redemption to our silent *Amidah* (*"semichat geulah l'tefillah"*).

Rav Schwab quotes the *siddur* of Rav Pinchas ben Rav Yehudah Palatchik, who writes that Chazal modeled our *tefillot* in the style of the prayers of our forefathers at the crossing of the Yam Suf.[41] B'nei Yisrael praised God in song and in jubilation at the Yam Suf; so too we, at our moment of longing for redemption after the recitation of *Shema*, express song, praise, and jubilation.

Rav Pinchas also demonstrates that embedded in this prayer is an abbreviated summary of our entire *Shacharit* service. *"V'natnu yedidim*—Our Sages instituted"*:

- *Zemirot*—refers to *Pesukei D'Zimra*
- *Shirot*—refers to *Az Yashir*
- *V'tishbachot*—refers to *Yishtabach*
- *Berachot*—refers to *Birkat Yotzeir Ohr*
- *V'hoda'ot*—refers to *Ahavah Rabbah*
- *La'melech Keil chai v'kayam*—refers to *Shema* and the *Amidah*

After studying and analyzing the *Shacharit* service, we can see a strong and repetitive focus on *yetziat Mitzrayim*. We complete *Pesukei D'Zimra* with *Az Yashir*, we remember *yetziat Mitzrayim* in the third paragraph of *Shema*, and and we review *yetziat Mitzrayim* in *Ezrat Avoteinu*.

---

40 *Berachot* 9b.
41 *Rav Schwab on Prayer*, p. 393.

Why is it that we place such a large emphasis on *yetziat Mitzrayim* each and every day in the morning as well as in the evening prayers?

The basic answer is because the genesis of our nation originates at *yetziat Mitzrayim*. At that time, God willed unprecedented open miracles and led us to Har Sinai in order for us to become a holy nation and receive His Torah. We are able to approach God daily **because** of *yetziat Mitzrayim* itself. In our *tefillot*, we review *yetziat Mitzrayim* and express prayers of gratitude and pride about this event because it serves as our foundation stone and pathway to Torah, mitzvot, and all of Jewish history as we know it.

A deeper answer is that before we humbly approach God in prayer, we contemplate and somewhat relive the fear, anxiety, and eventual euphoria that our forefathers experienced in Egypt and at the Yam Suf. With the Egyptians closing in on our backs and the roaring sea in front of us, we launched powerful outbursts of prayer and soon advanced onto the dry bed of the miraculously split sea. Chazal intended that we approach our daily prayers with the backdrop of our salvation from Egypt and the Egyptians and recognize that our lives and all of our challenges are similarly supported and guided from God in heaven. Just as the sea split for our ancestors, so too God can and will help us navigate through our sea of life experiences as well.

A DIVINE APPROACH: Although we review story of *yetziat Mitzrayim* thoroughly on Pesach at the Seder, every day we are obligated to consider and remember *yetziat Mitzrayim* and how it impacts us until today.

Amidah of *Shacharit*: The First Three Blessings

See page 53 for commentary.

After the third blessing, we recite *Kedushah*, and then continue with the thematic body of the *Amidah*. The body of Shabbat *Shacharit* begins with "*Yismach Moshe*—Moshe will be joyous."

Kedushah for *Shacharit*

נְקַדֵּשׁ אֶת שִׁמְךָ בָּעוֹלָם כְּשֵׁם שֶׁמַּקְדִּישִׁים אוֹתוֹ בִּשְׁמֵי מָרוֹם כַּכָּתוּב עַל יַד נְבִיאֶךָ וְקָרָא זֶה אֶל זֶה וְאָמַר.	*We will sanctify Your Name in the world, similar to how they sanctify it in the Upper Heavens, as it is written by the hand of Your prophet: And they will call one to the other and say:*
קָדוֹשׁ קָדוֹשׁ קָדוֹשׁ ה' צְבָאוֹת מְלֹא כָל הָאָרֶץ כְּבוֹדוֹ.	*"Holy, Holy, Holy, God, the Master of Hosts, the entire earth is filled with His glory!"*
אָז בְּקוֹל רַעַשׁ גָּדוֹל אַדִּיר וְחָזָק מַשְׁמִיעִים קוֹל מִתְנַשְּׂאִים לְעֻמַּת שְׂרָפִים לְעֻמָּתָם בָּרוּךְ יֹאמֵרוּ.	*Then, with a powerful roaring sound, great and mighty, they make their voice heard, and rising toward the Seraphim, facing them, offer praise and say:*
בָּרוּךְ כְּבוֹד ה' מִמְּקוֹמוֹ:	*"Blessed be God's glory from His place!"*
מִמְּקוֹמְךָ מַלְכֵּנוּ תוֹפִיעַ וְתִמְלוֹךְ עָלֵינוּ כִּי מְחַכִּים אֲנַחְנוּ לָךְ מָתַי תִּמְלֹךְ בְּצִיּוֹן בְּקָרוֹב בְּיָמֵינוּ לְעוֹלָם וָעֶד תִּשְׁכּוֹן. תִּתְגַּדֵּל וְתִתְקַדֵּשׁ בְּתוֹךְ יְרוּשָׁלַיִם עִירְךָ לְדוֹר וָדוֹר וּלְנֵצַח נְצָחִים וְעֵינֵינוּ תִרְאֶינָה מַלְכוּתֶךָ כַּדָּבָר הָאָמוּר בְּשִׁירֵי עֻזֶּךָ עַל יְדֵי דָּוִד מְשִׁיחַ צִדְקֶךָ.	*From Your place, our King, reveal Yourself, and reign over us, for we wait for You. When will You reign in Zion? Soon in our days, forever and ever, You shall rest there. May You be exalted and hallowed within Jerusalem Your city, for all generations and to all eternity. May our eyes behold Your Kingship, as it is said in the songs of Your power, by David, Your righteous anointed one:*
יִמְלֹךְ ה' לְעוֹלָם אֱלֹהַיִךְ צִיּוֹן לְדֹר וָדֹר הַלְלוּיָ-הּ.	*God shall reign forever; your God, of Zion, throughout all generations. Halleluyah.*
לְדוֹר וָדוֹר נַגִּיד גָּדְלֶךָ וּלְנֵצַח נְצָחִים קְדֻשָּׁתְךָ נַקְדִּישׁ וְשִׁבְחֲךָ אֱלֹהֵינוּ מִפִּינוּ לֹא יָמוּשׁ לְעוֹלָם וָעֶד כִּי אֵל מֶלֶךְ גָּדוֹל וְקָדוֹשׁ אָתָּה.	*From generation to generation we shall tell of Your greatness, and forever and ever Your sanctity we will sanctify, and Your praise, our God, will never cease from our lips, forever, for You are the Almighty, the great and holy King.*
בָּרוּךְ אַתָּה ה' הָאֵל הַקָּדוֹשׁ (בעשי"ת: הַמֶּלֶךְ הַקָּדוֹשׁ).	*Blessed are You, God, the Holy Almighty (during the Ten Days of Repentance: the Holy King).*

When davening with a minyan, after the third blessing, *HaKeil Ha'kadosh*, which is associated with Yaakov Avinu, we recite *Kedushah*—a sanctification of God's name. The reason we say it here is because Yaakov is associated with *kedushah*—holiness. The Kabbalistic sources even state that an image of Yaakov is actually located by the throne of God in heaven.

We have already explored the *Kedushah* recited before *Shema*, and we will again discuss *Kedushah* when we get to *Mussaf*. Here, during *Shacharit*, the traditional formula of *Kedushah* is invoked: *Nekadesh*; *Kadosh* three times and *Baruch kevod Hashem mimkomo*, and the concluding *Yimloch Hashem l'olam*.

One significant difference in this *Kedushah* is our use of the word *mimkomcha*, which means From **Your** place, God, **You** will reveal your Kingship. In all other times we pray that God reveals Himself during a *Kedushah*, it is in the third person, *mimkomo*—from **His** place.

Why is it different here?

- The *Matteh Moshe* explains that since Shabbat morning we are involved in praising Hashem in a much more elaborate *Pesukei D'Zimra* than any other time of the week, we achieve a loftier mind-space and therefore address Him directly with "*mimkomcha*—from Your Place."

- The *Anaf Yosef* explains that after the angels are befuddled and say, "*Baruch Kevod Hashem Mimkomo*—Blessed is God from His place," we beseech Hashem, asking Him to engage with us directly and rule over us, also on His earthly throne in Yerushalayim.

- Finally, it seems that Shabbat morning, as opposed to all other *tefillot*, is most fitting to address Hashem directly in the second person because it is the *tefillah* that reflects our direct interaction with Hashem at Har Sinai. Sinai is the only time in the history of the world that Hashem ever revealed Himself directly to millions of people. Therefore, it is specifically on Shabbat morning that we say "*mimkomcha*—from Your Place You will reveal Your Kingship."

A DIVINE APPROACH: The Talmud states that there are ten different words for prayer in Hebrew and each one of them connotes a different meaning and approach. Our sages have chosen the precise terminology for the particular *tefillah* we are reciting.

Yismach Moshe

יִשְׂמַח מֹשֶׁה בְּמַתְּנַת חֶלְקוֹ	*Moshe rejoiced in the gift of his portion, for You*
כִּי עֶבֶד נֶאֱמָן קָרָאתָ לּוֹ	*called him a faithful servant. You gave him a*
כְּלִיל תִּפְאֶרֶת בְּרֹאשׁוֹ נָתַתָּ	*beautiful crown for his head as he stood before*
לוֹ בְּעָמְדוֹ לְפָנֶיךָ עַל הַר סִינַי.	*You on Mount Sinai.*
וּשְׁנֵי לוּחוֹת אֲבָנִים הוֹרִיד	*And he brought down two stone Tablets in*
בְּיָדוֹ וְכָתוּב בָּהֶם שְׁמִירַת	*his hand, written on them the observance of*
שַׁבָּת וְכֵן כָּתוּב בְּתוֹרָתֶךָ.	*Shabbat; and so it is written in Your Torah:*
וְשָׁמְרוּ בְנֵי יִשְׂרָאֵל אֶת	*And the Children of Israel shall observe the*
הַשַּׁבָּת לַעֲשׂוֹת אֶת הַשַּׁבָּת	*Shabbat, establishing the Shabbat throughout*
לְדֹרֹתָם בְּרִית עוֹלָם בֵּינִי	*their generations as an everlasting covenant.*
וּבֵין בְּנֵי יִשְׂרָאֵל אוֹת הִיא	*Between Myself and the Children of Israel it is*
לְעֹלָם כִּי שֵׁשֶׁת יָמִים עָשָׂה	*an eternal sign, for in six days God made the*
ה' אֶת הַשָּׁמַיִם וְאֶת הָאָרֶץ	*Heavens and the earth, and on the seventh day*
וּבַיּוֹם הַשְּׁבִיעִי שָׁבַת וַיִּנָּפַשׁ.	*He ceased from work, and rested.*

Let's explore the opening phrases in order to derive a deeper meaning and understanding of our *tefillah* by asking a few questions:

- Why do we start with Moshe and the covenant at Sinai?
- What is meant by a crown on/in his head?
- Why are we recalling the moment that was diminished by the worshipping of the *Egel Zahav*—Golden Calf, and the breaking of the *Luchot*?

Answers:

- The Talmud teaches that the *Aseret Ha'dibrot* were transmitted **on** Shabbat morning. Therefore, we begin our Shabbat morning

Amidah recalling the covenant at Har Sinai. The commentaries also teach that long before Shabbat was commanded at Sinai, Moshe orchestrated a Shabbat day of rest in Egypt for B'nei Yisrael by advising Pharaoh that all slaves need a day off to re-energize themselves, and Moshe chose Shabbat as the day off.

- "A crown on/in his head": Chazal explain that the crown of Moshe was the radiance on his face after his encounter with God at Sinai. In *Shemot*, it states that when Moshe descended from the mountain, his face was radiant.[42] When Moshe was not communicating with God or teaching Torah to B'nei Yisrael, he would keep his radiant face covered with a mask. Rav Chaim Volozhiner explains that the reason the crown was "***b'rosho***—**in** his head," and not "***al*** *rosho*—**on** his head," is because the crown is Torah, which is spiritual and not physical.[43] A physical acquisition remains external, but a spiritual acquisition is inculcated in the core of the soul, hence *b'rosho*—**in** his head.

- Finally, we are not glorifying a moment that was overshadowed by the debacle of the *Egel Zahav*, i.e., the receiving of the first set of *Luchot*; rather, we are invoking the receiving of the second set of *Luchot* carved out by Moshe himself. Moshe descended from the mountain the third and final time on Yom Kippur in the year 2449 with the **second set** of *Luchot*, which B'nei Yisrael carried with them all forty years through the desert.

A DIVINE APPROACH: Every Shabbat morning during the *Shacharit Amidah*, we can reflect on the great Shabbat of Sinai. It was on that day of revelation that we became an eternal nation, a nation of royal priests charged with the vital task of bringing light, truth, and goodness to the world forever.

---

42   *Shemot* 34:19–35.
43   *Siddur HaGra*, p. 262.

V'Shamru B'nei Yisrael Et HaShabbat

וְשָׁמְרוּ בְנֵי יִשְׂרָאֵל אֶת הַשַּׁבָּת. לַעֲשׂוֹת אֶת הַשַּׁבָּת לְדֹרֹתָם בְּרִית עוֹלָם: בֵּינִי וּבֵין בְּנֵי יִשְׂרָאֵל אוֹת הִיא לְעֹלָם. כִּי שֵׁשֶׁת יָמִים עָשָׂה ה' אֶת הַשָּׁמַיִם וְאֶת הָאָרֶץ. וּבַיּוֹם הַשְּׁבִיעִי שָׁבַת וַיִּנָּפַשׁ:	*The Children of Israel must keep the Shabbat, observing the Shabbat in every generation as an everlasting covenant. It is a sign between Me and the Children of Israel for ever, for in six days God made the heavens and the earth, but on the seventh day He ceased work and refreshed Himself.*

V'Shamru is one of the most well-known passages in the Torah. It is chanted Friday nights before the Shabbat *Amidah* and it is also the opening passage of the Kiddush we recite Shabbat morning after services and before the meal. Over the centuries, beautiful melodies have been composed to express the grandeur of these *pesukim*.

Careful observation of this *tefillah* requires us to ask some compelling questions:

- We are taught in the Talmud that at Har Sinai, God stated simultaneously both "*Zachor*—Remember the Shabbat," as well as "*Shamor*—Guard the Shabbat." Why does our prayer only state *shamor*: "*V'shamru B'nei Yisrael*"?
- The prayer invokes the awe-inspiring transmission of the *Aseret Ha'dibrot* at Har Sinai, but quotes from a completely different passage in the Torah from *Ki Tisa*. Why doesn't the prayer simply quote *v'shamru* from the *Aseret Ha'dibrot*?

Answers:

- The *Anaf Yosef* explains that the first set of *Luchot* contain the word *zachor* and were broken, whereas the second set of *Luchot* that remained forever contain the phrase "*Shamor et yom ha-Shabbat*." It is therefore appropriate that the *tefillah* we recite today reflects the unbroken version—"*V'shamru B'nei Yisrael et haShabbat*."

- The *Iyun Tefillah* explains the reason for including *shamor* is because the Torah stresses *shamor* with much greater frequency than *zachor*. *Shamor*, which commands us to maintain and protect the sanctity of Shabbat by abstaining from prohibited labors, is mentioned seven times in the Torah, while *zachor*, which commands us in the positive mitzvot on Shabbat such as Kiddush and eating three meals, is only mentioned once.

- The *Iyun Tefillah* also writes that the reason the mitzvah of Shabbat is quoted from *Shemos* 31 and not from the *Aseret Ha'dibrot* themselves is to demonstrate that the *Aseret Ha'dibrot* are no more legally significant and authoritative than all other mitzvot.

A DIVINE APPROACH: Shabbat is our weekly reminder of the eternal relationship we share with our Creator. "*Ot hi*—It is an eternal sign." It is our task to read the sign each week and celebrate the gift of Shabbat.

V'Lo Netato Hashem Elokeinu L'Goyei Ha'aratzot

וְלֹא נְתַתּוֹ ה׳ אֱלֹהֵינוּ לְגוֹיֵי הָאֲרָצוֹת וְלֹא הִנְחַלְתּוֹ מַלְכֵּנוּ לְעוֹבְדֵי פְסִילִים וְגַם בִּמְנוּחָתוֹ לֹא יִשְׁכְּנוּ עֲרֵלִים כִּי לְיִשְׂרָאֵל עַמְּךָ נְתַתּוֹ בְּאַהֲבָה לְזֶרַע יַעֲקֹב אֲשֶׁר בָּם בָּחָרְתָּ	*And You, God, our Lord, did not give it [the Shabbat] to the nations of the world, nor did You, our King, grant it as a heritage to idol worshippers, nor can the uncircumcised participate in its rest—for to Israel, Your people, You have given it with love, to the descendants of Yaakov whom You have chosen.*
עַם מְקַדְּשֵׁי שְׁבִיעִי כֻּלָּם יִשְׂבְּעוּ וְיִתְעַנְּגוּ מִטּוּבֶךָ וּבַשְּׁבִיעִי רָצִיתָ בּוֹ וְקִדַּשְׁתּוֹ חֶמְדַּת יָמִים אוֹתוֹ קָרָאתָ זֵכֶר לְמַעֲשֵׂה בְרֵאשִׁית.	*A nation who sanctifies the seventh day, all of whom are satiated and touched by Your good, and the seventh day You desired and sanctified, the most desired of days You called it, a remembrance to Creation.*

"*V'lo netato Hashem Elokeinu l'goyei ha'aratzot*"—only to us!

1. Hashem did not give the Shabbat to the nations of the world.
2. He did not share the glory of Shabbat with idol worshippers.
3. The mitzvah to rest on Shabbat is not to be experienced by *areilim*—the uncircumcised.

The *Doveir Shalom* explains that the three different descriptions of those who did **not** receive the Shabbat represent the three famous Shabbatot in history:

1. The Shabbat of Creation
2. The Shabbat of Har Sinai
3. The future Shabbat of the Messianic era

"*Ki l'Yisrael amecha netato **b'ahavah**—*Rather it is unto the nation of Israel that Shabbat has been given with **love**."

Consider this story:

> As an adult, Daniel returned to his childhood bedroom in order to find memorable possessions from his youth. Aside from books, letters, stuffed animals, and old clothing, he found an old looking tie pin he had received from his late grandfather ten years prior. He knew that it was important and memorable, but he could not remember why. He took it home and placed it on the coffee table.
>
> Later that year, Uncle Shmuel came to the house for Yom Tov and saw the old tie pin. He shrieked with amazement and exclaimed, "Do you know what this is? This is the tie pin my late father received from his grandfather in Poland that was uniquely crafted in order to carry the synagogue key in their shtetl where there was no eiruv. Without this pin, they would not have been able to exit and enter the synagogue safely during those years. Zeide used to show us this tie pin all the time with pride, as a sign of the devotion and dedication of our family's commitment to Shabbat, Torah, and mitzvot, despite ongoing pressures of anti-Semitism.

"Your Zeide gave this to you because you now represent our family and our steadfast commitment to Shabbat, Torah, and mitzvot. It is because of your Zeide's love and confidence in you that he specifically placed this heirloom in your possession.

"From this day on, please pledge that every Shabbat you will don the historic pin that represents your family's remarkable loyalty and dedication to God and Torah throughout the generations, as a sign of pride and commitment to your family, history, and destiny. And every time you glance down at the tie pin, you will reflect on the great love and trust your Zeide showed by giving this pin to you."

The lesson we learn from this story is that although all believing Jews know that God gave us the Shabbat (as it is the fourth of the *Aseret Ha'dibrot*), we don't always consider the historic and cosmic significance of the gift of Shabbat and the love God demonstrated by His presenting it to us. The Talmud says that when celebrating Shabbat, one can access a taste of *Olam Haba*—eternity.[44] Shabbat is a central tenet of Judaism. A Jew who observes Shabbat is connected to eternity, and a Jew who does not, God forbid, is detached. A non-Jew is actually forbidden to observe Shabbat. This verse in the *tefillah* reminds us of the magnitude of the gift of Shabbat, *"Ki l'Yisrael amecha netato **b'ahavah**—*That it was unto the nation of Israel that Shabbat was given with **love**."

A DIVINE APPROACH: Research and review with your family some of the unique Shabbat and holiday customs that have been passed down through the generations, and then treasure them.

---

44   *Berachot 9.*

Retzeh Bi'menuchateinu

אֱלֹהֵינוּ וֵאלֹהֵי אֲבוֹתֵינוּ רְצֵה בִמְנוּחָתֵנוּ קַדְּשֵׁנוּ בְּמִצְוֹתֶיךָ וְתֵן חֶלְקֵנוּ בְּתוֹרָתֶךָ.	*Our Lord and Lord of our fathers, find favor in our rest, sanctify us with Your commandments and place our portion in Your Torah;*
שַׂבְּעֵנוּ מִטּוּבֶךָ וְשַׂמְּחֵנוּ בִּישׁוּעָתֶךָ וְטַהֵר לִבֵּנוּ לְעָבְדְּךָ בֶּאֱמֶת וְהַנְחִילֵנוּ ה׳ אֱלֹהֵינוּ בְּאַהֲבָה וּבְרָצוֹן שַׁבַּת קָדְשֶׁךָ וְיָנוּחוּ בוֹ יִשְׂרָאֵל מְקַדְּשֵׁי שְׁמֶךָ.	*satiate us with Your good, and gladden us with Your salvation, and purify our heart to serve You in truth; and bestow upon us, God, our Lord, with love and goodwill, Your holy Shabbat, and may all of Israel, who sanctify Your Name, rest on it.*
בָּרוּךְ אַתָּה ה׳ מְקַדֵּשׁ הַשַּׁבָּת.	*Blessed are You, God, who sanctifies the Shabbat.*

See page 58 for commentary.

The Last Three Blessings

רְצֵה ה׳ אֱלֹהֵינוּ בְּעַמְּךָ יִשְׂרָאֵל וּבִתְפִלָּתָם, וְהָשֵׁב אֶת הָעֲבוֹדָה לִדְבִיר בֵּיתֶךָ, וְאִשֵּׁי יִשְׂרָאֵל וּתְפִלָּתָם, בְּאַהֲבָה תְקַבֵּל בְּרָצוֹן, וּתְהִי לְרָצוֹן תָּמִיד עֲבוֹדַת יִשְׂרָאֵל עַמֶּךָ:	*Look with favor, God, our Lord, on Your people Israel and pay heed to their prayer; restore the service to Your Sanctuary and accept with love and favor Israel's fire-offerings and prayer, and may the service of Your people Israel always find favor.*
וְתֶחֱזֶינָה עֵינֵינוּ בְּשׁוּבְךָ לְצִיּוֹן בְּרַחֲמִים:	*May our eyes behold Your return to Zion in mercy.*
בָּרוּךְ אַתָּה ה׳ הַמַּחֲזִיר שְׁכִינָתוֹ לְצִיּוֹן:	*Blessed are You, God, who restores His Divine Presence to Zion.*
מוֹדִים אֲנַחְנוּ לָךְ, שָׁאַתָּה הוּא ה׳ אֱלֹהֵינוּ וֵאלֹהֵי אֲבוֹתֵינוּ לְעוֹלָם וָעֶד:	*We thankfully acknowledge that You are God, our Lord and Lord of our fathers, forever.*

צוּר חַיֵּינוּ, מָגֵן יִשְׁעֵנוּ אַתָּה הוּא לְדֹר וָדֹר:	*You are the strength of our life, the shield of our salvation in every generation.*
נוֹדֶה לְּךָ וּנְסַפֵּר תְּהִלָּתֶךָ, עַל חַיֵּינוּ הַמְּסוּרִים בְּיָדֶךָ, וְעַל נִשְׁמוֹתֵינוּ הַפְּקוּדוֹת לָךְ, וְעַל נִסֶּיךָ שֶׁבְּכָל יוֹם עִמָּנוּ, וְעַל נִפְלְאוֹתֶיךָ וְטוֹבוֹתֶיךָ שֶׁבְּכָל עֵת, עֶרֶב וָבֹקֶר וְצָהֳרָיִם:	*We will give thanks to You and recount Your praise, evening, morning, and noon, for our lives that are committed into Your hand, for our souls that are entrusted to You, for Your miracles that are with us daily, and for Your continual wonders and beneficences.*
הַטּוֹב, כִּי לֹא כָלוּ רַחֲמֶיךָ, וְהַמְרַחֵם, כִּי לֹא תַמּוּ חֲסָדֶיךָ, מֵעוֹלָם קִוִּינוּ לָךְ:	*You are the Beneficent One, for Your mercies never cease; the Merciful One, for Your kindnesses never end; for we always place our hope in You.*
וְעַל כֻּלָּם יִתְבָּרַךְ וְיִתְרוֹמַם שִׁמְךָ מַלְכֵּנוּ תָּמִיד לְעוֹלָם וָעֶד:	*And for all these, may Your Name, our King, be continually blessed, exalted, and extolled forever and all time.*
וְכֹל הַחַיִּים יוֹדוּךָ סֶּלָה, וִיהַלְלוּ אֶת שִׁמְךָ בֶּאֱמֶת, הָאֵל יְשׁוּעָתֵנוּ וְעֶזְרָתֵנוּ סֶּלָה:	*And all living things shall forever thank You, and praise Your great Name eternally, for You are good. God, You are our everlasting salvation and help, O benevolent God.*
בָּרוּךְ אַתָּה ה', הַטּוֹב שִׁמְךָ וּלְךָ נָאֶה לְהוֹדוֹת:	*Blessed are You, God, Beneficent is Your Name, and to You it is fitting to offer thanks.*
שִׂים שָׁלוֹם טוֹבָה וּבְרָכָה, חֵן וָחֶסֶד וְרַחֲמִים, עָלֵינוּ וְעַל כָּל יִשְׂרָאֵל עַמֶּךָ:	*Bestow peace, goodness and blessing, life, graciousness, kindness and mercy upon us and upon all Your people Israel.*
בָּרְכֵנוּ אָבִינוּ, כֻּלָּנוּ כְּאֶחָד בְּאוֹר פָּנֶיךָ, כִּי בְאוֹר פָּנֶיךָ נָתַתָּ לָנוּ ה' אֱלֹהֵינוּ, תּוֹרַת חַיִּים, וְאַהֲבַת חֶסֶד, וּצְדָקָה וּבְרָכָה וְרַחֲמִים, וְחַיִּים וְשָׁלוֹם:	*Bless us, our Father, all of us as one, with the light of Your countenance. For by the light of Your countenance You gave us, God, our Lord, the Torah of life and loving-kindness, righteousness, blessing, mercy, life, and peace.*

וְטוֹב בְּעֵינֶיךָ לְבָרֵךְ אֶת עַמְּךָ יִשְׂרָאֵל בְּכָל עֵת וּבְכָל שָׁעָה בִּשְׁלוֹמֶךָ:	*May it be favorable in Your eyes to bless Your people Israel, at all times and at every moment, with Your peace.*
בָּרוּךְ אַתָּה ה', הַמְבָרֵךְ אֶת עַמּוֹ יִשְׂרָאֵל בַּשָּׁלוֹם:	*Blessed are You, God, who blesses His people Israel with peace.*

See page 61 for commentary.

K'riat HaTorah

אֵין כָּמוֹךָ בָאֱלֹהִים אֲדֹנָי וְאֵין כְּמַעֲשֶׂיךָ.	*There is none like You among the Heavenly powers, God, and there is none who can perform Your deeds.*
מַלְכוּתְךָ מַלְכוּת כָּל עוֹלָמִים וּמֶמְשַׁלְתְּךָ בְּכָל דּוֹר וָדֹר:	*Your Kingship is an eternal kingship, and Your dominion is in every generation.*
ה' מֶלֶךְ ה' מָלָךְ ה' יִמְלֹךְ לְעוֹלָם וָעֶד:	*God rules, God ruled, God will rule forever and ever.*
ה' עֹז לְעַמּוֹ יִתֵּן ה' יְבָרֵךְ אֶת עַמּוֹ בַשָּׁלוֹם:	*God shall give strength to His nation, God shall bless His nation with peace.*
אַב הָרַחֲמִים הֵיטִיבָה בִרְצוֹנְךָ אֶת צִיּוֹן תִּבְנֶה חוֹמוֹת יְרוּשָׁלָיִם.	*Merciful Father, with Your will, do good to Zion; build the walls of Jerusalem.*
כִּי בְךָ לְבַד בָּטָחְנוּ מֶלֶךְ אֵל רָם וְנִשָּׂא אֲדוֹן עוֹלָמִים:	*For in You alone we have shown trust, King, elevated and exalted Almighty, Master of the worlds.*

The highlight and centerpiece of the Shabbat morning prayers is *k'riat haTorah*—the Torah reading service.

How many *aliyot* (when individuals are called up to recite blessings over a section of the Torah reading of the day) do we read?

- On Shabbat we read seven *aliyot*.
- On Yom Kippur we read six *aliyot*.

- On other Biblical holidays we read five *aliyot*.
- On Chol Hamoed and Rosh Chodesh we read four *aliyot*.
- During the week, as well as on fast days and on Shabbat afternoons, we read three *aliyot*.

The *k'riat haTorah* is meant to reflect the time when God revealed the Torah at Har Sinai. Therefore, there are many laws and customs that reflect the Sinai experience:

- The bimah is located in the center of the sanctuary surrounded by people, the same way B'nei Yisrael surrounded Har Sinai.
- When the Torah is brought out of the *aron kodesh*—the ark, we approach the Torah to kiss it, just as at Har Sinai, B'nei Yisrael approached the mountain as closely as they were permitted.
- The minimum amount of people at the bimah for *k'riat haTorah* is two, representing Hashem and Moshe who were front and center at the time of the transmission of the *Aseret Ha'dibrot*.
- Reverent decorum is required while the Torah is being read; many even remain standing throughout as a remembrance of the actual Torah transmission at Sinai.

Haftarah

After the Torah reading on Shabbat and holidays (as well as on fast days), a portion of *Nevi'im* (called the haftarah) is read that relates to that week's *parashah*.

There are two reasons why we recite a haftarah:

- When the Greeks ruled over Eretz Yisrael, they prohibited learning or reading from the Torah. Therefore, the rabbis instituted that we read a section of *Nevi'im* that contains a similar theme of the *parashah* that would have been read.
- The haftarah was instituted to stress our faith in the importance and undeniable truth of the prophecies that are in our *Tanach*.

The minimum number of *pesukim* in a haftarah is twenty-one. The reason for this is because the minimum number of *pesukim* in a Torah *aliyah* is three, and the number of *aliyot* we read on Shabbat is seven, so the minimum number of *pesukim* of a haftarah matches the minimum number of *pesukim* that could be read from the Torah on Shabbat.

Although the haftarah reading was instituted much later in history than the *k'riat haTorah*, it has become a great honor to be chosen to read the haftarah because the one who chants the haftarah recites five blessings in front of the congregation. There is a similar but different cantillation invoked for the reading of the haftarah.

A DIVINE APPROACH: The reason the *k'riat haTorah* is presented right in the middle of the overall service is because of its incredible import to the Jewish people. It is a mitzvah to listen carefully to every word of the reading. As we listen to the *k'riat haTorah*, as well as to the haftarah, let's remember that the reading of the Torah is simulating the teaching of God Himself, and the chanting of the haftarah is simulating the stirring words of the prophets of Israel.

Chapter Four

MUSSAF

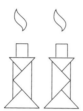

Yekum Purkan

יְקוּם פּוּרְקָן מִן שְׁמַיָּא חִנָּא וְחִסְדָּא וְרַחֲמֵי וְחַיֵּי אֲרִיכֵי וּמְזוֹנֵי רְוִיחֵי וְסִיַעְתָּא דִשְׁמַיָּא וּבַרְיוּת גּוּפָא וּנְהוֹרָא מַעַלְיָא זַרְעָא חַיָּא וְקַיָּמָא זַרְעָא דִּי לָא יִפְסוֹק וְדִי לָא יִבְטוֹל מִפִּתְגָּמֵי אוֹרַיְתָא.	*May deliverance arise from Heaven, in grace, kindness, compassion, long life, plentiful sustenance, Heavenly assistance, physical health, good vision, healthy and viable children, children who will not cease from, nor neglect, the words of Torah.*
לְמָרָנָן וְרַבָּנָן חֲבוּרָתָא קַדִּישְׁתָא דִּי בְאַרְעָא דְיִשְׂרָאֵל וְדִי בְּבָבֶל לְרֵישֵׁי כַלֵּי וּלְרֵישֵׁי גַלְוָתָא וּלְרֵישֵׁי מְתִיבָתָא וּלְדַיָּנֵי דִי בָבָא לְכָל תַּלְמִידֵיהוֹן וּלְכָל תַּלְמִידֵי תַלְמִידֵיהוֹן וּלְכָל מָן דְּעָסְקִין בְּאוֹרַיְתָא.	*To our masters and teachers, the holy company, who are in the Land of Israel and in Babylon, to the heads of the Torah assemblies and to the Exilarchs, to the heads of the yeshivos and to the judges at the gates, to all their disciples and to all the disciples of their disciples, and to all engrossed in Torah study.*

מַלְכָּא דְעָלְמָא יְבָרֵךְ יַתְהוֹן יַפִּישׁ חַיֵּיהוֹן וְיַסְגֵּא יוֹמֵיהוֹן וְיִתֵּן אַרְכָה לִשְׁנֵיהוֹן וְיִתְפָּרְקוּן וְיִשְׁתֵּזְבוּן מִן כָּל עָקָא וּמִן כָּל מַרְעִין בִּישִׁין.	*May the King of the universe bless you and prolong your lives, increase your days and give added length to your years; may you be delivered and protected from all distress and from all bad events.*
מָרָן דִּי בִשְׁמַיָּא יְהֵא בְּסַעֲדְּהוֹן כָּל זְמַן וְעִדָּן וְנֹאמַר אָמֵן.	*May our Master in Heaven be your support, at all times and seasons; and let us say, Amen.*
יְקוּם פּוּרְקָן מִן שְׁמַיָּא חִנָּא וְחִסְדָּא וְרַחֲמֵי וְחַיֵּי אֲרִיכֵי וּמְזוֹנֵי רְוִיחֵי וְסִיַּעְתָּא דִשְׁמַיָּא וּבַרְיוּת גּוּפָא וּנְהוֹרָא מַעַלְיָא.	*May deliverance arise from Heaven, in grace, kindness, compassion, long life, plentiful sustenance, Heavenly assistance, physical health, good vision,*
זַרְעָא חַיָּא וְקַיָּמָא זַרְעָא דִּי לָא יִפְסוּק וְדִי לָא יִבְטוּל מִפִּתְגָּמֵי אוֹרַיְתָא.	*healthy and viable children, children who will not cease from, nor neglect, the words of Torah.*
לְכָל קְהָלָא קַדִּישָׁא הָדֵין רַבְרְבַיָּא עִם זְעֵרַיָּא טַפְלָא וּנְשַׁיָּא.	*To this entire holy congregation, adults as well as children, infants and women.*
מַלְכָּא דְעָלְמָא יְבָרֵךְ יַתְכוֹן יַפִּישׁ חַיֵּיכוֹן וְיַסְגֵּא יוֹמֵיכוֹן וְיִתֵּן אַרְכָה לִשְׁנֵיכוֹן וְתִתְפָּרְקוּן וְתִשְׁתֵּזְבוּן מִן כָּל עָקָא וּמִן כָּל מַרְעִין בִּישִׁין.	*May the King of the universe bless you and prolong your lives, increase your days and give added length to your years; may you be delivered and protected from all distress and from all bad events.*
מָרָן דִּי בִשְׁמַיָּא יְהֵא בְּסַעֲדְכוֹן כָּל זְמַן וְעִדָּן וְנֹאמַר אָמֵן.	*May our Master in Heaven be your support, at all times and seasons; and let us say, Amen.*
מִי שֶׁבֵּרַךְ אֲבוֹתֵינוּ אַבְרָהָם יִצְחָק וְיַעֲקֹב הוּא יְבָרֵךְ אֶת כָּל הַקָּהָל הַקָּדוֹשׁ הַזֶּה עִם כָּל קְהִלּוֹת הַקֹּדֶשׁ הֵם וּנְשֵׁיהֶם וּבְנֵיהֶם וּבְנוֹתֵיהֶם וְכָל אֲשֶׁר לָהֶם	*May He who blessed our fathers, Avraham, Yitzchak, and Yaakov, may He bless this entire holy congregation, together with all the holy congregations—them and their wives, their sons and their daughters, and all that belongs to them.*

וּמִי שֶׁמְיַחֲדִים בָּתֵּי כְנֵסִיּוֹת לִתְפִלָּה וּמִי שֶׁבָּאִים בְּתוֹכָם לְהִתְפַּלֵּל וּמִי שֶׁנּוֹתְנִים נֵר לַמָּאוֹר וְיַיִן לְקִדּוּשׁ וּלְהַבְדָּלָה וּפַת לָאוֹרְחִים וּצְדָקָה לָעֲנִיִּים	*Those who establish synagogues for prayer and those who come there to pray, those who provide lights for illumination, wine for Kiddush and Havdalah, food for the wayfarers, and charity for the needy,*
וְכָל מִי שֶׁעוֹסְקִים בְּצָרְכֵי צִבּוּר בֶּאֱמוּנָה הַקָּדוֹשׁ בָּרוּךְ הוּא יְשַׁלֵּם שְׂכָרָם וְיָסִיר מֵהֶם כָּל מַחֲלָה וְיִרְפָּא לְכָל גּוּפָם וְיִסְלַח לְכָל עֲוֹנָם	*and all those who occupy themselves faithfully with the community's needs—may the Holy One, blessed be He, give them their reward, remove from them all sickness, heal their entire body, forgive all their sins,*
וְיִשְׁלַח בְּרָכָה וְהַצְלָחָה בְּכָל מַעֲשֵׂה יְדֵיהֶם עִם כָּל יִשְׂרָאֵל אֲחֵיהֶם. וְנֹאמַר אָמֵן.	*and send blessing and success to all their endeavors, together with all Israel their brethren, and let us say, Amen.*

I mmediately following the blessings recited after the haftarah, the *shaliach tzibbur* (cantor) ascends the bimah and leads the congregation in *Yekum Purkan*, "May There Be Success and Salvation."

Yekum Purkan is a two-paragraph Aramaic *tefillah*. It is in Aramaic because this was the spoken language of the masses at that time. The prayer begins by seeking God's blessings for the welfare and well-being of all Torah leaders of the generation, for the members of the congregation at large, as well as for those actually praying in the synagogue at that time. That is why the first paragraph is written in the third person, because it refers to the world's Torah leaders, while the second paragraph is written in the second person because it pertains to fellow congregants in the community. It was authored after the sealing of the Talmud roughly 1,500 years ago. Therefore, the leaders mentioned are the leaders of Israel as well as the Jewish community in Babylonia.

There is a third paragraph, which begins with the words *Mi She'beirach*, written in Hebrew (after Aramaic was no longer the spoken language) that acknowledges the love, loyalty, and dedication of the communal benefactors who dedicate their time, money, and effort toward the functioning of their synagogue. This beautiful *tefillah* is chanted publicly and harmoniously in order to express gratitude to the supporters and inspire the rest of the congregation to provide whatever support they can to maintain their spiritual home—the shul.

Since the latter two paragraphs refer specifically to the local congregation and speak directly to them, if for whatever reason a Jew is unable to pray in the synagogue on Shabbat morning, they should omit the second *Yekum Purkan* and the *Mi She'beirach*.

Why did the architects of our siddur include the *Yekum Purkan* trilogy at this point in the service?

Here are a few answers:

- Practically speaking, Shabbat morning is the time when the largest number of congregants are present in the sanctuary Shabbat morning.

- Since we recite *Mi She'beirach* prayers throughout the Torah service, it is appropriate to recite all of the *Mi She'beirach* prayers before returning the *Sefer Torah* to the *aron kodesh*.

- After the chanting of the Torah and the chanting of the haftarah, one could come to feel, God forbid, disconnected and alone. Our teacher Moshe is not living and able to teach us at Har Sinai. Yeshayahu, Yechezkel, Yirmiyahu and all other *nevi'im* are not here in person to share their prophecies as they did in yesteryear. So how are we to live fulfilling and relevant Torah lives that follow the will of God? Only through the vision and teachings of the Torah by the national and local leadership of Klal Yisrael, together with the support of the *parnassim*—benefactors, who sustain communal institutions and services so that Klal Yisrael can function until the time we will return again to Jerusalem.

A DIVINE APPROACH: We should feel and demonstrate appreciation to our leaders and teachers who provide the vision, instruction, and energy to support Klal Yisrael from day to day, year to year, and generation to generation.

Av Ha'rachamim

אַב הָרַחֲמִים שׁוֹכֵן מְרוֹמִים בְּרַחֲמָיו הָעֲצוּמִים הוּא יִפְקוֹד בְּרַחֲמִים הַחֲסִידִים וְהַיְשָׁרִים וְהַתְּמִימִים קְהִלּוֹת הַקֹּדֶשׁ שֶׁמָּסְרוּ נַפְשָׁם עַל קְדֻשַּׁת הַשֵּׁם.	*Merciful Father, who dwells on High: in His great mercy He will remember with mercy, the pious, upright, and the blameless, the holy communities, who offered their lives for the sanctification of His Name.*
הַנֶּאֱהָבִים וְהַנְּעִימִים בְּחַיֵּיהֶם וּבְמוֹתָם לֹא נִפְרָדוּ מִנְּשָׁרִים קַלּוּ וּמֵאֲרָיוֹת גָּבֵרוּ לַעֲשׂוֹת רְצוֹן קוֹנָם וְחֵפֶץ צוּרָם	*Loved and pleasant in their lives, and in death they were not parted. They were swifter than eagles and stronger than lions to carry out the will of their Maker and the desire of their steadfast Rock.*
יִזְכְּרֵם אֱלֹהֵינוּ לְטוֹבָה עִם שְׁאָר צַדִּיקֵי עוֹלָם וְיִנְקוֹם לְעֵינֵינוּ נִקְמַת דַּם עֲבָדָיו הַשָּׁפוּךְ כַּכָּתוּב בְּתוֹרַת מֹשֶׁה אִישׁ הָאֱלֹהִים הַרְנִינוּ גוֹיִם עַמּוֹ כִּי דַם עֲבָדָיו יִקּוֹם וְנָקָם יָשִׁיב לְצָרָיו וְכִפֶּר אַדְמָתוֹ עַמּוֹ.	*May God remember them for good, together with the other righteous of the world, and may He in front of our eyes avenge the vengeance of the spilled blood of His servants, as it is written in the Torah of Moshe, man of God, "Sing out praise, O you nations, for His people! For He will avenge the blood of His servants, inflict revenge upon His adversaries, and the land will appease its people."*
וְעַל יְדֵי עֲבָדֶיךָ הַנְּבִיאִים כָּתוּב לֵאמֹר וְנִקֵּיתִי דָּמָם לֹא נִקֵּיתִי וַה׳ שֹׁכֵן בְּצִיּוֹן.	*And through Your servants, the Prophets it is written, "Now though I cleanse, their blood I will not cleanse, when God dwells in Zion."*
וּבְכִתְבֵי הַקֹּדֶשׁ נֶאֱמַר לָמָּה יֹאמְרוּ הַגּוֹיִם אַיֵּה אֱלֹהֵיהֶם יִוָּדַע בַּגּוֹיִם לְעֵינֵינוּ נִקְמַת דַּם עֲבָדֶיךָ הַשָּׁפוּךְ.	*And in the Holy Writings it is said, "Why should the nations say, 'Where is their God?' Let it be known among the nations before our eyes the revenge of the spilt blood of Your servants."*

וְאוֹמֵר כִּי דוֹרֵשׁ דָּמִים אוֹתָם זָכָר לֹא שָׁכַח צַעֲקַת עֲנָוִים.	And it is said: "For He who avenges blood remembers them; He has not forgotten the cry of the humble."
וְאוֹמֵר יָדִין בַּגּוֹיִם מָלֵא גְּוִיּוֹת מָחַץ רֹאשׁ עַל אֶרֶץ רַבָּה מִנַּחַל בַּדֶּרֶךְ יִשְׁתֶּה עַל כֵּן יָרִים רֹאשׁ.	And it is said, "He will execute justice upon the nations [into] a heap of corpses; He crushed the head on a great land. From the stream on the way he would drink; therefore, he raised his head."

After *Yekum Purkan*, it is customary to recite the *tefillah* of *Av Ha'rachamim*, "Father of Compassion," in memory of the Jewish souls that were martyred and gave their life to sanctify God's name. *Av Ha'rachamim* is reputed to have been written after 1096 in response to the First Crusade. Originally, it was only recited on the Shabbat before Shavuot. Later, it became popular to recite it every Shabbat, unless an additional ritual celebration was taking place, such as *birkat ha'chodesh*, an *aufruf* celebration, or a *brit milah*. However, if the joyous event occurs during the *sefirah* period, which is the time period when the Crusades occurred, *Av Ha'rachamim* is still recited.

It has been a long and arduous exile with so many losses along the way. Chazal instituted that throughout the year, as well as at every joyous Jewish occasion, we reflect on our nation's history, both the tragic, as well as the glorious. A few examples:

- A *chattan* breaks a glass and sprinkles ashes on his forehead under the *chuppah* on the happiest day of his life to remember that we are still in exile and the Beit Hamikdash has not yet been rebuilt in Jerusalem.
- We say *Yizkor* on all the major festivals and remember those family members that are no longer present to celebrate Yom Tov with us.
- We devote nearly a month each summer remembering the beauty and spiritual grandeur of Zion and pray for the return of God's presence to Jerusalem.

There is a legend that upon entering a synagogue on Tisha b'Av morning, seeing Jewish men and women mourning on the floor, Napoleon the Great declared: "A nation that mourns the destruction of its empire from thousands of years ago will certainly see its eventual rebuilding." Napoleon was actually quoting the Talmud without realizing it. "*Kol ha'mitabel al Yerushalayim zocheh v'ro'eh b'simchatah*—He who mourns for Jerusalem will merit and see her future joy."[1]

In addition to mourning those who perished while sanctifying God's name, reciting *Av Ha'rachamim* bolsters our hope and faith that the God of Israel is just, and responds with positive, as well as negative consequences, according to our deeds. It has been passed down through tradition that each time a Jew is tormented and killed for simply being Jewish, God feels the pain as well, and douses His proverbial Divine cloak with droplets of blood to match. One day, when God metes out retribution toward our enemies, He will wear this holy cloak. The message of this teaching is that every Jewish soul is dear to our Father in Heaven and that each and every soul will forever be remembered.

As Jews, we must know that our history provides a reflection toward our eventual destiny. Our origins began with our Avot and Imahot; then the *Nevi'im*, *Shoftim*, and *Anshei Knesset Hagedolah*; and later continued with the *Geonim*, *Rambam*, *Rashi*, and all the great leaders until today. We continue carrying the torch that they lit and carried for so many generations. In *Av Ha'rachamim*, we honor the men, women, and children who preceded us and paved the way with their lives for our existence and survival. Before we recite the communal *Mussaf* prayer, we remember the holy Jewish martyrs who gave their lives for us to be able to *daven* in shul.

A DIVINE APPROACH: As we recite our *tefillot*, have in mind that our prayers echo the prayers of millions of others who are no longer here. They recited the same *tefillot*, perhaps chanting the same melodies to our compassionate Father in Heaven. We should also hope and pray that our children and grandchildren will maintain that eternal connection throughout the generations.

---

1   *Taanit* 30b.

Ashrei

אַשְׁרֵי יוֹשְׁבֵי בֵיתֶךָ עוֹד יְהַלְלוּךָ סֶּלָה אַשְׁרֵי הָעָם שֶׁכָּכָה לּוֹ אַשְׁרֵי הָעָם שֶׁה׳ אֱלֹהָיו.	*Fortunate are those who remain in Your house; they will continually praise You forever. Praiseworthy is the people that has this; praiseworthy is the people of whom God is their Lord.*
תְּהִלָּה לְדָוִד אֲרוֹמִמְךָ אֱלוֹהַי הַמֶּלֶךְ וַאֲבָרְכָה שִׁמְךָ לְעוֹלָם וָעֶד.	*A praise of David. I shall exalt You, my God the King, and I shall bless Your Name forever and ever.*
בְּכָל יוֹם אֲבָרְכֶךָּ וַאֲהַלְלָה שִׁמְךָ לְעוֹלָם וָעֶד.	*Every day I shall bless You, and I shall praise Your Name forever and ever.*
גָּדוֹל ה׳ וּמְהֻלָּל מְאֹד וְלִגְדֻלָּתוֹ אֵין חֵקֶר.	*God is great and very much praised, and His greatness cannot be comprehended.*
דּוֹר לְדוֹר יְשַׁבַּח מַעֲשֶׂיךָ וּגְבוּרֹתֶיךָ יַגִּידוּ.	*Generation to generation will praise Your works, and they will recite Your mighty deeds.*
הֲדַר כְּבוֹד הוֹדֶךָ וְדִבְרֵי נִפְלְאֹתֶיךָ אָשִׂיחָה.	*Of the majesty of the glory of Your splendor and the words of Your wonders I shall speak.*
וֶעֱזוּז נוֹרְאֹתֶיךָ יֹאמֵרוּ וּגְדוּלָּתְךָ אֲסַפְּרֶנָּה.	*And the strength of Your awesome deeds they will tell, and Your greatness I shall sing.*
זֵכֶר רַב טוּבְךָ יַבִּיעוּ וְצִדְקָתְךָ יְרַנֵּנוּ.	*Of the remembrance of Your abundant goodness they will speak, and of Your righteousness they will sing.*
חַנּוּן וְרַחוּם ה׳ אֶרֶךְ אַפַּיִם וּגְדָל חָסֶד.	*God is gracious and compassionate, slow to anger and of great kindness.*
טוֹב ה׳ לַכֹּל וְרַחֲמָיו עַל כָּל מַעֲשָׂיו.	*God is good to all, and His mercy is on all His works.*
יוֹדוּךָ ה׳ כָּל מַעֲשֶׂיךָ וַחֲסִידֶיךָ יְבָרְכוּכָה.	*All Your works will thank You, God, and Your pious ones will bless You.*
כְּבוֹד מַלְכוּתְךָ יֹאמֵרוּ וּגְבוּרָתְךָ יְדַבֵּרוּ.	*They will tell the glory of Your kingdom, and they will speak of Your might.*

לְהוֹדִיעַ לִבְנֵי הָאָדָם גְּבוּרֹתָיו וּכְבוֹד הֲדַר מַלְכוּתוֹ.	*To make known to the children of men His mighty deeds and the glory of the majesty of His kingdom.*
מַלְכוּתְךָ מַלְכוּת כָּל עֹלָמִים וּמֶמְשַׁלְתְּךָ בְּכָל דּוֹר וָדֹר.	*Your kingdom is a kingdom of all times, and Your dominion is throughout every generation.*
סוֹמֵךְ ה׳ לְכָל הַנֹּפְלִים וְזוֹקֵף לְכָל הַכְּפוּפִים.	*God supports all of the fallen and straightens all the bent.*
עֵינֵי כֹל אֵלֶיךָ יְשַׂבֵּרוּ וְאַתָּה נוֹתֵן לָהֶם אֶת אָכְלָם בְּעִתּוֹ.	*Everyone's eyes look to You with hope, and You give them their food in its time.*
פּוֹתֵחַ אֶת יָדֶךָ וּמַשְׂבִּיעַ לְכָל חַי רָצוֹן.	*You open Your hand and satisfy every living thing [with] its desire.*
צַדִּיק ה׳ בְּכָל דְּרָכָיו וְחָסִיד בְּכָל מַעֲשָׂיו.	*God is righteous in all His ways and kind in all His deeds.*
קָרוֹב ה׳ לְכָל קֹרְאָיו לְכֹל אֲשֶׁר יִקְרָאֻהוּ בֶאֱמֶת.	*God is near to all who call Him, to all who call Him with sincerity.*
רְצוֹן יְרֵאָיו יַעֲשֶׂה וְאֶת שַׁוְעָתָם יִשְׁמַע וְיוֹשִׁיעֵם.	*He does the will of those who fear Him, and He hears their cry and saves them.*
שׁוֹמֵר ה׳ אֶת כָּל אֹהֲבָיו וְאֵת כָּל הָרְשָׁעִים יַשְׁמִיד.	*God guards all who love Him, and He destroys all the wicked.*
תְּהִלַּת ה׳ יְדַבֶּר פִּי וִיבָרֵךְ כָּל בָּשָׂר שֵׁם קָדְשׁוֹ לְעוֹלָם וָעֶד.	*My mouth will speak God's praises, and all flesh will bless His holy Name forever and ever.*
וַאֲנַחְנוּ נְבָרֵךְ יָהּ מֵעַתָּה וְעַד עוֹלָם הַלְלוּיָהּ.	*But we shall bless God from now until everlasting, Halleluyah!*

The Talmud proclaims, "Anyone who recites *Ashrei*, *Tehillim* 145, three times a day is a *ben Olam Haba*—one who is fit for eternal reward in the World to Come."[2] During the week, *Ashrei* is found twice in *Shacharit* and once in *Minchah*. It is evident that Chazal intended to

---

2   *Berachot* 4b.

connect *Ashrei* with the reciting of *Kedushah*, because *Kedushah* always follows *Ashrei:*

- The first *Ashrei* is in *Pesukei D'Zimra*, which precedes the *Kedushah* of *Et Sheim* and the *Kedushah* of *Shemoneh Esreh*.
- The second *Ashrei* is located before *U'Va L'Tzion*, which contains the final *Kedushah* of *Shacharit*.
- The third *Ashrei* starts the prayer of *Minchah*, which leads into the *Amidah* and *Kedushah*.

Since *Maariv* was originally an optional prayer and does not contain a *Kedushah*, we do not recite *Ashrei*.

Why should it be that one who recites *Ashrei* daily receives eternal reward? What is so significant about this prayer that it contains within it the potential for eternity?

The uniqueness of this prayer is that it is written as an acrostic, presenting words of praise to Hashem in alphabetical order. This implies that when saying *Ashrei*, we praise God in every possible way, with every letter of the alphabet.

How is this sufficient to merit a guaranteed space in *Olam Haba*?

Rav Schwab explains that the twenty-one *pesukim* in the *perek* of *Ashrei* can be divided into two parts:[3]

1. From the first *Ashrei* until *potei'ach et yadecha* is a description of *Olam Haba*, where everything is good.
2. *Potei'ach et yadecha* until the end represents the realities in this world: *"Potei'ach et yadecha u'masbia' l'chol chai ratzon*—God, You open Your hand and satisfy all according to their desires," i.e., in this world.

Although we do not recite *Ashrei* at night, the fact that we say it three times a day is symbolic of the three times a day that we do pray. Chazal explain that praying at different times of the day represents different times in our lives:

---

3 *Rav Schwab On Prayer*, p. 170.

- Davening *Shacharit* when the day begins is comparable to praising God when life feels hopeful and we are faced with new opportunities holding great promise.
- Davening *Minchah* as the sun begins to set represents praising God when life presents times of uncertainty.
- Davening *Maariv* when it is dark outside is symbolic of praying to God even when one faces the darkness of difficult challenges.

Perhaps this is why the Talmud states that one who recites *Ashrei* three times a day merits the World to Come. One who expresses prayers and praises to Hashem throughout every part of life, in good times, as well as challenging times, is deserving of eternal reward in *Olam Haba*.

A DIVINE APPROACH: Just as *Ashrei* utilizes the entire alphabet to recognize and praise God, so too can we discover and recognize God and His benevolence in all aspects of our lives, each and every day. As stated in the *Kedushah*: "*Hashem tzevakot, melo kol ha'aretz kevodo*—The whole world is filled with His glory."

Yehallelu Et Shem Hashem

חַזָּן: יְהַלְלוּ אֶת שֵׁם ה' כִּי נִשְׂגָּב שְׁמוֹ לְבַדּוֹ.	*Chazzan: Praise God's Name, for His Name alone is elevated!*
קהל: הוֹדוֹ עַל אֶרֶץ וְשָׁמָיִם וַיָּרֶם קֶרֶן לְעַמּוֹ תְּהִלָּה לְכָל חֲסִידָיו לִבְנֵי יִשְׂרָאֵל עַם קְרֹבוֹ הַלְלוּי-הּ.	*Congregation: His splendor is on earth and Heaven. He raised up a horn for His people, praise to all His pious ones, to the Children of Israel, the people close to Him, Halleluyah!*

After the chazzan concludes *Ashrei*, he takes hold of the *Sefer Torah* that was just read, clutches it in his right shoulder and chants, "*Yehallelu et Shem Hashem ki nisgav Shemo levado*—They shall praise the name of God because His name **alone** is exalted."[4] The congregation then joins

---

4   *Tehillim* 148:13.

in unison and sings, "*Hodo al eretz v'shamayim*—His glory is over the earth and the heavens."

This is a unique section of our prayers, unlike any other in that the chazzan chants out loud the first part of a verse and the congregation responds and chants the latter part of the same verse. This is an anomaly because normative practice is to recite full Biblical *pesukim* and not partial ones. The *Iyun Tefillah* explains this phenomenon, remarking that since the chazzan is truly an emissary of the congregation and not simply a voice of leadership, it is actually considered as if the entire congregation does recite the entire verse.

The commentaries also explain why this *pasuk* from *Tehillim* is chanted specifically after the Torah reading has concluded. Seeing the awe and pageantry of the Torah service is a spiritual experience, as the congregation gathers to kiss the *Sefer Torah* as it passes through the congregation. It is read from the elevated bimah, located in the center of the synagogue, recreating a Sinai-like revelation. When one ascends the bimah for an *aliyah*, the individual kisses the *Sefer Torah* with the tallit and even bows when reciting the blessing beginning with *Barchu*. At the conclusion of the reading of the Torah portion of the week, the *Sefer Torah* is raised for all to see, taken around the synagogue again, and returned to the *aron kodesh*.

Because of all this grandeur, there is a concern that one could focus only on the holiness of the Torah and lose sight of from Whom it comes. We read what the Torah says, we quote the *pesukim* of the Torah, we adhere to the mitzvot of the Torah, but if we are not careful, we could lose focus that the Torah is the living word of God. Therefore, immediately following the Torah reading, we chant, "*Yehallelu et Shem Hashem ki nisgav Shemo levado*—They shall praise the name of God because His name **alone** is exalted." Without God, there would be no Torah, mitzvot, or life itself.

As the *Sefer Torah* returns to the *aron kodesh*, the congregation recites, "*U'venucho yomar shuva Hashem revivot alfei Yisrael*—And when it rested, Moshe would say, 'May *Hashem* return to the multitude of thousands of Israel.'"

During each *k'riat haTorah*, we literally reenact the events at Sinai in the way in which we take out the *Sefer Torah* and where and how we read it. At the conclusion of the reading, when we travel from the bimah and return the *Sefer Torah* to the *aron kodesh*, we chant *pesukim* reflecting the journey of B'nei Yisrael from Har Sinai through the desert for forty years.

> A DIVINE APPROACH: Throughout the day when we daven, study Torah, and fulfill the mitzvot, it is critical to remember that every fulfillment of a mitzvah and halachah is an act of dedication to Hashem and a fulfillment of His will: "*Yehallelu et Shem Hashem ki nisgav Shemo levado.*"

Mizmor L'David and *L'David Mizmor*

מִזְמוֹר לְדָוִד: הָבוּ לַה׳ בְּנֵי אֵלִים הָבוּ לַה׳ כָּבוֹד וָעֹז.	*A song of David. Prepare for God, [you] sons of the mighty; prepare for God glory and might.*
הָבוּ לַה׳ כְּבוֹד שְׁמוֹ הִשְׁתַּחֲווּ לַה׳ בְּהַדְרַת קֹדֶשׁ.	*Prepare for God the glory due His name; prostrate yourselves to God in the place beautified with sanctity.*
קוֹל ה׳ עַל הַמָּיִם: אֵל הַכָּבוֹד הִרְעִים ה׳ עַל מַיִם רַבִּים.	*The voice of God is upon the waters; the God of glory thunders; God is over the vast waters.*
קוֹל ה׳ בַּכֹּחַ קוֹל ה׳ בֶּהָדָר.	*The voice of God is in strength; the voice of God is in beauty.*
קוֹל ה׳ שֹׁבֵר אֲרָזִים וַיְשַׁבֵּר ה׳ אֶת אַרְזֵי הַלְּבָנוֹן.	*The voice of God breaks the cedars, yea, God breaks the cedars of Lebanon.*
וַיַּרְקִידֵם כְּמוֹ עֵגֶל לְבָנוֹן וְשִׂרְיֹן כְּמוֹ בֶן רְאֵמִים.	*He causes them to dance like a calf, Lebanon and Sirion like a young wild ox.*
קוֹל ה׳ חֹצֵב לַהֲבוֹת אֵשׁ.	*The voice of God cleaves with flames of fire.*
קוֹל ה׳ יָחִיל מִדְבָּר יָחִיל ה׳ מִדְבַּר קָדֵשׁ.	*The voice of God causes the desert to quake; God causes the desert of Kadesh to quake.*

קוֹל ה׳ יְחוֹלֵל אַיָּלוֹת וַיֶּחֱשֹׂף יְעָרוֹת: וּבְהֵיכָלוֹ כֻּלּוֹ אֹמֵר כָּבוֹד.	*The voice of God will frighten the hinds and strip the forests, and in His Temple, everyone speaks of His glory.*
ה׳ לַמַּבּוּל יָשָׁב וַיֵּשֶׁב ה׳ מֶלֶךְ לְעוֹלָם.	*God sat [enthroned] at the flood; God sat as King forever.*
ה׳ עֹז לְעַמּוֹ יִתֵּן ה׳ יְבָרֵךְ אֶת עַמּוֹ בַשָּׁלוֹם.	*God shall grant strength to His people; God shall bless His people with peace.*
בְּיוֹ״ט כְּשֶׁחָל בְּחוֹל:	*On a festival occurring on a weekday this passage is said:*
לְדָוִד מִזְמוֹר לַה׳ הָאָרֶץ וּמְלוֹאָהּ תֵּבֵל וְיֹשְׁבֵי בָהּ:	*Of David, a song. To God are the land and the fullness of what it contains; the world and those who dwell within it.*
כִּי הוּא עַל יַמִּים יְסָדָהּ וְעַל נְהָרוֹת יְכוֹנְנֶהָ:	*For He founded it upon seas and established it upon rivers.*
מִי יַעֲלֶה בְהַר ה׳ וּמִי יָקוּם בִּמְקוֹם קָדְשׁוֹ:	*Who will ascend upon God's mountain, and who will stand in His Holy place?*
נְקִי כַפַּיִם וּבַר לֵבָב אֲשֶׁר לֹא נָשָׂא לַשָּׁוְא נַפְשִׁי וְלֹא נִשְׁבַּע לְמִרְמָה:	*He who has clean hands and a pure heart, who has not taken My Name in vain, and has not sworn deceitfully.*
יִשָּׂא בְרָכָה מֵאֵת ה׳ וּצְדָקָה מֵאֱלֹהֵי יִשְׁעוֹ:	*He shall receive a blessing from God and charity from the God of his salvation.*
זֶה דּוֹר דֹּרְשָׁיו מְבַקְשֵׁי פָנֶיךָ יַעֲקֹב סֶלָה:	*This is the generation of those who seek Him, who seek Your presence, Yaakov, forever.*
שְׂאוּ שְׁעָרִים רָאשֵׁיכֶם וְהִנָּשְׂאוּ פִּתְחֵי עוֹלָם וְיָבוֹא מֶלֶךְ הַכָּבוֹד:	*Lift your heads, O gates, and be uplifted, O everlasting portals, and the King of glory may enter.*
מִי זֶה מֶלֶךְ הַכָּבוֹד ה׳ עִזּוּז וְגִבּוֹר ה׳ גִּבּוֹר מִלְחָמָה:	*Who is this King of glory? God, powerful and mighty, God, mighty warrior.*

שְׂאוּ שְׁעָרִים רָאשֵׁיכֶם וְשְׂאוּ פִּתְחֵי עוֹלָם וְיָבֹא מֶלֶךְ הַכָּבוֹד:	*Lift your heads, O gates, and become elevated, everlasting portals, so that the King of glory may enter.*
מִי הוּא זֶה מֶלֶךְ הַכָּבוֹד ה' צְבָאוֹת הוּא מֶלֶךְ הַכָּבוֹד סֶלָה:	*Who is this King of glory? God, Master of Hosts—He is the King of glory, forever.*

When returning the *Sefer Torah* to the *aron kodesh*, we recite *Mizmor L'David*.[5] This prayer is also included in our liturgy as the sixth *perek* taken from *Tehillim* that is recited on Friday night prior to the singing of *Lechah Dodi*. Due to the importance and holiness of the prayer, we always stand when reciting it.

The *Tur* explains that there are two reasons why we recite *Mizmor L'David* before returning the *Sefer Torah* to the *aron kodesh* on Shabbat:[6]

- It contains several references to the transmission of Torah at Har Sinai, which originally took place on Shabbat.
- In the prayer, we mention seven Divine *Kolot*—voices of God: **Kol** *Hashem al ha'mayim*, **Kol** *Hashem ba'koach*, **Kol** *Hashem b'hadar*, **Kol** *Hashem chotzev lehavot aish*, **Kol** *Hashem yachel ba'midbar*, **Kol** *Hashem shoveir arazim*, **Kol** *Hashem yecholel ayalot*—His voice over the water, with strength, with beauty, which pierces fire, causes the desert to tremor, breaks the cedar trees, and astounds animal life. The number seven is significant to us because, like the seven vocal expressions of God, there are also seven blessings in the Shabbat *Mussaf*.

Since this *perek* reflects the seven blessings of Shabbat *Mussaf*, we recite it only when returning the *Sefer Torah* on Shabbat morning before *Mussaf*, and not any other time that we remove and return the Torah to the *aron kodesh*. When we return the Torah to the *aron kodesh* on other days, we recite the *perek* of *L'David Mizmor*,[7] which

---

5   *Tehillim* 29.
6   Rav Yaakov ben Asher (1270–1340).
7   *Tehillim* 24.

reveals God's all-powerful strength, creativity, and dominion over the world.

The Talmud explains that the *pasuk* in *Tehillim* 24, "*Se'u she'arim roshei-chem*—Let the gates open, so the honorable King may pass through," is a prophetic reference to the time when Shlomo HaMelech, the son of David HaMelech, attempted to transport the *Aron* into the newly built Beit Hamikdash in Jerusalem. After an initial delay, God opened the gates specifically in the merit of his father, David HaMelech. In our service, we reenact the Psalmist's description of the opening of the gates of the Beit Hamikdash that accept the holy *Aron*. Therefore, we open the synagogue *aron kodesh* and return the *Sefer Torah*, the living word of God, to its place of honor.

A DIVINE APPROACH: There is great wisdom and meaning not only in the chosen words of our prayers, but in the choreography of the service as well. Reciting *Mizmor L'David* and *L'David Mizmor* are two great examples of the choreography.

U'Venucho Yomar

וּבְנֻחֹה יֹאמַר שׁוּבָה ה׳ רִבְבוֹת אַלְפֵי יִשְׂרָאֵל:	*And when it came to rest, he would say: Rest, God, among the myriads of thousands of Israel.*
קוּמָה ה׳ לִמְנוּחָתֶךָ אַתָּה וַאֲרוֹן עֻזֶּךָ:	*Arise, God, to Your resting place, You and the Ark of Your might.*
כֹּהֲנֶיךָ יִלְבְּשׁוּ צֶדֶק וַחֲסִידֶיךָ יְרַנֵּנוּ:	*Let Your priests be clothed with righteousness, and let Your devout ones sing praises.*
בַּעֲבוּר דָּוִד עַבְדֶּךָ אַל תָּשֵׁב פְּנֵי מְשִׁיחֶךָ:	*For the sake of David Your servant, turn not away the face of Your anointed.*
כִּי לֶקַח טוֹב נָתַתִּי לָכֶם תּוֹרָתִי אַל תַּעֲזֹבוּ:	*For I gave you good teaching; forsake not My Torah.*
עֵץ חַיִּים הִיא לַמַּחֲזִיקִים בָּהּ וְתֹמְכֶיהָ מְאֻשָּׁר:	*It is a tree of life for those who grasp it, and those who support it are fortunate.*

דְּרָכֶיהָ דַרְכֵי נֹעַם וְכָל	*Its ways are ways of pleasantness, and all its*
נְתִיבֹתֶיהָ שָׁלוֹם:	*paths are peace.*

הֲשִׁיבֵנוּ ה' אֵלֶיךָ וְנָשׁוּבָה	*Restore us to You, God, that we may be*
חַדֵּשׁ יָמֵינוּ כְּקֶדֶם:	*restored! Renew our days as of old.*

The paragraph of *U'Venucho Yomar* is a symphony of *pesukim* taken from *Bamidbar*,[8] *Tehillim*,[9] *Mishlei*,[10] and *Eichah*.[11] What a mix!

The first *pasuk*, "*U'venucho yomar*—And when it came to rest," is the *pasuk* in the Torah that describes what would occur at the conclusion of each travel period in the desert when the *Aron* would be placed back into the *Kodesh Hakodashim*, in the *Mishkan*—Tabernacle. We know there were forty-two stops during the forty years in the desert. At each stop Moshe would say, "*Shuvu Hashem revivot alfei Yisrael*—Return, God, to the many thousands of Israel." The *tefillah* continues and invokes the great aura of the Beit Hamikdash, where God's presence rested specifically by the *Aron*. "*Kohanecha yilbeshu tzedek v'chasidecha yeraneinu*," i.e., the Temple is the place where the Kohanim wear their holy vestments and the Levites sing during the services. The *tefillah* then describes the Torah, which of course is in the *Aron*: "*Eitz chaim hi l'machazikim bah v'tomcheha me'ushar*—It is a tree of life for those that grasp onto it, and those that support Torah will be joyous," because, "*Deracheha darchei noam*—All of [the Torah's] ways are ways of peace." The prayer concludes with the last *pasuk* of *Eichah*: "*Hashiveinu Hashem eilecha v'nashuva chadesh yameinu k'kedem*—Bring us back to You, God, and we will return, so that we will renew our relationship together as in the days of old."

In *U'Venucho Yomar*, the progression of the *pesukim* is quite logical. While we return the *Sefer Torah* to the *aron kodesh*, we begin by referencing and modeling when B'nei Yisrael in the desert returned the *Aron* to its place in the *Mishkan*. We continue with a description of what it

---

8   *Bamidbar* 10:36.
9   *Tehillim* 132:8–10.
10 *Mishlei* 4:2, 3:18, 3:17.
11 *Eichah* 5:21.

was like in the Beit Hamikdash with the Kohanim and Leviim. We then mention the Torah, the source of all of our mitzvot, and declare that all the ways of Torah are good and peaceful.

At this point, we recognize that although we have a *Sefer Torah*, an *aron kodesh*, and a local synagogue, our world is in a state of exile and therefore we are without the overt Shechinah. Therefore, we end (usually in beautiful song) and ask Hashem sincerely: "*Hashiveinu Hashem eilecha*—Return us to You, God," we long for the light of Your presence to illuminate the darkness in our world. The *Etz Yosef* writes that we ask Hashem to restore the world and all of us to our original state of perfection, as we were at Creation, in the Gan Eden.

> A DIVINE APPROACH: While we aim to fulfill all the mitzvot during the *tefillah* of *Shema*, *Shemoneh Esreh*, and Torah reading, we must always remember that before the Beit Hamikdash was destroyed, our services were very different. When Mashiach comes and the world is perfected, our service will adjust again to reflect this new reality.

Kaddish

יִתְגַּדַּל וְיִתְקַדַּשׁ שְׁמֵהּ רַבָּא. (קהל: אָמֵן.)	*May His Great Name be made great, and sanctified. (Congregation: Amen.)*
בְּעָלְמָא דִּי בְרָא כִרְעוּתֵה וְיַמְלִיךְ מַלְכוּתֵה, בְּחַיֵּיכוֹן וּבְיוֹמֵיכוֹן, וּבְחַיֵּי דְכָל בֵּית יִשְׂרָאֵל, בַּעֲגָלָא וּבִזְמַן קָרִיב. וְאִמְרוּ אָמֵן.	*In the world which He has created according to His will, and may He rule in His Kingdom, in your lifetime and during your days, and within the life of the entire House of Israel, speedily and soon; and say, Amen.*
(קהל: אָמֵן. יְהֵא שְׁמֵהּ רַבָּא מְבָרַךְ לְעָלַם וּלְעָלְמֵי עָלְמַיָּא.)	*(Congregation: Amen. May His great Name be blessed forever and to all eternity.)*

יְהֵא שְׁמֵהּ רַבָּא מְבָרַךְ	*May His great Name be blessed forever and*
לְעָלַם וּלְעָלְמֵי עָלְמַיָּא.	*to all eternity. Blessed and praised, glorified*
יִתְבָּרַךְ וְיִשְׁתַּבַּח וְיִתְפָּאַר	*and exalted, extolled and honored, adored and*
וְיִתְרוֹמַם וְיִתְנַשֵּׂא וְיִתְהַדָּר	*lauded be the Name of the Holy One, blessed be*
וְיִתְעַלֶּה וְיִתְהַלָּל שְׁמֵהּ	*He. (*Congregation: *Blessed be He.)*
דְּקֻדְשָׁא בְּרִיךְ הוּא.	
(קהל: בְּרִיךְ הוּא.)	
לְעֵלָּא מִן כָּל (בעשרת	*Beyond (*During the Ten Days of Repentance:
ימי תשובה: וּלְעֵלָּא	*and above and beyond) all the blessings and*
מִכָּל) בִּרְכָתָא וְשִׁירָתָא	*hymns, praises, and consolations that are*
תֻּשְׁבְּחָתָא וְנֶחֱמָתָא	*ever spoken in the world; and say, Amen.*
דַּאֲמִירָן בְּעָלְמָא. וְאִמְרוּ	*(*Congregation: *Amen.)*
אָמֵן: (קהל: אָמֵן.)	

Before and after we recite *Mussaf*, the chazzan leads us in one of the most well-known prayers to Jews worldwide: the *Kaddish*. The word *Kaddish* is actually Aramaic and means *kadosh*, holy. There are several types of *Kaddish*. We will explore the core text found in every *Kaddish*.

Chazal discuss why such an important prayer is recited in Aramaic, and not in Hebrew, like the majority of our *tefillot*. Here are some explanations:

- The *Tur* writes that it is because angels do not understand Aramaic. We are concerned that the angels who praise God continuously in the heavens should not be jealous that humans have the capacity to say such a magnificent prayer to praise Hashem, and therefore we say it in Aramaic.
- *Tosafot* explains that one of the times *Kaddish* is said is after the rabbis would study Torah with the people. Since the studying was in Aramaic and many of the students did not understand Hebrew, the prayer following the study was also in Aramaic.
- The *Shibolei Haleket* explains that originally, *Kaddish* was in Hebrew and was outlawed by our enemies. Therefore, it was translated and recited in Aramaic because our enemies did not understand Aramaic.

The chazzan chants: "*Yitgadal v'yitkadesh Shemei rabba*—May His [God's] Name be made great and sanctified." After an initial Amen, the congregation responds with a thunderous "*Amen yehei Shemei rabba mevorach l'olam u'l'almei almaya*—May God's great name be blessed forever and ever in this world and beyond."

What does it mean that God's name should be sanctified and made great? Isn't it already sanctified and great?

The commentators explain that this phrase alludes to the prophecy of Zechariah that depicts the pre-Messianic war of Gog and Magog, when the greatness of God will be clear and felt by all.[12]

Finding God

In everyday life, experiencing God and Godliness is a challenge for everyone. In fact, the Hebrew word for world is *olam*, which is directly related to the word *ne'elam*, which means hidden. This implies that truth and Godliness are hidden from the naked eye in this world. It is our challenge to discover and experience Godliness in our lives. This is achieved through prayer, the study of Torah, as well as the performance of mitzvot.

At the end of *Parashat Beshalach* we read of the war between B'nei Yisrael and Amalek. In *Shemot*, the *pasuk* states, "*Va'yomer ki yad al keis Kah milchamah l'Hashem ba'Amalek mi'dor dor*—The hand of Amalek remains on the throne of God for generations."[13] Note, that God's name here is written in a diminished form, with only the first two letters and missing the latter two letters. This means that even today, as long as the ways of Amalek are present in the world, God's presence and holiness are partially hidden from everyone. Therefore, we pray every day, "*Yitgadal v'yitkadesh Shemei rabba*—May His [God's] Name be made great and sanctified," and "*Yehei Shemei rabba mevorach l'olam u'l'almei almaya*—May God's great name be blessed forever and ever in this world and beyond," expressing our longing for the time when God's presence and holiness will be felt and recognized by all.

---

12 *Zechariah* 14:9.
13 *Shemot* 17:16.

A DIVINE APPROACH: When reciting and answering the *Kaddish*, we should include in our thoughts our fervent hope that Hashem should reveal His grandeur, sanctity, and presence to the world in all of His glory.

Amidah of *Mussaf:* The First Three Blessings
See page 53 for commentary.

Kedushah for *Mussaf*

נַעֲרִיצְךָ וְנַקְדִּישְׁךָ כְּסוֹד שִׂיחַ שַׂרְפֵי קֹדֶשׁ הַמַּקְדִּישִׁים שִׁמְךָ בַּקֹּדֶשׁ כַּכָּתוּב עַל יַד נְבִיאֶךָ וְקָרָא זֶה אֶל זֶה וְאָמַר.	*We will glorify You and we will sanctify You, like the innermost speech of the holy Seraphim, who sanctify Your Name in Holiness, as is written by the hand of Your Prophet:*
קָדוֹשׁ קָדוֹשׁ קָדוֹשׁ ה' צְבָאוֹת מְלֹא כָל הָאָרֶץ כְּבוֹדוֹ.	*"Holy, Holy, Holy, God, the Master of Hosts, the entire earth is filled with His glory!"*
כְּבוֹדוֹ מָלֵא עוֹלָם מְשָׁרְתָיו שׁוֹאֲלִים זֶה לָזֶה אַיֵּה מְקוֹם כְּבוֹדוֹ לְעֻמָּתָם בָּרוּךְ יֹאמֵרוּ.	*His glory fills the world, His attendants ask one from the other, "Where is the place of His glory?" Those facing them say, "Blessed!"*
בָּרוּךְ כְּבוֹד ה' מִמְּקוֹמוֹ.	*Blessed is God's glory from His place!*
מִמְּקוֹמוֹ הוּא יִפֶן בְּרַחֲמִים וְיָחֹן עַם הַמְיַחֲדִים שְׁמוֹ עֶרֶב וָבֹקֶר בְּכָל יוֹם תָּמִיד פַּעֲמַיִם בְּאַהֲבָה שְׁמַע אוֹמְרִים.	*From His place He turns with mercy and acts compassionately to the nation who declare the Oneness of His Name, evening and morning, every day, constantly, twice a day, with love, they say, "Shema."*
שְׁמַע יִשְׂרָאֵל ה' אֱלֹהֵינוּ ה' אֶחָד.	*Hear, O Israel, God is our Lord, God is One!*

הוּא אֱלֹהֵינוּ הוּא אָבִינוּ	*He is our God, He is our Father, He is our King,*
הוּא מַלְכֵּנוּ הוּא מוֹשִׁיעֵנוּ	*He is our Savior. And He, in His compassion,*
וְהוּא יַשְׁמִיעֵנוּ בְּרַחֲמָיו	*will let us hear a second time, in the sight of all*
שֵׁנִית לְעֵינֵי כָּל חָי לִהְיוֹת	*living beings, that He will be for us a God.*
לָכֶם לֵאלֹהִים.	

אֲנִי ה׳ אֱלֹהֵיכֶם.	*I am God your Lord!*

וּבְדִבְרֵי קָדְשְׁךָ	*And in Your holy words it is written, saying,*
כָּתוּב לֵאמֹר.	

יִמְלֹךְ ה׳ לְעוֹלָם אֱלֹהַיִךְ	*"God shall reign forever; your God, of Zion,*
צִיּוֹן לְדֹר וָדֹר הַלְלוּיָ-הּ.	*throughout all generations. Halleluyah."*

לְדֹר וָדֹר נַגִּיד גָּדְלֶךָ וּלְנֵצַח	*From generation to generation we shall tell*
נְצָחִים קְדֻשָּׁתְךָ נַקְדִּישׁ	*of Your greatness, and forever and ever Your*
וְשִׁבְחֲךָ אֱלֹהֵינוּ מִפִּינוּ לֹא	*sanctity we will sanctify, and Your praise, our*
יָמוּשׁ לְעוֹלָם וָעֶד כִּי אֵל	*God, will never cease from our lips, forever, for*
מֶלֶךְ גָּדוֹל וְקָדוֹשׁ אָתָּה.	*You are the Almighty, the great and holy King.*

בָּרוּךְ אַתָּה ה׳ הָאֵל	*Blessed are You, God, the Holy Almighty* (*during*
(בעשרת ימי תשובה: הַמֶּלֶךְ)	*the Ten Days of Repentance: the Holy King*).
הַקָּדוֹשׁ:	

The Shabbat *Mussaf* service symbolizes the sacrificial *Mussaf* that was offered in the Temple:

- Just as the *Mussaf* offering was brought before the seventh hour of the day, so too our *Mussaf* prayers are recited before the seventh hour of the day.
- Just as the *Mussaf* offering was brought between the daily morning sacrifice and the daily afternoon sacrifice, so too the *Mussaf* prayer is recited between the morning and afternoon prayers.

A highlight of the Shabbat *Mussaf* is the *Kedushah*, a communal prayer expressing our longing for God's holiness. The *Kedushah*, like *Kaddish*, *Barchu*, and the Torah reading, may only be recited in the presence of a minyan.

We recite *Kedushah* every day in the morning and afternoon prayers during the reader's repetition of the *Amidah*. Although the Shabbat benedictions are shorter than the rest of the week, the Shabbat *Kedushah* is longer than the weekday *Kedushah* and includes a more detailed description of the fascinating actions and reactions of the angels above when they praise God, as described by the prophets Yechezkel and Yeshayahu.

We will now explore the structure and content of *Kedushah* of Shabbat *Mussaf*:

"Naaritzecha v'nakdishecha k'sod siach sarfei kodesh—**We will express our awe of You and sanctify You just as the angels do in heaven."**

The commentaries explain that the double language of *"Naaritzecha v'nakdishecha*—We will express our awe of You and sanctify You" is because although God's fingerprints, so to speak, are on so many striking and beautiful parts of the world in front of our eyes, we understand that there is **so much** about God and His actions that we cannot and will never understand. Therefore, we recite both *"Naaritzecha v'nakdishecha,"* as an expression of our awe and recognition that there is so much more about God that we cannot see.

We then model the angels and recite:

"Kadosh Kadosh Kadosh Hashem tzevakot melo chol ha'aretz kevodo—**Holy, Holy, Holy is God that fills the world with His honor."**

The verse implies that God's abundant and universal holiness fills every crevice of our world. There is nowhere that God's holiness does not reach.

At this point, the ministering angels are puzzled as to where God's holiness emanates from. *"Ayeh mekom kevodo*—**Where does His holiness come from?"**

We then model the angels once again and answer:

"Baruch kevod Hashem mimkomo—**Blessed is the glory of Hashem from His place."**

The *Doveir Shalom* explains that unlike above (*"Kadosh...chol ha'aretz Kevodo"*), where it states that God's holiness fills the entire world, here it states that the honor of God emanates from His own place—*mimkomo*. This demonstrates that God is not in the world, rather, the world is in God. Therefore, God's holiness can be found everywhere.

The *Kedushah* then continues with:

"*Mimkomo hu yifen b'rachamim*—From His place He will turn with compassion."

After we have spoken the holy words of the *Navi*, we pray with humility and hope that God indeed will turn to us in mercy and listen to our praises and declarations of His oneness:

"*Shema Yisrael...v'hu yashmi'einu b'rachamav sheinit l'einei kol chai*—Hear O Israel...Then God will reveal Himself and His glory as He did by the exodus from Egypt and pronounce, *Ani Hashem Elokeichem*—I am God, your Lord.*"

The commentators discuss why the *Shema* is included in our *Mussaf Kedushah*. It is explained that there was a fifth-century Persian king named Yezdegerd that forbade the recitation of the *Shema*. The Jews, therefore, did not recite the *Shema* in *Shacharit*, but when the guards departed from the synagogue, they recited the *Shema* in *Mussaf* instead. Even once the decree was removed, Chazal maintained the *Shema* in the *Mussaf Kedushah* as a reminder of the evil decree and our deliverance from it.

The concluding phrase is:

"*Yimloch Hashem l'olam...l'dor v'dor Halleluyah*—May God reign over us for all eternity...throughout all generations, Halleluyah."

A DIVINE APPROACH: During *Kedushah* we praise and sanctify Hashem. We may wonder, are we actually fit and able to properly praise and sanctify Hashem? It is Hashem who creates, blesses, and provides sanctity for us and the world around us! The answer is a resounding YES. *Klal Yisrael* has been granted the privilege of *Kedushah* to praise and sanctify the King of kings, Hashem. We actually say the same words and phrases as the angels above. We are literally singing the songs of heaven.

Tikanta Shabbat

תִּכַּנְתָּ שַׁבָּת רָצִיתָ	*You have prepared the Shabbat, desired its*
קָרְבְּנוֹתֶיהָ צִוִּיתָ פֵּרוּשֶׁיהָ	*offerings, prescribed the details pertaining to*
עִם סִדּוּרֵי נְסָכֶיהָ מְעַנְּגֶיהָ	*it together with the order of its wine-offerings.*
לְעוֹלָם כָּבוֹד יִנְחָלוּ טוֹעֲמֶיהָ	*Those who delight in it will inherit everlasting*
חַיִּים זָכוּ וְגַם הָאוֹהֲבִים	*glory; those who savor it will merit eternal life;*
דְּבָרֶיהָ גְּדֻלָּה בָּחָרוּ אָז	*even those who love its principles have chosen*
מִסִּינַי נִצְטַוּוּ עָלֶיהָ.	*greatness, from then, at Sinai, they were*
	charged regarding it,
וַתְּצַוֵּנוּ ה' אֱלֹהֵינוּ לְהַקְרִיב	*when God, our Lord, commanded us, to offer on*
בָּהּ קָרְבַּן מוּסַף שַׁבָּת	*it, a Shabbat-mussaf offering, as appropriate.*
כָּרָאוּי.	
יְהִי רָצוֹן מִלְּפָנֶיךָ ה' אֱלֹהֵינוּ	*May it be Your will, God, our God and God of*
וֵאלֹהֵי אֲבוֹתֵינוּ שֶׁתַּעֲלֵנוּ	*our fathers, to bring us up in joy to our land and*
בְשִׂמְחָה לְאַרְצֵנוּ וְתִטָּעֵנוּ	*to plant us within its borders, and there we will*
בִּגְבוּלֵנוּ וְשָׁם נַעֲשֶׂה לְפָנֶיךָ	*offer to You our obligatory sacrifices, the daily*
אֶת קָרְבְּנוֹת חוֹבוֹתֵינוּ	*burnt-offerings according to their order, and*
תְּמִידִים כְּסִדְרָם וּמוּסָפִים	*the mussaf-offerings according to their rule;*
כְּהִלְכָתָם.	
וְאֶת מוּסַף יוֹם הַשַּׁבָּת	*and the mussaf-offering of this Shabbat day*
הַזֶּה נַעֲשֶׂה וְנַקְרִיב לְפָנֶיךָ	*we will prepare and offer to You with love in*
בְּאַהֲבָה כְּמִצְוַת רְצוֹנֶךָ כְּמוֹ	*accordance with the command of Your will, as*
שֶׁכָּתַבְתָּ עָלֵינוּ בְּתוֹרָתֶךָ	*You have written for us in Your Torah, through*
עַל יְדֵי מֹשֶׁה עַבְדֶּךָ מִפִּי	*Moshe, Your servant, from Your Holy utterance,*
כְּבוֹדֶךָ כָּאָמוּר.	*as it is stated.*

The first thing to note regarding *Tikanta Shabbat* is that it is a reverse acrostic. The prayer begins with *taf* and each word continues backward through the alphabet until *alef*. Reverse acrostics are quite rare in our liturgy. An additional prayer where we see a reverse acrostic is in the *tefillah* of *tal*—dew, on Pesach.

A reverse acrostic implies a time beyond the natural order, i.e., the time of the ultimate redemption, the Messianic era, when all the great problems in life will be solved and all the hard questions will finally be answered. Only at the end of days will all the mysteries throughout the history of the world be revealed. By seeing the end of days, we will understand why and how we got to where we did, and how God has been guiding us every step of the way. This is why the *tefillah* begins at the end of the alphabet and ends at the beginning, as if to say that from the clarity of the conclusion we will be able to grasp and embrace all the times that have led up to it.

Since Shabbat is *m'ein Olam Haba*—tantamount to the next world, we get a glimpse of what that world will look like. Through our prayers, studies, and celebrations of Shabbat, we aim to experience this piece of heaven on earth.

How in fact do we celebrate Shabbat? The *tefillah* teaches us:

- "*Me'angeha l'olam kavod yinchalu*—Those who delight in Shabbat will receive honor."
- "*To'ameha chaim zachu*—Those who savor it merit eternal life."
- "*Ha'ohavim devareha gedulah bacharu*—Those who love its teachings have chosen greatness."

There are three levels of experience:

1. Delight and celebration
2. Tasting and experiencing
3. Anticipating and pursuing the celebration of Shabbat

On a basic level, one may "keep Shabbat." On a deeper level, one can actually "taste the Shabbat." At the highest level, one can literally live from Shabbat to Shabbat and pray for and look forward to the time when the state of the world will be *kulo Shabbat*—the time of redemption.

A DIVINE APPROACH: In the Torah, in our *tefillot*, and in life, it is not just what is said, it is **how** it is said. The architects of our siddur were scholars, prophets, and kabbalists. Let's take note of what they wrote, and **how** they wrote it, such as in this *tefillah*, where it was written as a reverse acrostic, in order to recognize the different layers of knowledge and inspiration.

U'V'Yom HaShabbat and *Yismechu B'Malchutecha*

וּבְיוֹם הַשַּׁבָּת שְׁנֵי כְבָשִׂים בְּנֵי שָׁנָה תְּמִימִם וּשְׁנֵי עֶשְׂרֹנִים סֹלֶת מִנְחָה בְּלוּלָה בַשֶּׁמֶן וְנִסְכּוֹ, עֹלַת שַׁבַּת בְּשַׁבַּתּוֹ עַל עֹלַת הַתָּמִיד וְנִסְכָּהּ.	On the Shabbat day, two first-year male lambs without blemish, two-tenths of an ephah of fine flour mixed with oil as a meal-offering, and its wine-offering; this is the burnt-offering for Shabbat, on each Shabbat, aside from the daily burnt-offering and its wine-offering.
יִשְׂמְחוּ בְמַלְכוּתְךָ שׁוֹמְרֵי שַׁבָּת וְקוֹרְאֵי עֹנֶג, עַם מְקַדְּשֵׁי שְׁבִיעִי, כֻּלָּם יִשְׂבְּעוּ וְיִתְעַנְּגוּ מִטּוּבֶךָ, וּבַשְּׁבִיעִי רָצִיתָ בּוֹ וְקִדַּשְׁתּוֹ, חֶמְדַּת יָמִים אוֹתוֹ קָרָאתָ, זֵכֶר לְמַעֲשֵׂה בְרֵאשִׁית.	They shall rejoice in Your Kingship, those who observe the Shabbat and call it a delight; the nation which hallows the seventh day—all of them shall be satiated and touched with Your goodness, and the seventh day You desired and sanctified it; You called it the most desirable of days, a remembrance of the work of Creation.

The heart of the *Mussaf* prayer is the reciting of the actual Divine command of the offering, which is a quote from *Sefer Bamidbar*: "And on the Shabbat day, you shall bring two first-year male lambs."[14]

The Shabbat *Mussaf* offering is smaller than all the other holiday *Mussaf* offerings. On Rosh Chodesh, in addition to bulls and a ram, there are seven lambs brought. On Pesach, Shavuot, Sukkot, Rosh Hashanah, and Yom Kippur, there are also seven lambs.

So why on Shabbat are we commanded to only bring two?

The *Ohr Hachaim* explains that the *Mussaf* offering reflects the gift of the *lechem mishnah*, the "double portion" of Shabbat. For forty years in the desert, every Friday, the Jews received a double portion of *mann* for Shabbat. So too, in the Beit Hamikdash, the *Mussaf* offering is double the rest of the week. During the rest of the week, we bring a daily morning sacrifice called the *Tamid Shel Shachar* and a daily evening

---

14   *Bamidbar* 28:9–10.

sacrifice, called the *Tamid Shel Bein Ha'arbayim*. On Shabbat, we double the amount and offer an additional two lambs as the *Mussaf*.

The gift of the *lechem mishnah* teaches us that while during the rest of the week we are responsible to be productive and creative to build and maintain the world around us, on Shabbat we leave behind those struggles and challenges and enter the realm of Shabbat, the palace of the Almighty where God takes care of us and all of His creation with abundance.

In the next paragraph, "*Yismechu b'malchutecha shomrei Shabbat* — They **will** rejoice in Your majesty," the phrase is conspicuously in the future tense. All the other *tefillot* in *Mussaf* are in the present or past tense. Why is *Yismechu* in the future tense?

The *Otzar Hatefillot* writes that while even today on Shabbat there exists a sense of family, serenity, and tranquility, when celebrating Shabbat with care and exactitude in the time of Mashiach, a time of universal Shabbat, then "*yismechu b'malchutecha* — we **will** rejoice to the fullest in Your majesty."

A DIVINE APPROACH: There was a Torah outreach seminar where a rabbi was lecturing about self-introspection, improvement, and growth. An attendee spoke up and stated, "The ideas you propose are wonderful and inspirational, but who has time for them in our busy world? What we really need is one day a week to return to ourselves and do a spiritual inventory before advancing into the week ahead." The rabbi said, "We have that day. It is called Shabbat."

Retzeh Bi'menuchateinu

אֱלֹהֵינוּ וֵאלֹהֵי אֲבוֹתֵינוּ	*Our Lord and Lord of our fathers, find favor in*
רְצֵה בִמְנוּחָתֵנוּ קַדְּשֵׁנוּ	*our rest, sanctify us with Your commandments*
בְּמִצְוֹתֶיךָ וְתֵן חֶלְקֵנוּ	*and place our portion in Your Torah;*
בְּתוֹרָתֶךָ.	

שַׂבְּעֵנוּ מִטּוּבֶךְ וְשַׂמְּחֵנוּ	*satiate us with Your good, and gladden us*
בִּישׁוּעָתֶךְ וְטַהֵר לִבֵּנוּ	*with Your salvation, and purify our heart to*
לְעׇבְדְּךָ בֶּאֱמֶת וְהַנְחִילֵנוּ	*serve You in truth; and bestow upon us, God,*
ה׳ אֱלֹהֵינוּ בְּאַהֲבָה וּבְרָצוֹן	*our Lord, with love and goodwill, Your holy*
שַׁבַּת קׇדְשֶׁךָ וְיָנוּחוּ בוֹ	*Shabbat, and may all of Israel, who sanctify*
יִשְׂרָאֵל מְקַדְּשֵׁי שְׁמֶךָ.	*Your Name, rest on it.*

| בָּרוּךְ אַתָּה ה׳ מְקַדֵּשׁ | *Blessed are You, God, who sanctifies* |
| הַשַּׁבָּת. | *the Shabbat.* |

See page 58 for commentary.

The Last Three Blessings

רְצֵה ה׳ אֱלֹהֵינוּ בְּעַמְּךָ	*Look with favor, God, our Lord, on Your people*
יִשְׂרָאֵל וּבִתְפִלָּתָם, וְהָשֵׁב	*Israel and pay heed to their prayer; restore the*
אֶת הָעֲבוֹדָה לִדְבִיר בֵּיתֶךָ,	*service to Your Sanctuary and accept with love*
וְאִשֵּׁי יִשְׂרָאֵל וּתְפִלָּתָם,	*and favor Israel's fire-offerings and prayer, and*
בְּאַהֲבָה תְקַבֵּל בְּרָצוֹן,	*may the service of Your people Israel always*
וּתְהִי לְרָצוֹן תָּמִיד עֲבוֹדַת	*find favor.*
יִשְׂרָאֵל עַמֶּךָ:	

| וְתֶחֱזֶינָה עֵינֵינוּ בְּשׁוּבְךָ | *May our eyes behold Your return to Zion* |
| לְצִיּוֹן בְּרַחֲמִים: | *in mercy.* |

| בָּרוּךְ אַתָּה ה׳, הַמַּחֲזִיר | *Blessed are You, God, who restores His Divine* |
| שְׁכִינָתוֹ לְצִיּוֹן: | *Presence to Zion.* |

מוֹדִים אֲנַחְנוּ לָךְ, שָׁאַתָּה	*We thankfully acknowledge that You are God,*
הוּא ה׳ אֱלֹהֵינוּ וֵאלֹהֵי	*our Lord and Lord of our fathers, forever.*
אֲבוֹתֵינוּ לְעוֹלָם וָעֶד:	

| צוּר חַיֵּינוּ, מָגֵן יִשְׁעֵנוּ אַתָּה | *You are the strength of our life, the shield of our* |
| הוּא לְדֹר וָדֹר: | *salvation in every generation.* |

נוֹדֶה לְּךָ וּנְסַפֵּר תְּהִלָּתֶךָ, עַל חַיֵּינוּ הַמְּסוּרִים בְּיָדֶיךָ, וְעַל נִשְׁמוֹתֵינוּ הַפְּקוּדוֹת לָךְ, וְעַל נִסֶּיךָ שֶׁבְּכָל יוֹם עִמָּנוּ, וְעַל נִפְלְאוֹתֶיךָ וְטוֹבוֹתֶיךָ שֶׁבְּכָל עֵת, עֶרֶב וָבֹקֶר וְצָהֳרָיִם:	*We will give thanks to You and recount Your praise, evening, morning, and noon, for our lives that are committed into Your hand, for our souls that are entrusted to You, for Your miracles that are with us daily, and for Your continual wonders and beneficences.*
הַטּוֹב, כִּי לֹא כָלוּ רַחֲמֶיךָ, וְהַמְרַחֵם, כִּי לֹא תַמּוּ חֲסָדֶיךָ, מֵעוֹלָם קִוִּינוּ לָךְ:	*You are the Beneficent One, for Your mercies never cease; the Merciful One, for Your kindnesses never end; for we always place our hope in You.*
וְעַל כֻּלָּם יִתְבָּרַךְ וְיִתְרוֹמַם שִׁמְךָ מַלְכֵּנוּ תָּמִיד לְעוֹלָם וָעֶד:	*And for all these, may Your Name, our King, be continually blessed, exalted, and extolled forever and all time.*
וְכֹל הַחַיִּים יוֹדוּךָ סֶּלָה, וִיהַלְלוּ אֶת שִׁמְךָ בֶּאֱמֶת, הָאֵל יְשׁוּעָתֵנוּ וְעֶזְרָתֵנוּ סֶלָה:	*And all living things shall forever thank You, and praise Your great Name eternally, for You are good. God, You are our everlasting salvation and help, O benevolent God.*
בָּרוּךְ אַתָּה ה', הַטּוֹב שִׁמְךָ וּלְךָ נָאֶה לְהוֹדוֹת:	*Blessed are You, God, Beneficent is Your Name, and to You it is fitting to offer thanks.*
שִׂים שָׁלוֹם טוֹבָה וּבְרָכָה, חֵן וָחֶסֶד וְרַחֲמִים, עָלֵינוּ וְעַל כָּל יִשְׂרָאֵל עַמֶּךָ:	*Bestow peace, goodness and blessing, life, graciousness, kindness and mercy upon us and upon all Your people Israel.*
בָּרְכֵנוּ אָבִינוּ, כֻּלָּנוּ כְּאֶחָד בְּאוֹר פָּנֶיךָ, כִּי בְאוֹר פָּנֶיךָ נָתַתָּ לָּנוּ ה' אֱלֹהֵינוּ, תּוֹרַת חַיִּים, וְאַהֲבַת חֶסֶד, וּצְדָקָה וּבְרָכָה וְרַחֲמִים, וְחַיִּים וְשָׁלוֹם:	*Bless us, our Father, all of us as one, with the light of Your countenance. For by the light of Your countenance You gave us, God, our Lord, the Torah of life and loving-kindness, righteousness, blessing, mercy, life, and peace.*
וְטוֹב בְּעֵינֶיךָ לְבָרֵךְ אֶת עַמְּךָ יִשְׂרָאֵל בְּכָל עֵת וּבְכָל שָׁעָה בִּשְׁלוֹמֶךָ:	*May it be favorable in Your eyes to bless Your people Israel, at all times and at every moment, with Your peace.*
בָּרוּךְ אַתָּה ה', הַמְבָרֵךְ אֶת עַמּוֹ יִשְׂרָאֵל בַּשָּׁלוֹם:	*Blessed are You, God, who blesses His people Israel with peace.*

The concluding three blessings of *Retzeh*, *Modim* and *V'Al Kulam*, *and Sim Shalom* are the same as during the week. They represent the thanksgiving section of the *Amidah* in which we ask Hashem to receive our prayers as He would an offering in the Beit Hamikdash, make an overall statement of gratitude for all the gifts of life Hashem prepares and shares with us every minute, and conclude with a prayer for peace.

Rabbi Joseph B. Soloveitchik explained that the concluding three blessings of thanksgiving are a reflection of the first three blessings of praise, albeit in the opposite order:

- The blessing of *Magen Avraham* mirrors *Sim Shalom*. In *Sim Shalom*, we state that God presented to us the Torah, love of kindness, charity, blessings, life, and peace. It was our forefathers, Avraham, Yitzchak, and Yaakov, who brought these principles to the world.

- *Mechayeh Meitim* corresponds to *V'Al Kulam*. In *V'Al Kulam*, we state that "all of life" will thank You, and *Mechalkel Chaim B'Chessed* is the blessing that introduces life in this world and the next world—i.e., "all of life."

- *HaKeil Ha'kadosh* is the blessing wherein we recognize that every day, people and angels sanctify God's name through prayer, and *Retzeh* asks that our prayers be accepted as if they were sacrificial offerings.

These six blessings are constant in every *Amidah* we recite all year long.

Aleinu L'Shabei'ach

Every single *tefillah* concludes with *Aleinu L'Shabei'ach*, which literally means "It is upon us to praise."

עָלֵינוּ לְשַׁבֵּחַ לַאֲדוֹן	*It is our duty to praise the Master of all, to*
הַכֹּל לָתֵת גְּדֻלָּה לְיוֹצֵר	*acclaim the greatness of the One who forms*
בְּרֵאשִׁית שֶׁלֹּא עָשָׂנוּ	*all creation. For God did not make us like the*
כְּגוֹיֵי הָאֲרָצוֹת וְלֹא שָׂמָנוּ	*nations of other lands and did not make us the*
כְּמִשְׁפְּחוֹת הָאֲדָמָה.	*same as other families of the earth.*

שֶׁלֹּא שָׂם חֶלְקֵנוּ כָּהֶם וְגוֹרָלֵנוּ כְּכָל הֲמוֹנָם. (שֶׁהֵם מִשְׁתַּחֲוִים לְהֶבֶל וָרִיק וּמִתְפַּלְלִים אֶל אֵל לֹא יוֹשִׁיעַ.)	*God did not place us in the same situations as others, and our destiny is not the same as anyone else's. (For they worship vanity and emptiness and pray to a god who cannot save.)*
וַאֲנַחְנוּ כּוֹרְעִים וּמִשְׁתַּחֲוִים וּמוֹדִים לִפְנֵי מֶלֶךְ מַלְכֵי הַמְּלָכִים הַקָּדוֹשׁ בָּרוּךְ הוּא.	*And we bend our knees, and bow down, and give thanks, before the Ruler, the Ruler of Rulers, the Holy One, blessed be He.*
שֶׁהוּא נוֹטֶה שָׁמַיִם וְיֹסֵד אֶרֶץ וּמוֹשַׁב יְקָרוֹ בַּשָּׁמַיִם מִמַּעַל וּשְׁכִינַת עֻזּוֹ בְּגָבְהֵי מְרוֹמִים.	*The One who spread out the heavens, and made the foundations of the earth, and whose precious dwelling is in the heavens above, and whose powerful Presence is in the highest heights.*
הוּא אֱלֹהֵינוּ אֵין עוֹד.	*God is our Lord, there is no one else.*
אֱמֶת מַלְכֵּנוּ אֶפֶס זוּלָתוֹ כַּכָּתוּב בְּתוֹרָתוֹ:	*Our God is truth, and nothing else compares. As it is written in Your Torah:*
וְיָדַעְתָּ הַיּוֹם וַהֲשֵׁבֹתָ אֶל לְבָבֶךָ כִּי ה׳ הוּא הָאֱלֹהִים בַּשָּׁמַיִם מִמַּעַל וְעַל הָאָרֶץ מִתָּחַת אֵין עוֹד:	*"And you shall know today, and take to heart, that God is the Lord, in the heavens above and on earth below. There is no other."*
וְעַל כֵּן נְקַוֶּה לְךָ ה׳ אֱלֹהֵינוּ לִרְאוֹת מְהֵרָה בְּתִפְאֶרֶת עֻזֶּךָ לְהַעֲבִיר גִּלּוּלִים מִן הָאָרֶץ וְהָאֱלִילִים כָּרוֹת יִכָּרֵתוּן לְתַקֵּן עוֹלָם בְּמַלְכוּת שַׁדַּי.	*Therefore, we put our hope in You, God, our Lord, to soon see the glory of Your strength, to remove all idols from the earth, and to completely cut off all false gods; to repair the world, Your holy empire.*
וְכָל בְּנֵי בָשָׂר יִקְרְאוּ בִשְׁמֶךָ לְהַפְנוֹת אֵלֶיךָ כָּל רִשְׁעֵי אָרֶץ. יַכִּירוּ וְיֵדְעוּ כָּל יוֹשְׁבֵי תֵבֵל כִּי לְךָ תִּכְרַע כָּל בֶּרֶךְ תִּשָּׁבַע כָּל לָשׁוֹן.	*And for all living flesh to call Your name, and for all the wicked of the earth to turn to You. May all the world's inhabitants recognize and know that to You every knee must bend, and every tongue must swear loyalty.*

לְפָנֶיךָ ה׳ אֱלֹהֵינוּ יִכְרְעוּ וְיִפֹּלוּ וְלִכְבוֹד שִׁמְךָ יְקָר יִתֵּנוּ. וִיקַבְּלוּ כֻלָּם אֶת עֹל מַלְכוּתֶךָ וְתִמְלֹךְ עֲלֵיהֶם מְהֵרָה לְעוֹלָם וָעֶד.	*Before You, God, our Lord, may all bow down, and give honor to Your precious name, and may all take upon themselves the yoke of Your rule. And may You reign over them soon and forever and always.*
כִּי הַמַּלְכוּת שֶׁלְּךָ הִיא וּלְעוֹלְמֵי עַד תִּמְלֹךְ בְּכָבוֹד. כַּכָּתוּב בְּתוֹרָתֶךָ: ה׳ יִמְלֹךְ לְעֹלָם וָעֶד.	*Because all rule is Yours alone, and You will rule in honor forever and ever. As it is written in Your Torah: "God will reign forever and ever."*
וְנֶאֱמַר: וְהָיָה ה׳ לְמֶלֶךְ עַל כָּל הָאָרֶץ בַּיּוֹם הַהוּא יִהְיֶה ה׳ אֶחָד וּשְׁמוֹ אֶחָד:	*And it is said: "God will be Ruler over the whole earth, and on that day, God will be One, and God's name will be One."*

See page 66 for commentary.

Chapter Five

MINCHAH

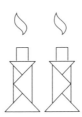

Ashrei

אַשְׁרֵי יוֹשְׁבֵי בֵיתֶךָ עוֹד יְהַלְלוּךָ סֶּלָה אַשְׁרֵי הָעָם שֶׁכָּכָה לוֹ אַשְׁרֵי הָעָם שֶׁה׳ אֱלֹהָיו.	*Fortunate are those who remain in Your house; they will continually praise You forever. Praiseworthy is the people that has this; praiseworthy is the people of whom God is their Lord.*
תְּהִלָּה לְדָוִד אֲרוֹמִמְךָ אֱלוֹהַי הַמֶּלֶךְ וַאֲבָרְכָה שִׁמְךָ לְעוֹלָם וָעֶד.	*A praise of David. I shall exalt You, my God the King, and I shall bless Your Name forever and ever.*
בְּכָל יוֹם אֲבָרְכֶךָ וַאֲהַלְלָה שִׁמְךָ לְעוֹלָם וָעֶד.	*Every day I shall bless You, and I shall praise Your Name forever and ever.*
גָּדוֹל ה׳ וּמְהֻלָּל מְאֹד וְלִגְדֻלָּתוֹ אֵין חֵקֶר.	*God is great and very much praised, and His greatness cannot be comprehended.*
דּוֹר לְדוֹר יְשַׁבַּח מַעֲשֶׂיךָ וּגְבוּרֹתֶיךָ יַגִּידוּ.	*Generation to generation will praise Your works, and they will recite Your mighty deeds.*

הֲדַר כְּבוֹד הוֹדֶךָ וְדִבְרֵי נִפְלְאוֹתֶיךָ אָשִׂיחָה.	*Of the majesty of the glory of Your splendor and the words of Your wonders I shall speak.*
וֶעֱזוּז נוֹרְאֹתֶיךָ יֹאמֵרוּ וּגְדֻלָּתְךָ אֲסַפְּרֶנָּה.	*And the strength of Your awesome deeds they will tell, and Your greatness I shall sing.*
זֵכֶר רַב טוּבְךָ יַבִּיעוּ וְצִדְקָתְךָ יְרַנֵּנוּ.	*Of the remembrance of Your abundant goodness they will speak, and of Your righteousness they will sing.*
חַנּוּן וְרַחוּם ה׳ אֶרֶךְ אַפַּיִם וּגְדָל חָסֶד.	*God is gracious and compassionate, slow to anger and of great kindness.*
טוֹב ה׳ לַכֹּל וְרַחֲמָיו עַל כָּל מַעֲשָׂיו.	*God is good to all, and His mercy is on all His works.*
יוֹדוּךָ ה׳ כָּל מַעֲשֶׂיךָ וַחֲסִידֶיךָ יְבָרְכוּכָה.	*All Your works will thank You, God, and Your pious ones will bless You.*
כְּבוֹד מַלְכוּתְךָ יֹאמֵרוּ וּגְבוּרָתְךָ יְדַבֵּרוּ.	*They will tell the glory of Your kingdom, and they will speak of Your might.*
לְהוֹדִיעַ לִבְנֵי הָאָדָם גְּבוּרֹתָיו וּכְבוֹד הֲדַר מַלְכוּתוֹ.	*To make known to the children of men His mighty deeds and the glory of the majesty of His kingdom.*
מַלְכוּתְךָ מַלְכוּת כָּל עֹלָמִים וּמֶמְשַׁלְתְּךָ בְּכָל דּוֹר וָדֹר.	*Your kingdom is a kingdom of all times, and Your dominion is throughout every generation.*
סוֹמֵךְ ה׳ לְכָל הַנֹּפְלִים וְזוֹקֵף לְכָל הַכְּפוּפִים.	*God supports all of the fallen and straightens all the bent.*
עֵינֵי כֹל אֵלֶיךָ יְשַׂבֵּרוּ וְאַתָּה נוֹתֵן לָהֶם אֶת אָכְלָם בְּעִתּוֹ.	*Everyone's eyes look to You with hope, and You give them their food in its time.*
פּוֹתֵחַ אֶת יָדֶךָ וּמַשְׂבִּיעַ לְכָל חַי רָצוֹן.	*You open Your hand and satisfy every living thing [with] its desire.*
צַדִּיק ה׳ בְּכָל דְּרָכָיו וְחָסִיד בְּכָל מַעֲשָׂיו.	*God is righteous in all His ways and kind in all His deeds.*
קָרוֹב ה׳ לְכָל קֹרְאָיו לְכֹל אֲשֶׁר יִקְרָאֻהוּ בֶאֱמֶת.	*God is near to all who call Him, to all who call Him with sincerity.*

רְצוֹן יְרֵאָיו יַעֲשֶׂה וְאֶת שַׁוְעָתָם יִשְׁמַע וְיוֹשִׁיעֵם.	*He does the will of those who fear Him, and He hears their cry and saves them.*
שׁוֹמֵר ה' אֶת כָּל אֹהֲבָיו וְאֵת כָּל הָרְשָׁעִים יַשְׁמִיד.	*God guards all who love Him, and He destroys all the wicked.*
תְּהִלַּת ה' יְדַבֶּר פִּי וִיבָרֵךְ כָּל בָּשָׂר שֵׁם קָדְשׁוֹ לְעוֹלָם וָעֶד.	*My mouth will speak God's praises, and all flesh will bless His holy Name forever and ever.*
וַאֲנַחְנוּ נְבָרֵךְ יָהּ מֵעַתָּה וְעַד עוֹלָם הַלְלוּיָהּ.	*But we shall bless God from now until everlasting, Halleluyah!*

See page 129 for commentary.

U'Va L'Tzion

וּבָא לְצִיּוֹן גּוֹאֵל וּלְשָׁבֵי פֶשַׁע בְּיַעֲקֹב נְאֻם ה' וַאֲנִי זֹאת בְּרִיתִי אוֹתָם אָמַר ה' רוּחִי אֲשֶׁר עָלֶיךָ וּדְבָרַי אֲשֶׁר שַׂמְתִּי בְּפִיךָ לֹא יָמוּשׁוּ מִפִּיךָ וּמִפִּי זַרְעֲךָ וּמִפִּי זֶרַע זַרְעֲךָ אָמַר ה' מֵעַתָּה וְעַד עוֹלָם.	*And a redeemer shall come to Zion and to those in Yaakov who repent of transgression, says God. And as for Me, this is My covenant with them, says God, "My spirit which is upon you and My words which I have put in your mouth shall not depart from your mouth, nor from the mouth of your children, nor from the mouth of your children's children, declares God, from now to eternity."*
וְאַתָּה קָדוֹשׁ יוֹשֵׁב תְּהִלּוֹת יִשְׂרָאֵל וְקָרָא זֶה אֶל זֶה וְאָמַר קָדוֹשׁ קָדוֹשׁ קָדוֹשׁ ה' צְבָאוֹת מְלֹא כָל הָאָרֶץ כְּבוֹדוֹ	*And You, Holy One, are enthroned upon the praises of Israel. And [the angels] call to one another and say, "Holy, holy, holy is God, Master of Hosts; the whole earth is full of His glory."*
וּמְקַבְּלִין דֵּין מִן דֵּין וְאָמְרִין קַדִּישׁ בִּשְׁמֵי מְרוֹמָא עִלָּאָה בֵּית שְׁכִינְתֵּהּ קַדִּישׁ עַל אַרְעָא עוֹבַד גְּבוּרְתֵּהּ קַדִּישׁ לְעָלַם וּלְעָלְמֵי עָלְמַיָּא ה' צְבָאוֹת מַלְיָא כָל אַרְעָא זִיו יְקָרֵהּ.	*And they receive permission one from the other, and say, "Holy in the loftiest, most sublime heavens, the abode of His Divine Presence; holy upon earth, the work of His might; holy forever and to all eternity—is God, Master of Hosts; the whole earth is filled with the radiance of His glory."*

וַתִּשָּׂאֵנִי רוּחַ וָאֶשְׁמַע אַחֲרַי קוֹל רַעַשׁ גָּדוֹל בָּרוּךְ כְּבוֹד ה׳ מִמְּקוֹמוֹ.	*And a wind lifted me, and I heard behind me a great, roaring, sound, "Blessed be the glory of the God from His place."*
וּנְטָלַתְנִי רוּחָא וּשְׁמָעִית בַּתְרַי קָל זִיעַ סַגִּיא דִמְשַׁבְּחִין וְאָמְרִין בְּרִיךְ יְקָרָא דַה׳ מֵאֲתַר בֵּית שְׁכִינְתֵּהּ. ה׳ יִמְלֹךְ לְעָלַם וָעֶד.	*And a wind lifted me, and I heard behind me a mighty, thunderous sound of those who utter praises and say, "Blessed be the glory of God from the place, the abode of His Divine Presence. God will reign forever and ever."*
ה׳ מַלְכוּתֵהּ קָאֵם לְעָלַם וּלְעָלְמֵי עָלְמַיָּא.	*God's sovereignty is established forever, and to all eternity.*
ה׳ אֱלֹהֵי אַבְרָהָם יִצְחָק וְיִשְׂרָאֵל אֲבוֹתֵינוּ. שָׁמְרָה זֹּאת לְעוֹלָם לְיֵצֶר מַחְשְׁבוֹת לְבַב עַמֶּךָ וְהָכֵן לְבָבָם אֵלֶיךָ.	*God, Lord of Avraham, Yitzchak, and Yisrael our forefathers, keep this forever as the desire, the intention, of the hearts of Your people, and turn their hearts to You.*
וְהוּא רַחוּם יְכַפֵּר עָוֹן וְלֹא יַשְׁחִית וְהִרְבָּה לְהָשִׁיב אַפּוֹ וְלֹא יָעִיר כָּל חֲמָתוֹ.	*And He, being compassionate, pardons iniquity, and does not destroy; He repeatedly turns away His anger, and does not arouse all His wrath.*
כִּי אַתָּה אֲדֹנָי טוֹב וְסַלָּח וְרַב חֶסֶד לְכָל קֹרְאֶיךָ.	*For You, God, are good and forgiving, and abounding in kindness to all who call upon You.*
צִדְקָתְךָ צֶדֶק לְעוֹלָם וְתוֹרָתְךָ אֱמֶת.	*Your righteousness is everlasting righteousness, Your Torah is truth.*
תִּתֵּן אֱמֶת לְיַעֲקֹב חֶסֶד לְאַבְרָהָם אֲשֶׁר נִשְׁבַּעְתָּ לַאֲבֹתֵינוּ מִימֵי קֶדֶם.	*Show faithfulness to Yaakov, kindness to Avraham, as You have sworn to our forefathers from the days of yore.*
בָּרוּךְ אֲדֹנָי יוֹם יוֹם יַעֲמָס לָנוּ הָאֵל יְשׁוּעָתֵנוּ סֶלָה, ה׳ צְבָאוֹת עִמָּנוּ מִשְׂגָּב לָנוּ אֱלֹהֵי יַעֲקֹב סֶלָה ה׳ צְבָאוֹת אַשְׁרֵי אָדָם בֹּטֵחַ בָּךְ ה׳ הוֹשִׁיעָה הַמֶּלֶךְ יַעֲנֵנוּ בְיוֹם קָרְאֵנוּ.	*Blessed is God who each day loads us [with blessing], the God who is our deliverance forever. God, Master of Hosts, is with us; the God of Yaakov is our eternal stronghold. God, Master of Hosts, happy is the man who trusts in You. God, deliver us; may the King answer us on the day we call.*

בָּרוּךְ הוּא אֱלֹהֵינוּ שֶׁבְּרָאָנוּ	*Blessed is He, our God, who has created us for*
לִכְבוֹדוֹ וְהִבְדִּילָנוּ מִן	*His glory, and has set us apart from those who*
הַתּוֹעִים וְנָתַן לָנוּ תּוֹרַת	*go astray, has given us the Torah of truth, and*
אֱמֶת וְחַיֵּי עוֹלָם נָטַע	*has implanted eternal life within us. May He*
בְּתוֹכֵנוּ הוּא יִפְתַּח לִבֵּנוּ	*open our heart to His Torah, instill in our heart*
בְּתוֹרָתוֹ וְיָשֵׂם בְּלִבֵּנוּ	*love toward Him and awe of Him, and [instill*
אַהֲבָתוֹ וְיִרְאָתוֹ וְלַעֲשׂוֹת	*in our heart] to do His will and serve Him with*
רְצוֹנוֹ וּלְעָבְדוֹ בְּלֵבָב שָׁלֵם	*a perfect heart, so that we shall not labor for*
לְמַעַן לֹא נִיגַע לָרִיק וְלֹא	*nothingness, nor produce [nothing but] panic.*
נֵלֵד לַבֶּהָלָה.	

יְהִי רָצוֹן מִלְּפָנֶיךָ ה' אֱלֹהֵינוּ	*May it be Your will, God, our Lord and Lord of*
וֵאלֹהֵי אֲבוֹתֵינוּ שֶׁנִּשְׁמֹר	*our fathers, that we observe Your statutes in*
חֻקֶּיךָ בָּעוֹלָם הַזֶּה וְנִזְכֶּה	*this world, and merit, and live, and see, and*
וְנִחְיֶה וְנִרְאֶה וְנִירַשׁ טוֹבָה	*inherit the goodness and blessing of the years*
וּבְרָכָה לִשְׁנֵי יְמוֹת הַמָּשִׁיחַ	*of the Messianic era and the life of the World*
וּלְחַיֵּי הָעוֹלָם הַבָּא לְמַעַן	*to Come. So that my soul shall sing to You,*
יְזַמֶּרְךָ כָבוֹד וְלֹא יִדֹּם ה'	*and not be silent; God my Lord, I will thank*
אֱלֹהַי לְעוֹלָם אוֹדֶךָּ.	*You forever.*

בָּרוּךְ הַגֶּבֶר אֲשֶׁר יִבְטַח	*Blessed is the man who trusts in God, and God*
בַּה' וְהָיָה ה' מִבְטַחוֹ.	*will be his security.*

בִּטְחוּ בַה' עֲדֵי עַד כִּי בְּיָהּ	*Trust in God forever and ever, for in God is the*
ה' צוּר עוֹלָמִים.	*strength of the worlds.*

וְיִבְטְחוּ בְךָ יוֹדְעֵי שְׁמֶךָ כִּי	*Those who know Your Name put their trust*
לֹא עָזַבְתָּ דֹרְשֶׁיךָ ה'.	*in You, for You have not abandoned those who*
	seek You, God.

ה' חָפֵץ לְמַעַן צִדְקוֹ יַגְדִּיל	*God desired, for the sake of Israel's*
תּוֹרָה וְיַאְדִּיר.	*righteousness, to make the Torah great*
	and glorious.

U'Va L'Tzion begins with a declaration that God will be sending a redeemer to Tzion, and to all those who grow closer to Him. It then states that our covenant with God is eternal and includes our children, grandchildren, great-grandchildren, and so on.

U'Va L'Tzion also contains *Kedushah*. We call this *Kedushah D'Sidra*—the *Kedushah* of order. Just like the other two places in *Shacharit*, i.e., before *Shema* and during the repetition of the *Amidah*, as well as in every other *Minchah* after the silent *Amidah*, this *Kedushah* contains an introduction, "*Kadosh Kadosh Kadosh, baruch kevod Hashem mimkomo*," and "*Hashem yimloch l'olam va'ed*." Unlike the other versions of *Kedushah*, here there is also an Aramaic translation that follows. The question is, why do we say *Kedushah* during *U'Va L'Tzion* at all, and why the Aramaic translation?

The siddur *Otzar Hatefillot* answers that there was a time in history when the authorities of the land banned the recitation of *Kedushah*. In response, Chazal instituted that we wait until after *Shacharit* and *Mussaf* and recite *Kedushah* twice in a subsequent prayer after the officials would have left the synagogue. The translation in Aramaic was also added to demonstrate our great love and affection to Hashem and how much we long to sanctify His Name.

On Shabbat afternoon, the holiest time of Shabbat, after *Ashrei*, we recite *U'Va L'Tzion* together with *Kedushah*, right before we open the *aron kodesh* to bring out and read from the *Sefer Torah*. After a full day of Shabbat prayers and celebration, we reflect on repentance and invoke the *Kedushah* one final time during the day.

Just imagine the following parable: A young man and women are deeply in love and committed to one another for life but are forced to be apart due to unforeseen circumstances. The impending separation is so devastating; not only because they will be apart, but because the amount of time they will be apart is uncertain. Imagine the declarations of love, fidelity, and commitment pledged to one another before they separate? After the separation, imagine the potency of the letters sent one to another with emotion and great anticipation of the time when they will be together again? The longing for reconnection is palpable.

These are the images that come to mind when we read and chant the next nine *pesukim* of *U'Va L'Tzion*. Yet the couple is not a young man and woman; it is rather Hashem and His beloved children, Yisrael.

The section after the *Kedushah D'Sidra* of *U'Va L'Tzion* quotes nine *pesukim* from throughout *Tanach*. There is a *pasuk* from *Divrei*

Hayamim when David HaMelech delivers a farewell address to the Jewish People, as well as several *pesukim* from *Tehillim*. Although the *pesukim* are quoted from different *sefarim* and *perakim*, there is one theme that exists throughout all of them; namely, the unbreakable and inextricable connection that God has and will maintain with Am Yisrael forever.

The *pesukim* refer to God's infinite patience and compassion, and that He is forgiving of iniquity and does not destroy. We invoke His promises of truth and goodness that were sworn unto Avraham and Yaakov, and that God is our salvation and will answer us on the day that we call upon Him.

After we recite the *Kedushah D'Sidra* and declare our loving commitment to God, the conclusion of *U'Va L'Tzion* describes the unbelievable opportunity and privilege we have been afforded by God to receive, learn, and fulfill the precepts of the Torah.

The Gap between Inspired Expression and Defined Commitment

Many years ago, Rav Shimon Schwab stated in front of a group of rabbinical students who were running a summer program for *baalei teshuvah*—returnees to Jewish tradition, that all Jews should be *baalei teshuvah*; Jews of all backgrounds need to continuously strive to grow closer to Hashem and fulfill the Torah better.

There is an interesting phenomenon that can develop when a Jew finds his way back to the traditions of Torah. The journey begins with fascination and inspiration. Each new mitzvah taken on is exhilarating, both in its performance, and in adding another slice of holiness to one's life. Then one day, through study and/or experience, a realization sets in that if one does **not** keep the Torah and mitzvot, they may face the Biblical warnings and punishments therein. The *baal teshuvah* then does a double take and thinks, "Wait a minute, I took on (for example) Shabbat because it's enjoyable, holy, and a great idea for family...now you're telling me that I **must** keep it?!" This is a reality check faced by many newly observant Jews each year. When they succeed in crossing that threshold with positivity, they arrive at observance and commitment to halachic Judaism.

This experience is mirrored in the final *pesukim* of *U'Va L'Tzion*: "*Baruch Elokeinu she'baranu lichvodo*—Blessed is our God who has created us for His glory, separated us from the sinners, and presented us with the eternal truths of the Torah and implanted eternity within us." The prayer continues with a *pasuk* from *Yeshayahu*: "*Hu yiftach libeinu b'Torato...u'l'avdo b'leivav shaleim l'maan lo nigah la'rik v'lo neiled l'behalah*—May God open our hearts to Torah...so that we may serve Him with full hearts and not decline toward emptiness and pursue futility."[1]

The first phrase demonstrates the unparalleled greatness God created us for. The second phrase from *Yeshayahu* states clearly that the lack of pursuit toward a life of truth and mitzvot will determine a life, God forbid, that leads toward emptiness and futility. What a contrast!

U'Va L'Tzion concludes with a request that God protect us in this world and the next world, where we will praise God with our souls, greet the Mashiach, and experience the World to Come. The final *pesukim* from *Tehillim* and *Yeshayahu* punctuate this theme of our eternal relationship with God.

A DIVINE APPROACH: It is our task, challenge, and privilege to develop a relationship with Hashem. One of the pathways to that relationship is prayer. All good relationships require attention and effort. Reciting *U'Va L'Tzion* with concentration and focusing on the layers of meaning reinforces and enriches our relationship with Hashem.

Va'ani Tefilati

וַאֲנִי תְפִלָּתִי לְךָ ה' עֵת
רָצוֹן אֱלֹהִים בְּרָב חַסְדֶּךָ
עֲנֵנִי בֶּאֱמֶת יִשְׁעֶךָ.

As for me, may my prayer to You, God, be accepted at this auspicious time; Elokim, with Your abundance of kindness, answer me with Your truthful deliverance.

---

1   *Yeshayahu* 65:23.

This *pasuk* from *Tehillim*[2] is chanted by the congregation during Shabbat afternoon *Minchah*, after *U'Va L'Tzion*. The *Shaarei Teshuvah* states that it is specifically at the moment this *pasuk* is recited that the leader should don his tallit.[3] The *Mishneh Berurah* there notes that it is recited only during Shabbat *Minchah* and not Yom Tov *Minchah* because it is only on Shabbat that we take out the *Sefer Torah* to read, and it is therefore an *eit ratzon*—auspicious time. However, on Yom Tov *Shacharit*, we do say this *pasuk* together with the Thirteen Attributes of Mercy, which is another auspicious moment associated with *k'riat haTorah*. The question is, why is Shabbat *Minchah* such a significant and merciful time?

The *Aruch Hashulchan* gives two different reasons:

- The *Zohar* in *Parashat Terumah* states that during the week, the late afternoon is a time of Heavenly judgment, but on Shabbat, Hashem demonstrates a unique Divine compassion; therefore, Shabbat *Minchah* is the time to engage and entreat the Almighty.

- The *Tur* brings a *Midrash Tehillim* that contrasts our Shabbat celebration to a standard earthly celebration. He writes that when we say *Va'ani Tefilati*, we call out to Hashem and proclaim that even after we eat, drink, and celebrate on Shabbat, we return to Him in prayer and service. This is as opposed to ordinary celebrations where after an abundance of food and wine is consumed, the participants behave with fewer inhibitions and might pursue mundane pleasures.[4]

A DIVINE APPROACH: The recitiation of *Va'ani Tefilati* demonstrates that Shabbat *Minchah* and the time afterward are a unique and holy time of Shabbat. It is not a time for leisure where we simply wait for Shabbat to conclude, but rather it is a time for song, praise to God, and Torah study in order to embrace the heights of Shabbat and grasp onto it before it ebbs away.

---

2   69:14.
3   *Orach Chaim* 292.
4   *Tur* 292.

Shabbat *Minchah* continues with *k'riat haTorah*, which was instituted by Moshe himself. We read three *aliyot* from the *parashah* of the upcoming week. After returning the Torah to the *aron kodesh* and reciting *L'David Mizmor*, the reader continues with half *Kaddish*, and we recite the silent *Amidah*.

Amidah of Minchah: The First Three Blessings

See page 53 for commentary.

Atah Echad V'Shimcha Echad

אַתָּה אֶחָד וְשִׁמְךָ אֶחָד וּמִי כְּעַמְּךָ יִשְׂרָאֵל גּוֹי אֶחָד בָּאָרֶץ תִּפְאֶרֶת גְּדֻלָּה וַעֲטֶרֶת יְשׁוּעָה יוֹם מְנוּחָה וּקְדֻשָּׁה לְעַמְּךָ נָתָתָּ.	*You are One and Your Name is One, and who is like Your People Israel, one nation on earth? You have given Your People the beauty of greatness and crown of salvation, a day of rest and holiness.*
אַבְרָהָם יָגֵל יִצְחָק יְרַנֵּן יַעֲקֹב וּבָנָיו יָנוּחוּ בוֹ מְנוּחַת אַהֲבָה וּנְדָבָה מְנוּחַת אֱמֶת וֶאֱמוּנָה מְנוּחַת שָׁלוֹם וְשַׁלְוָה וְהַשְׁקֵט וָבֶטַח מְנוּחָה שְׁלֵמָה שָׁאַתָּה רוֹצֶה בָּהּ יַכִּירוּ בָנֶיךָ וְיֵדְעוּ כִּי מֵאִתְּךָ הִיא מְנוּחָתָם וְעַל מְנוּחָתָם יַקְדִּישׁוּ אֶת שְׁמֶךָ.	*Avraham rejoices, Yitzchak exults, Yaakov and his sons rest on it; a rest of love and generosity, a rest of truth and faithfulness, a rest of peace, serenity, and security, a complete rest with which You find favor. May Your children recognize and know, that from You is their rest, and by their rest they sanctify Your Name.*

There are a few questions related to this *berachah*:

- What is the oneness we refer to throughout the *tefillah*?
- Why is the oneness of the nation of Israel mentioned alongside the oneness of God and His name?
- What is the theme behind the entire *tefillah* in general?

The Theme

We have previously explained that the three different time segments of Shabbat (Friday night, Shabbat morning, and Shabbat afternoon) reflect three historic Shabbatot in world history.

- Friday night corresponds to the Shabbat of Creation; therefore, the theme of the prayer is *"Atah kidashta et yom hashevi'i tachlit maaseh shamayim va'aretz*—You sanctified the seventh day as the culmination of **Creation**."

- Shabbat morning corresponds to the Shabbat of the revelation at Har Sinai; therefore, the theme of the prayer is *"Yismach Moshe b'matnat chelko…klil tiferet natata lo…al Har Sinai*—Moshe will rejoice upon his future reward, crowns of splendor he adorned when he stood at **Har Sinai**."

- Shabbat *Minchah* corresponds to Shabbat in the **Messianic era**—may it come soon in our days—when all of life will be Shabbat-like: *"Yom she'kulo Shabbat."* At that time, God's presence will be recognized and appreciated by all nations on earth and there will be only **one God** perceived by all.

The Words of the Prayer

- *Atah echad*—At that time, all the mysteries of You, God, and the universe will be uncovered, and all the unanswerable questions will be answered. Then Your oneness will be proclaimed and understood.

- *V'Shimcha echad*—Your Name, meaning your multifaceted impact on all aspects of the universe, will be understood clearly as all emanating from You, the Divine one and only one.

- *U'mi k'amcha Yisrael goy echad ba'aretz*—At that time, Your nation Israel will also be one. There will be no more internal infighting and turf wars, as well as no more external threats of anti-Semitism and extermination, because Israel will achieve its destiny as the one nation of the one God.

The Oneness

The Talmud records an incredible question that the rabbis raised about God's tefillin.[5]

---

5   *Berachot* 6b.

The content written on the parchment of our tefillin is "*Shema Yisrael Hashem Elokeinu Hashem Echad*—Hear O Israel, God is our Lord, God is **One**." Rav Nachman bar Isaac asks which words are written on the parchment of God's tefillin? Rav Chiya bar Avin answers that they are words from this prayer! "*Mi k'amcha Yisrael goy echad ba'aretz*—Who is like Your nation Israel, **one nation** on earth?"

It is noteworthy that just as we literally bind God's name to our bodies, so too, God binds our name, Israel, to Himself. We observe God's oneness, and God recognizes when Israel is one. We proclaim this symmetrical celebration of oneness now at Shabbat *Minchah*, the holiest time of Shabbat, when we envision a perfected world at the time of Mashiach.

The *Siach Yitzchak* in the *Siddur HaGra* actually demonstrates how this *tefillah* corresponds to the three famous Shabbatot in Jewish history and destiny.

Shabbat is the:

- "*Tiferet gedulah*—Splendor of greatness." Shabbat is the culmination of **Creation**.
- "*V'ateret yeshuah*—The crown of salvation." This refers to the crowns worn by B'nei Yisrael on the Shabbat at **Har Sinai**.
- "*Yom menuchah u'kedushah l'amcha natata*—A day of contentment and holiness You have given Your people." This refers to the time when Mashiach comes and it will be *kulo Shabbat*.

At that time:

- "*Avraham yagel*—Avraham will rejoice;"
- "*Yitzchak yeranen*—Yitzchak will exult;"
- (because) "*Yaakov u'vanav yanuchu vo*—Yaakov and all of his descendants will rest and celebrate Shabbat.

The prayer then describes the multidimensional *menuchah*—spiritual tranquility of Shabbat:

- "*Menuchat ahavah u'nedavah...emet v'emunah*—A rest of love and magnanimity, truth and faith." This reflects **Creation** when God demonstrated unconditional loving-kindness by creating the world.

- *"Menuchat shalom v'shalvah v'hashkeit va'vetach—*A rest of peace, serenity, tranquility, and security." This reflects the Shabbat of **Har Sinai**, because Torah is the pathway to peace.
- *"Menuchah sheleimah she'atah rotzeh bah—*A perfect rest in which You find favor." This refers to the time when there will be perfection in the world: the **Messianic era**.

Finally, *"Yakiru vanecha v'yeidu ki me'itcha hi menuchatam v'al menuchatam yakdishu et Shemecha—*At that time, Your children will know that from You comes this rest and that by resting they sanctify Your name."

> A DIVINE APPROACH: The *Avudraham* explains that as opposed to so many other mitzvot like charity, donning tefillin, and eating kosher, whereby we fulfill the commands of God, on Shabbat we actually emulate God by resting and taking pleasure in His Divine rest. Keeping Shabbat is literally walking in the spiritual footsteps of God.

Retzeh Bi'menuchateinu

אֱלֹהֵינוּ וֵאלֹהֵי אֲבוֹתֵינוּ רְצֵה בִמְנוּחָתֵנוּ קַדְּשֵׁנוּ בְּמִצְוֹתֶיךָ וְתֵן חֶלְקֵנוּ בְּתוֹרָתֶךָ.	*Our Lord and Lord of our fathers, find favor in our rest, sanctify us with Your commandments and place our portion in Your Torah;*
שַׂבְּעֵנוּ מִטּוּבֶךָ וְשַׂמְּחֵנוּ בִּישׁוּעָתֶךָ וְטַהֵר לִבֵּנוּ לְעָבְדְּךָ בֶּאֱמֶת וְהַנְחִילֵנוּ ה' אֱלֹהֵינוּ בְּאַהֲבָה וּבְרָצוֹן שַׁבַּת קָדְשֶׁךָ וְיָנוּחוּ בוֹ יִשְׂרָאֵל מְקַדְּשֵׁי שְׁמֶךָ. בָּרוּךְ אַתָּה ה' מְקַדֵּשׁ הַשַּׁבָּת.	*satiate us with Your good, and gladden us with Your salvation, and purify our heart to serve You in truth; and bestow upon us, God, our Lord, with love and goodwill, Your holy Shabbat, and may all of Israel, who sanctify Your Name, rest on it. Blessed are You, God, who sanctifies the Shabbat.*

See page 58 for commentary.

The Last Three Blessings

רְצֵה ה׳ אֱלֹהֵינוּ בְּעַמְּךָ יִשְׂרָאֵל וּבִתְפִלָּתָם, וְהָשֵׁב אֶת הָעֲבוֹדָה לִדְבִיר בֵּיתֶךָ, וְאִשֵּׁי יִשְׂרָאֵל וּתְפִלָּתָם, בְּאַהֲבָה תְקַבֵּל בְּרָצוֹן, וּתְהִי לְרָצוֹן תָּמִיד עֲבוֹדַת יִשְׂרָאֵל עַמֶּךָ:	*Look with favor, God, our Lord, on Your people Israel and pay heed to their prayer; restore the service to Your Sanctuary and accept with love and favor Israel's fire-offerings and prayer, and may the service of Your people Israel always find favor.*
וְתֶחֱזֶינָה עֵינֵינוּ בְּשׁוּבְךָ לְצִיּוֹן בְּרַחֲמִים:	*May our eyes behold Your return to Zion in mercy.*
בָּרוּךְ אַתָּה ה׳, הַמַּחֲזִיר שְׁכִינָתוֹ לְצִיּוֹן:	*Blessed are You, God, who restores His Divine Presence to Zion.*
מוֹדִים אֲנַחְנוּ לָךְ, שָׁאַתָּה הוּא ה׳ אֱלֹהֵינוּ וֵאלֹהֵי אֲבוֹתֵינוּ לְעוֹלָם וָעֶד:	*We thankfully acknowledge that You are God, our Lord and Lord of our fathers, forever.*
צוּר חַיֵּינוּ, מָגֵן יִשְׁעֵנוּ אַתָּה הוּא לְדוֹר וָדוֹר:	*You are the strength of our life, the shield of our salvation in every generation.*
נוֹדֶה לְּךָ וּנְסַפֵּר תְּהִלָּתֶךָ, עַל חַיֵּינוּ הַמְּסוּרִים בְּיָדֶךָ, וְעַל נִשְׁמוֹתֵינוּ הַפְּקוּדוֹת לָךְ, וְעַל נִסֶּיךָ שֶׁבְּכָל יוֹם עִמָּנוּ, וְעַל נִפְלְאוֹתֶיךָ וְטוֹבוֹתֶיךָ שֶׁבְּכָל עֵת, עֶרֶב וָבֹקֶר וְצָהֳרָיִם:	*We will give thanks to You and recount Your praise, evening, morning, and noon, for our lives that are committed into Your hand, for our souls that are entrusted to You, for Your miracles that are with us daily, and for Your continual wonders and beneficences.*
הַטּוֹב, כִּי לֹא כָלוּ רַחֲמֶיךָ, וְהַמְרַחֵם, כִּי לֹא תַמּוּ חֲסָדֶיךָ, מֵעוֹלָם קִוִּינוּ לָךְ:	*You are the Beneficent One, for Your mercies never cease; the Merciful One, for Your kindnesses never end; for we always place our hope in You.*
וְעַל כֻּלָּם יִתְבָּרַךְ וְיִתְרוֹמַם שִׁמְךָ מַלְכֵּנוּ תָּמִיד לְעוֹלָם וָעֶד:	*And for all these, may Your Name, our King, be continually blessed, exalted, and extolled forever and all time.*

וְכָל הַחַיִּים יוֹדוּךָ סֶּלָה, וִיהַלְלוּ אֶת שִׁמְךָ בֶּאֱמֶת, הָאֵל יְשׁוּעָתֵנוּ וְעֶזְרָתֵנוּ סֶלָה:	*And all living things shall forever thank You, and praise Your great Name eternally, for You are good. God, You are our everlasting salvation and help, O benevolent God.*
בָּרוּךְ אַתָּה ה', הַטּוֹב שִׁמְךָ וּלְךָ נָאֶה לְהוֹדוֹת:	*Blessed are You, God, Beneficent is Your Name, and to You it is fitting to offer thanks.*
שִׂים שָׁלוֹם טוֹבָה וּבְרָכָה, חֵן וָחֶסֶד וְרַחֲמִים, עָלֵינוּ וְעַל כָּל יִשְׂרָאֵל עַמֶּךָ:	*Bestow peace, goodness and blessing, life, graciousness, kindness and mercy upon us and upon all Your people Israel.*
בָּרְכֵנוּ אָבִינוּ, כֻּלָּנוּ כְּאֶחָד בְּאוֹר פָּנֶיךָ, כִּי בְאוֹר פָּנֶיךָ נָתַתָּ לָּנוּ ה' אֱלֹהֵינוּ, תּוֹרַת חַיִּים, וְאַהֲבַת חֶסֶד, וּצְדָקָה וּבְרָכָה וְרַחֲמִים, וְחַיִּים וְשָׁלוֹם:	*Bless us, our Father, all of us as one, with the light of Your countenance. For by the light of Your countenance You gave us, God, our Lord, the Torah of life and loving-kindness, righteousness, blessing, mercy, life, and peace.*
וְטוֹב בְּעֵינֶיךָ לְבָרֵךְ אֶת עַמְּךָ יִשְׂרָאֵל בְּכָל עֵת וּבְכָל שָׁעָה בִּשְׁלוֹמֶךָ:	*May it be favorable in Your eyes to bless Your people Israel, at all times and at every moment, with Your peace.*
בָּרוּךְ אַתָּה ה', הַמְבָרֵךְ אֶת עַמּוֹ יִשְׂרָאֵל בַּשָּׁלוֹם:	*Blessed are You, God, who blesses His people Israel with peace.*

See page 61 for commentary.

Tzidkatecha Tzedek L'Olam

After the chazzan concludes the repetition of the *Amidah* for Shabbat *Minchah*, on most weeks the congregation recites these three *pesukim* from *Tehillim*:

צִדְקָתְךָ צֶדֶק לְעוֹלָם וְתוֹרָתְךָ אֱמֶת.	*Your righteousness is everlasting righteousness, and Your Torah is Truth.*
וְצִדְקָתְךָ אֱלֹהִים עַד מָרוֹם אֲשֶׁר עָשִׂיתָ גְדֹלוֹת אֱלֹהִים מִי כָמוֹךָ.	*And Your righteousness, God, is up to the heights, for You have done great things. God, who is like You?*

צִדְקָתְךָ כְּהַרְרֵי אֵל	*Your righteousness is like the mighty*
מִשְׁפָּטֶךָ תְּהוֹם רַבָּה אָדָם	*mountains; Your judgments are like the vast*
וּבְהֵמָה תוֹשִׁיעַ ה'.	*deep. You save both man and beast, God.*

- *Tzidkatecha*—Your righteousness is everlasting and Your Torah is truth.
- *Tzidkatecha*—Your righteousness reaches the heavens and You demonstrate greatness.
- *Tzidkatecha*—Your righteousness is like the mountains, and Your judgment is like the deep waters; unto man and beast You are their salvation.

This short prayer that emphasizes God's righteousness seems similar to a solemn prayer that is recited at funerals called *Tzidduk Ha'din*, "The righteousness of God's justice." Additionally, *Tzidkatecha* is said straight after the *Amidah*, which is the same place that during the week we recite *Tachanun*, mournful supplications.

What is the significance of these associations? Why would Chazal institute a *tefillah* on Shabbat that is connected to mourning? Aren't public demonstrations of mourning forbidden on Shabbat? Why, then, do we say *Tzidkatecha*?

Some answers:

- The *Eliyahu Rabbah* quotes the *Zohar*, which states the reason is because Moshe Rabbeinu, Yosef HaTzaddik, and David HaMelech all died during the time period of Shabbat *Minchah*. Therefore, a brief "memorial prayer" is offered at this time.
- The *Arugot Habosem* writes that the choice of these particular *pesukim* from *Tehillim* actually reflects the untimely passing of these three great Biblical Jewish leaders.
- In acknowledging the death of Moshe Rabbeinu when he asked Hashem if he could live beyond 120 years and enter Eretz Yisrael, we say: "*Tzidkatecha tzedek l'olam v'toratecha emet*—Your righteousness is everlasting and Your Torah is true," only God decides the lifespan of each person."

- In acknowledging the death of Yosef at the earlier age of 110, which the Talmud explains was a result of him living a life of leadership and authority, we recite: "*Tzidkatecha Elokim ad marom asher asita gedolot Elokim mi kamocha*—Your righteousness is as high as the heavens, You have done great things, and You, God, are the only true authority."
- In acknowledging the death of David HaMelech, who requested not to die on Shabbat, we recite: "*Tzidkatecha k'harerei Keil mishpatecha tehom rabbah adam u'behemah toshia Hashem*—Your righteousness is as mighty as the mountains and as vast as the deep waters." Hashem decides the time when one king descends from the throne and another ascends.
- The *Rosh* in *Pesachim*, as well as the *Avudraham*, provide a different idea. They write that we recite *Tzidkatecha* at the end of Shabbat *Minchah*, often around the time of sunset, because we are taught that although after death a soul may need to achieve an atonement for its sins through time spent in Gehinnom, all souls are given reprieve and are invited out one day a week for Shabbat. Toward the end of Shabbat, we recite *Tzidkatecha* because it is now time for these souls to return to Gehinnom for the coming week as Shabbat departs.

Those who occasionally daven in different shuls, such as Ashkenazic, Chassidic, Yemenite, Sephardic, etc., have surely noticed that *Tzidkatecha* is not always recited in the same order. In Ashkenazic shuls, the order is based on the siddur of Rav Amram Gaon as we saw above:

- *Tzidkatecha tzedek l'olam*
- *Tzidkatecha Elokim ad marom*
- *Tzidkatecha k'harerei Keil mishpatecha tehom rabbah adam u'behemah toshia Hashem*

In Sephardic and Yemenite shuls, the order is the opposite. The reason for the difference in custom rests on whether the three *pesukim* from different *perakim* in *Tehillim* need to be recited in the order in which they are written (e.g. *Tehillim* 36, then 72, and then 119), or if the *pesukim* can be reordered. The Sephardim and Yemenites say them in order, while the Ashkenazic custom does not require the recitation to be in the order of the *perakim*.

The final *pasuk* Ashkenazim recite is *"Tzidkatecha k'harerei Keil mishpatecha tehom rabbah adam u'behemah toshia Hashem*—Your righteousness is as mighty as the mountains and as vast as the deep waters." They then say, *"Adam u'beheimah toshia Hashem*—Man and beast you save, God."

What does "Man and beast You save" mean? The three *pesukim* of *Tzidkatecha* describe God's infinite righteousness and kindness, and the inimitable truth of His Torah. What does a beast have to do with this?

- *Rashi* explains that wise men approach God with humility, as if they were no better than a beast, and God provides them with salvation.

- The *Malbim* explains that every person is made up of both the animal self combined with the spiritual self. A person is greater than a beast only because of his soul. Therefore we state: *"Adam u'behemah toshia Hashem*—Man and beast You save, God," meaning that it is only because of our uniquely human souls, which provide spirituality for our otherwise animalistic selves, that God provides salvation.

A DIVINE APPROACH: Every human being is comprised of both body and soul. We are given the choice by God whether to live our lives focusing primarily on the body, or live our lives focusing on our souls. Shabbat is the perfect time of the week to attend to and nourish our souls.

Aleinu L'Shabei'ach

Every single *tefillah* concludes with *Aleinu L'Shabei'ach*, which literally means "It is upon us to praise."

עָלֵינוּ לְשַׁבֵּחַ לַאֲדוֹן הַכֹּל לָתֵת גְּדֻלָּה לְיוֹצֵר בְּרֵאשִׁית שֶׁלֹּא עָשָׂנוּ כְּגוֹיֵי הָאֲרָצוֹת וְלֹא שָׂמָנוּ כְּמִשְׁפְּחוֹת הָאֲדָמָה.	*It is our duty to praise the Master of all, to acclaim the greatness of the One who forms all creation. For God did not make us like the nations of other lands and did not make us the same as other families of the earth.*
שֶׁלֹּא שָׂם חֶלְקֵנוּ כָּהֶם וְגֹרָלֵנוּ כְּכָל הֲמוֹנָם. (שֶׁהֵם מִשְׁתַּחֲוִים לְהֶבֶל וָרִיק וּמִתְפַּלְּלִים אֶל אֵל לֹא יוֹשִׁיעַ.)	*God did not place us in the same situations as others, and our destiny is not the same as anyone else's. (For they worship vanity and emptiness and pray to a god who cannot save.)*
וַאֲנַחְנוּ כּוֹרְעִים וּמִשְׁתַּחֲוִים וּמוֹדִים לִפְנֵי מֶלֶךְ מַלְכֵי הַמְּלָכִים הַקָּדוֹשׁ בָּרוּךְ הוּא.	*And we bend our knees, and bow down, and give thanks, before the Ruler, the Ruler of Rulers, the Holy One, blessed be He.*
שֶׁהוּא נוֹטֶה שָׁמַיִם וְיֹסֵד אָרֶץ וּמוֹשַׁב יְקָרוֹ בַּשָּׁמַיִם מִמַּעַל וּשְׁכִינַת עֻזּוֹ בְּגָבְהֵי מְרוֹמִים.	*The One who spread out the heavens, and made the foundations of the earth, and whose precious dwelling is in the heavens above, and whose powerful Presence is in the highest heights.*
הוּא אֱלֹהֵינוּ אֵין עוֹד.	*God is our Lord, there is no one else.*
אֱמֶת מַלְכֵּנוּ אֶפֶס זוּלָתוֹ כַּכָּתוּב בְּתוֹרָתוֹ:	*Our God is truth, and nothing else compares. As it is written in Your Torah:*
וְיָדַעְתָּ הַיּוֹם וַהֲשֵׁבֹתָ אֶל לְבָבֶךָ כִּי ה׳ הוּא הָאֱלֹהִים בַּשָּׁמַיִם מִמַּעַל וְעַל הָאָרֶץ מִתָּחַת אֵין עוֹד:	*"And you shall know today, and take to heart, that God is the Lord, in the heavens above and on earth below. There is no other."*
וְעַל כֵּן נְקַוֶּה לְךָ ה׳ אֱלֹהֵינוּ לִרְאוֹת מְהֵרָה בְּתִפְאֶרֶת עֻזֶּךָ לְהַעֲבִיר גִּלּוּלִים מִן הָאָרֶץ וְהָאֱלִילִים כָּרוֹת יִכָּרֵתוּן לְתַקֵּן עוֹלָם בְּמַלְכוּת שַׁדַּי.	*Therefore, we put our hope in You, God, our Lord, to soon see the glory of Your strength, to remove all idols from the earth, and to completely cut off all false gods; to repair the world, Your holy empire.*

וְכָל בְּנֵי בָשָׂר יִקְרְאוּ בִשְׁמֶךָ לְהַפְנוֹת אֵלֶיךָ כָּל רִשְׁעֵי אָרֶץ. יַכִּירוּ וְיֵדְעוּ כָּל יוֹשְׁבֵי תֵבֵל כִּי לְךָ תִּכְרַע כָּל בֶּרֶךְ תִּשָּׁבַע כָּל לָשׁוֹן.	*And for all living flesh to call Your name, and for all the wicked of the earth to turn to You. May all the world's inhabitants recognize and know that to You every knee must bend, and every tongue must swear loyalty.*
לְפָנֶיךָ ה׳ אֱלֹהֵינוּ יִכְרְעוּ וְיִפֹּלוּ וְלִכְבוֹד שִׁמְךָ יְקָר יִתֵּנוּ. וִיקַבְּלוּ כֻלָּם אֶת עֹל מַלְכוּתֶךָ וְתִמְלֹךְ עֲלֵיהֶם מְהֵרָה לְעוֹלָם וָעֶד.	*Before You, God, our Lord, may all bow down, and give honor to Your precious name, and may all take upon themselves the yoke of Your rule. And may You reign over them soon and forever and always.*
כִּי הַמַּלְכוּת שֶׁלְּךָ הִיא וּלְעוֹלְמֵי עַד תִּמְלֹךְ בְּכָבוֹד. כַּכָּתוּב בְּתוֹרָתֶךָ: ה׳ יִמְלֹךְ לְעֹלָם וָעֶד.	*Because all rule is Yours alone, and You will rule in honor forever and ever. As it is written in Your Torah: "God will reign forever and ever."*
וְנֶאֱמַר: וְהָיָה ה׳ לְמֶלֶךְ עַל כָּל הָאָרֶץ בַּיּוֹם הַהוּא יִהְיֶה ה׳ אֶחָד וּשְׁמוֹ אֶחָד:	*And it is said: "God will be Ruler over the whole earth, and on that day, God will be One, and God's name will be One."*

See page 66 for commentary.

Chapter Six

HOLIDAY PIECES

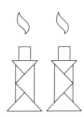

Blessing the New Moon

יְהִי רָצוֹן מִלְפָנֶיךָ ה׳ אֱלֹהֵינוּ וֵאלֹהֵי אֲבוֹתֵינוּ שֶׁתְּחַדֵּשׁ עָלֵינוּ אֶת הַחוֹדֶשׁ הַזֶּה לְטוֹבָה וְלִבְרָכָה.	*May it be Your will, God, our Lord and Lord of our fathers, that you renew this new month for us, for good and for blessing.*
וְתִתֶּן לָנוּ חַיִּים אֲרוּכִים חַיִּים שֶׁל שָׁלוֹם חַיִּים שֶׁל טוֹבָה חַיִּים שֶׁל בְּרָכָה חַיִּים שֶׁל פַּרְנָסָה חַיִּים שֶׁל חִלּוּץ עֲצָמוֹת	*And may You give us long life, life of peace, life of good, life of blessing, life of livelihood, life with strong bones,*
חַיִּים שֶׁיֵּשׁ בָּהֶם יִרְאַת שָׁמַיִם וְיִרְאַת חֵטְא חַיִּים שֶׁאֵין בָּהֶם בּוּשָׁה וּכְלִמָּה חַיִּים שֶׁל עֹשֶׁר וְכָבוֹד	*life in which we have fear of Heaven and fear of sin, life in which we have no embarrassment or shame, life of wealth and honor,*

חַיִּים שֶׁתְּהֵא בָּנוּ אַהֲבַת תּוֹרָה וְיִרְאַת שָׁמַיִם חַיִּים שֶׁיְמַלֵּא ה' מִשְׁאֲלוֹת לִבֵּנוּ לְטוֹבָה אָמֵן סֶלָה.	*life in which we have a love of Torah and fear of Heaven, life which God fulfills the longings of our heart for good, Amen, forever.*
מִי שֶׁעָשָׂה נִסִּים לַאֲבוֹתֵינוּ וְגָאַל אוֹתָם מֵעַבְדוּת לְחֵרוּת הוּא יִגְאַל אוֹתָנוּ בְּקָרוֹב וִיקַבֵּץ נִדָּחֵינוּ מֵאַרְבַּע כַּנְפוֹת הָאָרֶץ חֲבֵרִים כָּל יִשְׂרָאֵל וְנֹאמַר אָמֵן.	*May He who performed miracles for our fathers, and redeemed them from slavery to freedom, may He speedily redeem us, and gather our dispersed people from the four comers of the earth, all Israel united, and let us say, Amen.*
רֹאשׁ חֹדֶשׁ (פלוני) יִהְיֶה בְּיוֹם (פלוני [וּלְמָחֳרָתוֹ בְּיוֹם פלוני]) הַבָּא עָלֵינוּ וְעַל כָּל יִשְׂרָאֵל לְטוֹבָה.	*Rosh Chodesh (say name of new month) will be on (say the days of the week on which Rosh Chodesh will occur), may it come upon us and upon all of Israel, for good.*
יְחַדְּשֵׁהוּ הַקָּדוֹשׁ בָּרוּךְ הוּא עָלֵינוּ וְעַל כָּל עַמּוֹ בֵּית יִשְׂרָאֵל לְטוֹבָה וְלִבְרָכָה לְשָׂשׂוֹן וּלְשִׂמְחָה לִישׁוּעָה וּלְנֶחָמָה לְפַרְנָסָה וּלְכַלְכָּלָה לְחַיִּים וּלְשָׁלוֹם לִשְׁמוּעוֹת טוֹבוֹת וְלִבְשׂוֹרוֹת טוֹבוֹת (בחורף: וְלִגְשָׁמִים בְּעִתָּם) וְלִרְפוּאָה שְׁלֵמָה וְלִגְאֻלָּה קְרוֹבָה, וְנֹאמַר אָמֵן.	*May the Holy One, blessed be He, renew upon ourselves and upon His entire nation, the House of Israel, for good and for blessing, for gladness and for joy, for salvation and for consolation, for livelihood and sustenance, for life and for peace, for good news and good tidings, (in the winter months: and for rain in its proper time), and for complete recovery, and for imminent redemption, and let us say, Amen.*

L et's consider the words in the middle section:
"*Mi she'asah nissim...Hu yigal otanu b'karov*—He who has done miracles for our forefathers and redeemed them from slavery, may He redeem us as well and gather us from the four corners of the earth." Then the prayer concludes enigmatically: "*Chaveirim kol Yisrael v'nomar Amen*—The Jewish People are all friends and let us say Amen."

Question: It is clear why we ask God for blessings and redemption as we begin a new month, but why the phrase about the brotherhood and collective friendship of the Jewish People?

Answer: The *Doveir Shalom* remarks that this little passage contains the **prerequisites** for the future redemption of Am Yisrael, may it come soon in our days.

- First, God will remove any oppression and oppressors from us.
- Then, God will gather us all to one place.
- Finally, when Am Yisrael become united in purpose and friendship, the *geulah*, the final redemption, will occur.

> A DIVINE APPROACH: When we are faced with national existential challenges such as terror, war, and hatred, we all ask ourselves, "What can we do about it?" So, we pray, and do mitzvot, and give *tzedakah*, but we must also follow the directions in this prayer: "*chaveirim kol Yisrael*," creating genuine and loving friendship within Am Yisrael. We must put this on the top of all agendas: our personal agenda, communal agenda, and national agenda. All differences aside, we must be *chaveirim*. In the merit of our efforts, may God deliver us from our enemies and bring forth peace to Eretz Yisrael, Am Yisrael, and the world generally. Amen.

And Let Us Say Amen

One of the most spoken words by all Jews in synagogues is "Amen." What does Amen mean anyway?

It is one of the first words we learn to say during davening. Throughout the *Yamim Norai'm*, it is quite a moving experience to participate in a thundering Amen response in a large *beit midrash* or shul. It is a spiritually powerful tool as well. The Talmud states: "Anyone who answers '*Amen. Yehei shemei rabba*' with all his strength merits to have opened in front of him the gates of Gan Eden."[1] Why?

---

1   *Shabbat* 119b.

The word Amen is associated with the word *emunah*, which means faith, belief, and loyalty. Reciting Amen to a blessing or a prayer demonstrates a statement of affirmation that the blessing is reliably true, as well as hope and confidence that the prayer will be heard in Heaven.

Amen is also an acronym. It stands for *"Keil melech ne'eman*—God is a true and faithful king." The halachah teaches that when praying alone, an individual says these three words before reciting the *Shema*.[2]

Rav Shlomo Wolbe, in his classic work *Alei Shur*, reveals deeper implications of the word Amen.[3] He explains that man's relationship with God is three-dimensional. We know Him through His creation, His revelation at Sinai, as well as His promise of redemption.

- Creation: We recognize God by His handiwork. A sunset, a rainbow, a glacier, the human body, and the animal kingdom all showcase God's artistry in His creation of this planet.
- Revelation: At Har Sinai over 3,300 years ago, Hashem called out from the heavens and uttered the first two commandments. The awesome encounter was a moment of national inspiration and prophesy when the infinite came directly in contact with the finite.
- Redemption: It says in *Yeshayahu*: "And on that day God will be one, and His name will be one."[4] We are promised that one day, all the nations of the world will recognize the one eternal God, and then evil and falsehood will be eradicated from the world.

These three concepts are all encapsulated in the word Amen:

- *Keil*: represents God's trait of kindliness with which He created the world.
- *Melech*: He is our King due to the Torah we have received from Him.
- *Ne'eman*: He is faithful and will one day reveal His grandeur to the world and bring redemption to all mankind.

---

2   *Orach Chaim* 61:3.
3   Vol. 2, p. 286.
4   8:10.

> A DIVINE APPROACH: Reciting Amen is incredibly powerful. There are great Jews who try to only recite blessings when there is another person to answer Amen. It is so simple, yet incredibly profound. Let's make the most of answering Amen.

Rainy Season

After we celebrate the *Yamim Nora'im* and advance toward the winter, we begin to recite "*Mashiv ha'ruach u'morid ha'geshem*—God makes the wind blow and makes the rain descend."

The word *geshem* is related to *gashmiyut*, which means physicality and earthliness.

Why are we instructed to begin saying this prayer at this time?

- Since at the end of Sukkot, the world is judged and rain is apportioned for that year, we now appropriately recite "*Mashiv ha'ruach u'morid ha'geshem*" because the rainy season has officially begun.
- After the hours and days that we spent in synagogue, at our tables, and in our sukkah involved in prayer, repentance, and kindness, now is the time to nurture our hopes, plans, and dreams for the year to come. Now is the time to pour water on the seeds we have planted during the months of Elul and Tishrei.

How many *Al Cheits* did we recite on Yom Kippur, promising that this year would be different? How many tears flowed from our eyes for past misdeeds together with a genuine hope that this year we would do better. For generations, on Yom Kippur, Jews have implored Hashem to grant them the opportunity for another year of life. They have made a thorough accounting of the past and formulated *kabbalot*—resolutions, setting goals for a brighter future.

"*Mashiv ha'ruach u'morid ha'geshem*" means let's move those plans off the drawing board and into our lives. Now is the time to be more careful about how we speak to and about our friends, relatives, and colleagues. Now is the time to put into effect increased time for Torah learning and other strategies for growth that we have been considering. Now is the time to strategize how to improve our *tefillah* with punctuality and increased concentration.

> A DIVINE APPROACH: When reciting *Mashiv ha'ruach u'morid ha'geshem*, let's remember that just like a farmer, after all of his efforts, knows that it is only Hashem who generates the winds and rains in order to bring forth growth, so too in our lives, we must do our part and exert efforts toward improvement. Then Hashem will bestow His blessings upon us and they will take root and blossom.

Chanukah Tips

מָעוֹז צוּר יְשׁוּעָתִי לְךָ נָאֶה לְשַׁבֵּחַ.	*O mighty stronghold of my salvation, to You praise is fitting.*
תִּכּוֹן בֵּית תְּפִילָתִי וְשָׁם תּוֹדָה נְזַבֵּחַ.	*Restore my House of Prayer and there we will bring a thanksgiving-offering.*
לְעֵת תָּכִין מַטְבֵּחַ מִצָּר הַמְנַבֵּחַ.	*When You will have prepared the slaughter for the blaspheming foe,*
אָז אֶגְמוֹר בְּשִׁיר מִזְמוֹר חֲנֻכַּת הַמִּזְבֵּחַ.	*Then I shall complete with a song of hymn the dedication of the Altar.*
רָעוֹת שָׂבְעָה נַפְשִׁי בְּיָגוֹן כֹּחִי כָּלָה.	*My soul had been sated with troubles, my strength has been consumed with grief.*
חַיַּי מֵרְרוּ בְּקוֹשִׁי בְּשִׁעְבּוּד מַלְכוּת עֶגְלָה.	*They had embittered my life with hardship, with the calf-like kingdom's bondage.*
וּבְיָדוֹ הַגְּדוֹלָה הוֹצִיא אֶת הַסְּגֻלָּה.	*But with His great power He brought forth the treasured ones,*
חֵיל פַּרְעֹה, וְכָל זַרְעוֹ יָרְדוּ כְּאֶבֶן בִּמְצוּלָה.	*Pharaoh's army and all his offspring Went down like a stone into the deep.*
דְּבִיר קָדְשׁוֹ הֱבִיאַנִי וְגַם שָׁם לֹא שָׁקַטְתִּי.	*To the holy abode of His Word He brought me. But there, too, I had no rest*

וּבָא נוֹגֵשׂ וְהִגְלַנִי כִּי זָרִים עָבַדְתִּי.	*And an oppressor came and exiled me. For I had served alien gods,*
וְיֵין רַעַל מָסַכְתִּי כִּמְעַט שֶׁעָבַרְתִּי.	*And had drunk poisonous wine. Scarcely had I departed*
קֵץ בָּבֶל, זְרֻבָּבֶל לְקֵץ שִׁבְעִים נוֹשָׁעְתִּי.	*At Babylon's end Zerubabel came. At the end of seventy years I was saved.*
כְּרוֹת קוֹמַת בְּרוֹשׁ בִּקֵּשׁ אֲגָגִי בֶּן הַמְּדָתָא.	*To sever the towering cypress sought the Agagite, son of Hamdasa,*
וְנִהְיְתָה לוֹ לְפַח וּלְמוֹקֵשׁ וְגַאֲוָתוֹ נִשְׁבָּתָה.	*But it became a snare and a stumbling block to him, and his arrogance was stilled.*
רֹאשׁ יְמִינִי נִשֵּׂאתָ וְאוֹיֵב שְׁמוֹ מָחִיתָ.	*The head of the Benjaminite You lifted and the enemy, his name You obliterated*
רֹב בָּנָיו וְקִנְיָנָיו עַל הָעֵץ תָּלִיתָ.	*His numerous progeny, and his possessions, on the gallows You hanged.*
יְוָנִים נִקְבְּצוּ עָלַי אֲזַי בִּימֵי חַשְׁמַנִּים.	*Greeks gathered against me then in Hasmonean days.*
וּפָרְצוּ חוֹמוֹת מִגְדָּלַי וְטִמְּאוּ כָּל הַשְּׁמָנִים.	*They breached the walls of my towers and they defiled all the oils;*
וּמִנּוֹתַר קַנְקַנִּים נַעֲשָׂה נֵס לַשּׁוֹשַׁנִּים.	*And from the remnant of the flasks a miracle was wrought for the roses.*
בְּנֵי בִינָה יְמֵי שְׁמוֹנָה קָבְעוּ שִׁיר וּרְנָנִים.	*Men of insight—eight days were established for song and jubilation*
חֲשֹׂף זְרוֹעַ קָדְשֶׁךָ וְקָרֵב קֵץ הַיְשׁוּעָה.	*Bare Your holy arm and hasten the End, the time for salvation—*
נְקֹם נִקְמַת דַּם עֲבָדֶיךָ מֵאֻמָּה הָרְשָׁעָה.	*Avenge the vengeance of Your servants' blood from the wicked nation.*
כִּי אָרְכָה לָּנוּ הַיְשׁוּעָה וְאֵין קֵץ לִימֵי הָרָעָה.	*For the salvation is too long delayed for us, and there is no end to days of evil,*
דְּחֵה אַדְמוֹן בְּצֵל צַלְמוֹן הָקֵם לָנוּ רוֹעִים שִׁבְעָה.	*Repel the Red One in the nethermost shadow and establish for us the Seven Shepherds.*

We sing *Ma'oz Tzur*, "Rock of Ages," every Chanukah. Let's explore the beautiful *pizmon*—song.

To identify the name of the author of *Ma'oz Tzur*, simply read the first letter of each stanza and you'll see his name: Mordechai. Very often, we can find the name of the author of *zemirot* and *pizmonim* woven into the fabric of the words themselves.

The content of *Ma'oz Tzur* charts our voyages through the long and often bitter exiles throughout the centuries. In it, we also pray to Hashem to return us to His house, the Beit Hamikdash where we will one day soon renew *avodah*, light the *Menorah*, and witness the return of God's presence and splendor in Jerusalem.

Each paragraph deals with a different Jewish experience in *galut*.

- After the opening praises to God, the second stanza, "*Ra'ot savah nafshi*," is about our stay in Egypt for 210 years, which culminated in *yetziat Mitzrayim*, with Pharaoh and his army drowning in the Yam Suf.
- "*D'vir kadsho*" tells of our exile in Babylon, where we stayed for seventy years until our return to Jerusalem, led by the great scribe, Ezra.
- "*Kerot komat*" refers to our frightening encounter with Achashverosh and Haman in Persia, which left Haman and his children ("*rov banav*") dangling from a tree.
- "*Yevanim nikbetzu*" refers to Chanukah. It is about our battle with the Greeks and its seductive culture, which concluded with the military victory by the Maccabees, as well as the miracle of the oil in the Beit Hamikdash.
- "*Chasof zeroa*" calls upon Hashem to literally bare His proverbial forearm and finally release us out of our current exile, *Galut Edom*, which has lasted over two thousand years, and bring comfort to the Jewish People through the rebuilding of Jerusalem.

The word *tzur*, which refers to God, is translated as a rock. The Torah, Talmud, and siddur refer to Hashem in tens of different ways—but a "rock"? How can we understand this?

The answer is that a rock symbolizes a support one can lean on no matter how unstable he or she feels. This is what Hashem is to every single one of us. No matter what predicament we find ourselves in, we have a "Rock" to lean on. In essence, this is the message of Chanukah, and also the message of *Ma'oz Tzur*. No matter what land we are in, no matter who our enemies are in any generation, Hashem, our "Rock," is there with us.

The word *tzur* is also found in the prayer of *Ein K'Elokeinu*. The verse reads: "*Ein tzur K'Elokeinu*," which is translated as "There is no Rock like our God." *Rashi* interprets the word *tzur* as related to the word *tzayar*, which means creator or artist, teaching that there is no artist like Hashem.[5] Who else could create the Swiss Alps, Hawaii, and the Grand Canyon? Who else could create a human being with all of its complexity and a heavenly soul within? Only Hashem, the greatest artist of all.

So, what is Hashem—a rock or a creative artist?

Of course, He is **both**! And we should study the paradox therein. A creative artist is often perceived as otherworldly, and possibly eccentric...but not necessarily stable and reliable. Only God Himself can be **the most creative Artist** in the history of the universe, yet also be the **Rock of Ages** that provides love, strength, and direction, and embraces our praises and prayers every day.

A DIVINE APPROACH: As we sing *Ma'oz Tzur*, let's pray that the Great Rock and Artist hears our prayers and creatively blesses us with the rebuilding of the Third Beit Hamikdash, soon in our days.

Parashat Zachor

It is not by chance that the same word *zachor*—remember, is used both in the Torah to command the remembrance of Amalek and by the Jewish world today to remember the atrocities of Hitler and the Holocaust.

---

5   *Shmuel 1–2:2.*

The question is what exactly should we remember and why should we remember it?

- Should we remember how brutal our enemies have been and that the world has never been a friendly place for Jews?
- Should we remember how powerless we were without our own country and our own army?
- Should we remember the sincerity and dedication of so many Jews throughout the generations—including the Holocaust—who stood strong against evil and remained faithful to God and the Torah?

We must remember all of the above.

Why exactly are we remembering Amalek and the Holocaust? I do not believe that the answer is simply, "So it will not happen again." Keeping the memories of tragedy fresh in our minds has not and will not prevent anti-Semitism. Today, only seventy-five years after the Holocaust, the world as a whole is again frighteningly unfriendly to the Jews. Despite the fact that we have our own homeland with a world-class army, we are still terrorized regularly with bombs, rockets, and political warfare. So, what exactly are we supposed to remember?

A vital lesson that is taught throughout the twenty-four books of the *Tanach*, as well as the Talmud, is that God is just and always metes out justice.[6] However, sometimes there are crimes, atrocities, and tragedies so horrific that we cannot imagine how these punishments are just. Therefore, the Torah tells us *zachor*—remember and do not forget that God will justly respond to the evil at the right time. "*Zachor v'al tishkach*"—eventually it will all be Divinely addressed. As Nitai HaArbely says in *Pirkei Avot*: "*Al titya'esh min ha'puraniyot*—Do not despair, indeed, retribution will come."[7]

Whether it was Pharaoh in Egypt, Haman in Persia, Hitler in Germany, or modern-day terrorists, in the end, Hashem, the Divine Judge remembers and executes pefect judgment.

---

6   *Devarim* 32:4.
7   *Pirkei Avot* 1:7.

> A DIVINE APPROACH: When reviewing *Parashat Zachor*, remember that just as God saved and supported Israel throughout history, we pray and are confident that eventually truth and justice will prevail.

Megillat Esther

While the story of the *Megillah* is replete with wisdom, insight, nuance, and has so much to teach in this piece, I'd like to focus on the mitzvah of *Megillah* reading itself. There are lessons to be learned from the actual form and structure of the *Megillah* reading.

- **Law**: One must listen to every single syllable of every word in order to fulfill the mitzvah of *Megillah*. This means that a person could attend *Megillah* readings all their life and, God forbid, never fulfill the mitzvah.

  Lesson: To succeed, one must be a good listener—to really hear what another is saying By paying attention, one will even be able to hear what is unspoken, and will be able to comprehend the underlying message.

- **Law**: When the name Haman is called out, we yell, stamp, and "boo" to demonstrate our hatred of Haman and Amalek, and our wish to erase what they stand for from the world.

  Lesson: To understand that there is real evil in the world that needs to be addressed. Left alone, Haman would have achieved the dream of all our enemies—to wipe us off the map. We must address evil both spiritually—by asking Hashem in heaven for assistance—and physically—by waging war against evil here in our world.

- **Law**: It is a special mitzvah to listen to the *Megillah* in a large congregational setting to publicize the miracles of Purim as much as possible.

  Lesson: Over the years, many well-meaning Jews have attempted to be creative and orchestrate different types and styles of readings to try to make the reading more enjoyable and personally meaningful. The Talmud and our *Shulchan Aruch* direct us otherwise. The best way to fulfill this mitzvah, like all others, is the way it was commanded to us: *"B'rov am hadrat Melech*—The larger the crowd, the more splendor for our King."

A DIVINE APPROACH: In every Jewish law, there is a lesson. When we observe the law, let's aim to learn the lesson as well.

Shoshanat Yaakov

At the conclusion of the *Megillah* reading, both at night and in the morning on Purim, we say a prayer called *Shoshanat Yaakov*, "Rose of Jacob." This small paragraph reiterates the conclusion of *Megillat Esther*, as well as restates the who's who of the heroes and villains of the Purim story.

As you would expect, the prayer refers to Mordechai the righteous and Haman the wicked, as well as Esther the heroine and vicious Vashti. The final phrase mentions a less famous character in the Purim story: Charvonah. "And Charvonah should be remembered for the good."

Who Was Charvonah?

Toward the end of the *Megillah*, Haman's world comes crashing down. To his humiliation, he has to lead Mordechai on the king's horse. King Achashverosh explodes with rage against him for a variety of reasons. Esther openly accuses Haman of attempting to destroy her people, the Jewish People. Next, Haman is seen lying on the sofa too close to Esther, and at that tense and telling moment, Charvonah chimes in and says, "And Haman built a gallows to hang your trustworthy servant, Mordechai."[8] That is the final straw. Achashverosh immediately orders the execution of Haman.

What a great story! But who was Charvonah?

The *Ibn Ezra* comments on the *pasuk* and writes that there are those that say that Charvonah was Eliyahu HaNavi, the angel who is always present at critical moments in Jewish life. He comes to every *brit milah* and every Pesach Seder table.

---

8   *Esther* 7:9.

The question is, why does he appear as a common soldier in the royal court of Achashverosh? Perhaps the lesson here is that God has many messengers that He sends to us on a regular basis. The problem is our antennae aren't always tuned in to recognize them. Everybody thought that Charvonah was just another Persian infantryman, but he was actually Eliyahu HaNavi.

This lesson is very fitting for the holiday of Purim, which is characterized as a holiday of hidden miracles. In fact, it is intriguing that in the entire *Megillat Esther*, God's name is not mentioned even once! This symbolizes the essence of the holiday of Purim and what we can learn from it. We need to keep our eyes open for all of the Charvonahs out there and pay attention to the messages they bring.

A DIVINE APPROACH: We naturally attend to the most outspoken and popular people that surround us, but sometimes, it is the less noticeable people that can make the biggest difference. The lesson of Charvonah is that *"harbeh shluchim l'Makom*—God has many agents," and each person has a significant role to play.

The Haggadah

The Seder night is our yearly exhibition of Jewish education in the home. We discuss the four types of children that make up Jewish families, their questions, and some answers.

As we sing and eat our way through the night, there are plenty of customs and rituals to give definition and meaning to the evening(s).

Let's focus on a poignant moment during the night. *Yachatz* (which means "dividing") is when the Seder leader breaks the middle matzah into two. The smaller piece is maintained on the matzah plate and eaten at the beginning of the meal, while the bigger one is hidden away and eaten after the meal, at the part of the Seder called *Tzafun* (which means "hidden"). This is the moment the children at the Seder have been waiting for since Chanukah. If they somehow manage to find the hidden piece called the *afikomen*, a present is traditionally promised in exchange for its return.

The traditional explanation for *Yachatz* is that it is a reminder that because we were slaves in Egypt, we ate broken scraps and impoverished bread; not fancy fresh loaves. But there is something much deeper we can learn from this as well.

Rav Shimon Schwab, in the name of his father, reveals a beautiful insight into *Yachatz*.[9]

He explains that the two broken pieces of matzah from *Yachatz* represent two entirely different worlds. The smaller piece on which we pronounce "the bread of affliction" represents *Olam Hazeh*, the everyday world that we live in. It is the world that has ups and downs, sickness and health, and a myriad of imperfections. The bigger piece that we are commanded to eat after we are sated (*"al ha'sovah"*) represents *Olam Haba*, the World to Come, the world we transition to after we die. The reward in *Olam Haba* is what we look forward to after a life filled with worthy tasks and productive behavior. Perhaps that is why we eat it after we are full.

The Seder night is unique because it is the only time that so many mitzvot are fulfilled during the nighttime hours. Aside from lighting Chanukah candles, which is not Biblically commanded, holiday mitzvot are reserved for the daytime. We shake a lulav during the day, blow a shofar during the day, etc. So why do we eat matzah and read the Haggadah specifically at night? Why is this night different?

The answer is because Pesach has a **redemptive** quality. It is the holiday that reminds us through ritual and prayer that our exile is only temporary. Our celebration of retelling and reexperiencing the events of *yetziat Mitzrayim* from over 3,300 years ago fortifies us and our belief that we will be redeemed again.

> A DIVINE APPROACH: As we sit at the Seder, let's strengthen our faith that we indeed will be redeemed, and that darkness will finally turn into light and night will turn into day. That is why we celebrate the Pesach Seder at night.

---

9   *Rav Schwab On Prayer*, p. 541.

Dayeinu

Perhaps the most well-known song in the Haggadah is *Dayeinu*, literally translated as "It would have been enough." Children around the world joyfully sing *Dayeinu* with their parents and grandparents. The refrain is so repetitive that after several stanzas, some families stop singing the chorus because *dayeinu*—it feels like it is enough!

There are a few key questions worth considering in *Dayeinu*:

- Why are there fifteen steps in *Dayeinu*?
- Is there significance to their order?
- Why do we repeat the entire sequence of events over again after *Dayeinu* in "*Al Achat Kamah*," but this time, we do not repeat *Dayeinu* between each event?

Rav Shmuel Ehrenfeld, known as the Mattersdorfer Rav, writes in his Haggadah that fifteen is a key number in Jewish life, and it demonstrates ascendency.

- Pesach is on the fifteenth of Nissan.
- There were fifteen steps that led from the *Ezrat Nashim* to the *Ezrat Yisrael* in the Beit Hamikdash.
- David HaMelech wrote fifteen *perakim* of *Tehillim* that begin with *Shir Ha'maalot*, "Song of Ascents."
- The moon waxes larger until the fifteenth of the lunar month.
- There are fifteen steps to the Seder.

All these fifteens represent transition and physical and spiritual ascent.

The *Maharal* writes that the fifteen steps of *Dayeinu* may be divided into three parts.

- 1–5 are connected with *yetziat Mitzrayim*.
- 6–10 are connected with the miracles at Yam Suf.
- 11–15 all reflect the unique and eternal relationship God maintains with Am Yisrael, as expressed through Shabbat, Eretz Yisrael, and the Beit Hamikdash, etc.

The *Darash Dovid* explains that when we sing *Dayeinu*, we are focusing on our gratitude to God and spiritual growth as a nation. Therefore, each one of the fifteen are worthy in their own merit and are reason to pause and thank God for His Divine love, protection, and intervention.

When we then recite *Al Achat Kamah*, we recite all fifteen steps without pausing to say *Dayeinu* between each stanza. Here we are celebrating our historic physical survival and development as a nation; it therefore would **not** have been enough to take us out of Egypt without helping us cross the sea, or to bring us to Har Sinai without giving us the Torah. We needed all of those fifteen steps to actualize ourselves as the Children of Israel.

> A DIVINE APPROACH: While the Seder focuses on children, it is not the night for children to simply share what they learned in school. It is the night for parents to educate and inspire their children—and this will be most effective with preparation. So take some time before Pesach to prepare a few passages from the Haggadah in depth and with age-appropriate explanations. Use the Seder as an opportunity to engage the participants and instill in them the wonder of Pesach and a deep connection to Torah and our rich heritage.

Shavuot

אַתָּה בְחַרְתָּנוּ מִכָּל הָעַמִּים	*You have chosen us from among all the nations,*
אָהַבְתָּ אוֹתָנוּ וְרָצִיתָ בָּנוּ	*You loved us and desired us, and elevated us*
וְרוֹמַמְתָּנוּ מִכָּל הַלְּשׁוֹנוֹת	*from all the languages, and sanctified us with*
וְקִדַּשְׁתָּנוּ בְּמִצְוֹתֶיךָ	*Your commandments, and brought us close, our*
וְקֵרַבְתָּנוּ מַלְכֵּנוּ לַעֲבוֹדָתֶךָ	*King, to Your service, and You have called us*
וְשִׁמְךָ הַגָּדוֹל וְהַקָּדוֹשׁ	*with Your great and holy Name.*
עָלֵינוּ קָרָאתָ.	

The *Amidah* we recite during every *tefillah* of Shavuot, Sukkot, and Pesach after the opening three blessings reads as follows:"*Atah vechartanu mi'kol ha'amim...v'kidashtanu b'mitzvotecha*—You have chosen us from all other nations...**and You have sanctified us with Your mitzvot.**"

The phrase "You have sanctified us with Your mitzvot" needs clarification. How does the performance of mitzvot sanctify us? We invoke this formula regularly in many blessings we recite each day: "*Asher kideshanu b'mitzvotav*—That He has sanctified us with His mitzvot." Understanding this concept can add meaning to every Yom Tov we celebrate, not to mention the mitzvot we perform and the *berachot* we recite daily.

Some approaches are as follows:

- The words "You have sanctified us with Your mitzvot" indicate that since mitzvot are commanded by God, and God is the eternal King of kings, our performance of the mitzvot are a connection to eternity and the Divine. Therefore, every mitzvah elevates us because we are living life with Godly direction.

- The *Etz Yosef* provides a different thought. God's laws are unlike the laws of human kings and governments. When a government passes a law, it is legislated for the benefit of the nation as a whole. For example, one pays taxes for the benefit of the society. The laws of Hashem—the mitzvot—are not only for the benefit of society, but for the growth, purification, and benefit of every person fulfilling the law as well. Chazal taught: "*Lo nitnah Torah elah l'tzaref et habriot*—The Torah was given in order to refine humanity."[10]

By connecting to God through His mitzvot, integrating them into our lives, and refining ourselves in the process, we become sanctified.

This provides special meaning to us as we prepare for Shavuot. It was on Shavuot, over 3,300 years ago, that we cried out, "*Naaseh v'nishmah*," and the Torah was transmitted to us at Sinai. Since that moment in time, the world has never been the same, because a world and a life with Torah as its guide is an illuminated world and life, filled with eternal wisdom, meaning, and blessings.

---

10   *Bereishit Rabbah* 44:1.

A DIVINE APPROACH: When studying Torah on Shavuot night, remember that Torah and mitzvot refine us and provide personal growth for all who attach themselves to them: *"Eitz chaim hi la'machazikim bah*—It is a Tree of Life for all who grasp onto it."[11]

Where Are the Kids on Shavuot?

Shavuot is arguably the most significant day on the calendar. As the great Rav Yosef of the Talmud said: "Were it not for that day when the Torah was given, I would have been like many other Yosefs wandering in the marketplace!"[12] Without the great Yom Tov of Shavuot, there would be no other holidays, no Shabbat, and no Jewish nation. While Shavuot may be best associated with eating dairy, ice-cream, and cheesecakes, the true hallmark of Shavuot is *Kabbalat HaTorah*—our receiving of the Torah from God at Har Sinai.

Despite the clear significance of the day, children can get lost and be left out of our celebrations. On Rosh Hashanah, the children dip the apple in the honey and look forward to the majestic blasts of the shofar. On Sukkot, our children help build, design, and decorate the Sukkah, and they eat and even sleep in it. And on Pesach, the crowning moments of the Seder are the children's singing, asking, discussing, and engaging in the mitzvah of *sippur yetziat Mitzrayim*—the retelling of the Exodus narrative. Where are the kids on Shavuot? They are sleeping during the all-night learning, they don't participate in the sunrise *Shacharit*, and many of them simply don't like cheesecake!

We are even taught in the midrash that before God granted us the Torah, He required a collateral. Only when B'nei Yisrael offered their children as the collateral did Hashem acquiesce and present the Torah to us. So, even though the entire holiday is because of our children and in honor of them, if we are not mindful, they could miss out on key celebrations of the day.

---

11   *Mishlei* 3:18.
12   *Pesachim* 68b.

Therefore, if you will be celebrating Shavuot with children, please be certain to explain the significance of the day: how children brought sacrifices at Sinai,[13] and that God invested in Avraham Avinu specifically because Avraham taught his children and household Torah.[14] Perhaps we should encourage the children to help decorate the house with greenery, symbolic of Har Sinai. Since Shavuot is the culmination of Pesach, let's discuss what it felt like to be the only nation in the history of the world to encounter God publicly. Shavuot is our time to model and demonstrate our historic national pride in being God's chosen nation by receiving the Torah.

> A DIVINE APPROACH: Without our past, we have no history, but without a future—committed children—we have no destiny.

---

13   *Shemot* 24:5.
14   *Bereishit* 18:19.

CONCLUDING THOUGHTS

All worthy pursuits in life must be approached with particular goals in mind. Once the goals are in place, the strategies can be formulated and executed. Davening is no different.

Which Jew, who davens on any type of regular basis, does not want to make their davening as meaningful as possible?

The goal of all davening is to:

- express praise and gratitude to Hashem,
- deepen our faith and connection to Hashem,
- unlock the Divine blessings in order to receive them.

Praising and giving gratitude are done best when we understand well what it is that we are saying. When we understand the words, meaning, and order of our *tefillot*, our faith and connection to Hashem can be strengthened.

Chazal ask the following question: Why is it that our Imahot were barren? They answer that it is because Hashem desires the prayers of the righteous.[1] Surely, we cannot understand this to mean that Hashem caused pain to our Imahot because He enjoys listening to their prayers to Him.

Rabbi Dr. Abraham Twerski explains that Hashem wanted our Imahot to become pregnant and bear children specifically amid heartfelt and

---

1 *Bereishit Rabbah* 45:4.

meaningful *tefillah*. Hashem wanted the building of Klal Yisrael to be fueled by the pleas and praises of the holy Mothers of Israel.

Our nation was born out of intense and heartfelt *tefillah*. It behooves all of us to follow in the footsteps of our Imahot and Avot and storm the heavens with meaningful *tefillah*.

We live in a world with no shortage of pain and suffering. Everyone has something to daven for.

So, let's fill the heavens with our meaningful *tefillot* together, and may Hashem hear and answer all of our prayers for the good.

Finally, may Hashem grant us all the opportunity soon to return to Yerushalayim and serve Him in the Beit Hamikdash, the House of ultimate prayer. May we see the comfort of Tzion and the rebuilding of Yerushalayim. Amen.

ABOUT THE AUTHOR

Rabbi Ephraim Epstein has been serving as the *rav* in Congregation Sons of Israel in Cherry Hill, New Jersey, since 2000. He received his rabbinic ordination from HaRav Berel Wein, *shlita*. Before serving in the rabbinate, he was a founder and educator at the Center Program located at Ohr Somayach International in Yerushalayim. Rabbi Epstein teaches regularly, not only in New Jersey but also globally on the popular website TorahAnytime.com. He holds a degree in marriage and family therapy and serves as a counselor and advisor to many regarding their family relationships and their relationship with Hashem.